# The Karmic Life
# of a Psychic Medium

### Brandi Wilson

The Karmic Life of a Psychic Medium
Copyright © 2024 Brandi Wilson
Published by Hebe Wynturr The Author LLC

Printed in the United States of America.

ISBN (paperback): 979-8-9893615-7-1

The events and conversations in this book have been set down to the best of the author's ability, although some names and details have been changed to protect the privacy of individuals.

www.nofilterspiritualcounseling.com

# Table of Contents

# Dedication

I dedicate this book to the Most High God, the highest form of energy. I thank you so much for all your help and guidance. Thank you so much for protecting me. I love you every day of my life. I know I'm very hard to deal with, but thank you for having patience with me. Thank you for loving me and showing me the way. Thank you for choosing me to write this book. We are going to make history. I love you always.

I thank Jesus for all his help. Thank you for protecting me from all those demons. Thank you for being so kind and gentle with me. The love we shared was incredible.

I thank archangel Michael for all his help. You have been with me for a while. I love you very much. Your energy is amazing. Your protection is strong. Thanks for guarding me and coming anytime I call.

I thank my spirit guides, angels, and ancestors. I know I'm a brat, but thanks for sticking in there with me.

## A Warning

This book is protected by the Most High God, archangel Michael, and Jesus. If anyone adds to or takes away the words from this book. You will have to deal with the Most High God and these other entities.

# Introduction

**D**ear Souls, it's time to wake up.

I am a victim of black magic. Some of you may not believe in it, but I am here to tell you that black magic is very real. I have lived through some of the most traumatic events on a spiritual level. I'm honestly surprised that I survived it all. I will take you on my spiritual journey of becoming a psychic medium, where I have encountered darkness and evil. I will share my experiences I've had with God, his holy angels, and Jesus who helped me through these hard times and helped me become the woman I am today.

You see, Souls, you are very lucky that you are able to read my story. It will make you rethink what you think you know. Everything written in this book is all true. The experiences are real, and the people are real. Names and places have been changed to protect the identity of the people. I hope this book will open your eyes to different ideas and teach you about the spiritual world. I know in my heart I was meant to write this book. This is my truth, my testimony, and my punishment. I hope you're ready to dive deep into your soul and relive my journey with me. You've been sleeping way too long. I'm here to wake you up.

# Chapter 1:
# A Touch of Lavender

**H**ave you ever had the feeling like you weren't from this planet?

I felt like this for most of my life. I always felt out of place, like I didn't fit in anywhere. Don't get me wrong, I had friends, but just a few from high school. After I graduated, I became antisocial. I really didn't like people that much to tell you the truth.

When I was twenty-one, I worked at a hotel gift shop. I was in community college, and I had my own apartment at the time. I didn't really know what I wanted to do with my life. I was very unhappy.

We were getting a new employee, and I was in charge of training the new staff. She went by the name Lavender. She was a year older than me, and she was a Scorpio. She came in with a smile on her face and was very bubbly. "You're pretty," she said.

It caught me off guard, but I appreciated the compliment. "Thank you," I said.

My boss's daughter was also there to help with the training. We went over a few things with Lavender. She seemed to be really interested in me. She just kept staring at me.

"Are you a virgin?" she blurted out.

Feeling completely embarrassed, I said, "Yes."

"You look like a virgin," she said.

Yes, I was a twenty-one-year-old virgin. But I *wanted* to have sex badly. My sex drive was through the roof! There wasn't anyone I liked at the time, though. Well, I did have my eye on a football player. See, working in a hotel gift shop, I was able to meet all kinds of celebrities. I had developed a crush on this guy, and he was quite a popular player. To be honest, I was obsessed. I just knew when he saw me, he would fall in love with me. I wanted him to take my virginity and I was determined to make it happen.

Well, I was quite delusional back then but hey, I was only twenty-one. I never had a boyfriend or even dated anybody. I figured working at that hotel was the perfect opportunity for me to meet someone famous. After all, I wanted to be famous too. I just didn't have any talent. I wanted to be a famous singer but I couldn't sing.

Lavender and I connected instantly. We started to get off-topic from work and started talking about our personal lives. I was venting and said, "I keep feeling like I'm an angel." I really felt that way for some reason. I felt angelic – like I was a real angel. I wasn't sure why I felt this way and it wasn't because I was a virgin.

She stopped and looked at me and said, "WHAT!" Her entire face rose with surprise. "I feel the same way. You are an angel and I'm an angel too."

Nobody had ever said that to me before. "That's crazy!" I was also a little confused because I didn't know anybody felt the same way. Not too many people thought they were angels. We oddly said at the same time that after we died, we would get our wings.

We continued to discuss our weird experiences. We had a lot in common. She told me she had spirit guides and they told her I was a virgin.

"Girl, how does someone look like a virgin?" I asked.

"My spirit guides told me. They said, 'She's cool, she's a virgin,'" she explained.

I thought it was really cool that she had spirit guides. I didn't think it was strange at all. I definitely believed in spirits and ghosts – all that spiritual stuff.

The next day, work started like any normal workday. Lavender was, of course, still in the training process. I was still showing her the ropes of the job. Two of my co-workers walked in while me and Lavender were deep in conversation. They both came to the register to check out. They were two white girls who thought they were black. They wore the weaves and big earrings, but they were cool as hell. Lavender was checking them out and out of nowhere one of the girls called Lavender a fucking bitch.

I was thinking, '*What just happened?*'

Lavender looked at me while laughing, "You hear this?" They had both tried to gang up on her, and I was caught completely off guard. So was Lavender. I tried to be the peacemaker and tried to calm everyone down. After rude words were exchanged, they left. "They usually aren't like that," I said.

"You did that," said Lavender.

"What?" I said.

"You did that, you made that happen."

"No, I didn't," I said. The way she said it was as if I was powerful and was able to cause such events to happen. I had no idea what she was talking about. I was wondering why she would be so excited at the fact that she thought I had caused two girls to argue with her. The rest of our time together started to get really strange after that.

Lavender had only been at the job for a week. We became really close. There were times when my shift was over, and I would stay and talk with her and vice versa. We talked about God a lot. She was very spiritual, but she didn't have any religion.

One time, I stayed with her during her whole shift. A customer came up to us to check out and interrupted our conversation and said, "You two seem like you're having fun," and walked away. We laughed because we were having such a great time. Lavender was telling me how much she was smitten by me. "You're a keeper," she said.

Another customer came up to us and said, "You are a keeper. I hope you don't mind me saying that." Lavender and I just laughed. We thought it was so strange that customers were responding to our conversations. It was almost like it wasn't them talking. It was like something else was taking over their bodies. We looked near the glass doors out in the hallway and saw a man with big eyes just staring at us.

"See, that's God doing that," I said. Me being the brat I was, I complained that God was just sending people to her; the people were only looking at her. Nobody was paying attention to me.

When her shift was over, we headed out the door of the hotel. A random guy came up to me specifically and asked where the bathroom was. I told him, but the guy didn't even go inside the hotel; he went in a different direction. I knew God sent that person to me because I was complaining. He didn't even look at Lavender.

We were so excited the weird things that were happening, and it seemed to only happen when we were together. Lavender shouted, "How did you find me?"

I said, "How did you find me?"

"I'm so happy I found you," she said.

We declared that we were soul sisters. We gave each other a hug and went home for the night.

We started writing each other letters and we would read them when we got to work. We would talk on the phone every day. She told me about her brother who was a local rapper. "Do you know my brother?"

"No, I've never heard of him."

"Well, he raps and next week he is coming here for the local Hip Hop Award Show. Nobody believes he's my brother," she said. She had told other co-workers about him.

I guess they thought she was lying because he was well-known, but she was telling the truth. She explained how she didn't trust the people around him. She didn't think they had his best interest. She told me about their family life. They moved around often. She didn't have the best relationship with them. She felt like her parents treated her brother better. He was the prize of the family. She felt sometimes they would all gang up on her, which had landed her in the emergency room from stress at one point. Either way, she loved her family and had their back no matter what, she said.

The day of the award show, her brother stopped by to say hello. He leaned over and gave Lavender a kiss on the cheek. He was a lot taller than her. Lavender introduced me to him. He was very polite and went to shake my hand, but I hesitated to shake his. After all, he was a stranger, and I wasn't friendly back then. He soon left and went to the show while me and Lavender stayed behind.

"Girl, why was you acting like that? He's family," she asked.

"I just didn't know him, that's all," I said.

Lavender slowly pulled out a couple of pictures of them when they were younger. She really loved him and wanted the best for him. We saw a girl standing in the hallway, "Look girl, that's the girl that be coming over to have sex with him. I heard her giving him head one day." We both giggled. Her brother already had little groupie chicks running around.

I noticed a lot of men were drawn to her. A random guy just came up to her and asked her to come upstairs with him into one of the hotel rooms. He was so blunt about it. I thought it was odd, but she said it happened all the time. She was able to make fortunate events happen too. She was so powerful.

There was a guy we worked with who had really bad acne. I came in to work one day and she said, "He owes me his face. I told him to drink water."

I had no clue what she was talking about. I quickly left the gift shop to find him, and when I did, I couldn't believe what I saw. I stood in front of him for a second in awe. His face was completely clear. I mean his skin had been really bad. He'd had red pimples that covered his whole face. I referred to him as 'Pizza Face', but now they were all gone. Anybody can drink water, but their face would not just clear up like that, and not that fast. I was amazed. It was unbelievable. He was so happy his face had cleared up, but he ended up giving me all the credit for it.

"What?" I said, "That was all Lavender."

He leaned over and gave me a hug. He was so excited. Another time, we had a co-worker who always bought scratch-off tickets but never won that much money. When she bought one from Lavender, she won $200. I looked at Lavender and said, "You did that."

"Calm down," she said. She knew what she was capable of.

"I'm gonna tell her you did that," I said.

"No, she will think I'm crazy," she said with a loud tone.

You see, Souls, I never gave a fuck what anybody thought about me or how crazy I looked. I was all for it, but I kept that information to myself.

We had so much fun together: sharing stories and talking about spiritual things. I never had someone to talk to about God, not like we did. The connection we had was amazing.

Then I started to hear strange rumors about her. A guy asked me if she was a man and he started to laugh. I was very confused. I said, "No, what the fuck are you talking about."

I heard many comments like that and was unaware where those accusations were coming from. More and more people were talking and asking me questions – questions I couldn't answer. It was ridiculous; clearly, she wasn't a man. I mean, she looked like a woman. She was a little muscular but nothing out of the ordinary. Her voice was girly. She was more girly than I was. I ignored what was being said. She was my friend, and I didn't care what anybody said about her.

A few weeks later we ended up having a disagreement. I honestly can't remember why, but when I stopped talking to her things got even weirder.

I was at work one night and I noticed the jewelry stand started to turn by itself. I stared at it for a minute to see if it was an illusion but no, I was pretty sure it turned by itself.

At my apartment, I was in the process of moving so I was up late packing. I couldn't wait to leave that apartment. I had been there for two years, but a family had moved into the apartment above me with at least five kids. It was only a two-bedroom. Their kids made noise every damn day and I couldn't get any sleep. I had argued with them for a while. It was horrible. I didn't understand why the woman had all those children, and she was pregnant again. That was my cue to get the fuck out.

I got a call at 12 am on the dot. "Hello, Brandi!"

"Yeah," I said sarcastically, "Who is this?" I wondered why someone was calling so late. It sounded like a white guy. I hadn't given any white guys my number. He told me his name, but I forgot what he said. I heard a lot of static in the background and the connection wasn't clear. After he said his name, he hung up. I dialed #69 to see what number he was calling from, but it wouldn't go through. The first thing that popped in my head was that Lavender had given my number to him.

A couple of days later, I was in the hallway at work. I heard a man call my name. I turned around and saw a short man wearing one of the shirts those who worked in the hotel bar area wore. I looked at him. He didn't say anything, just stared at me. I got really irritated.

Souls, did I mention I wasn't the friendliest person? Like, what the fuck did he call my name for? I continued walking down the hall.

I was curious about who the man was, so I started asking around. I thought he may have been a new employee at the bar, but when I asked, the supervisor of the bar said they didn't have anybody new.

A week later, I was at my mother's house and there was a knock at the door. I yelled several times, "Who is it?" but nobody answered. I slowly moved closer to the door and looked out the peephole and saw a woman standing there. "Who is it?" I yelled again. Still no answer. '*I ain't opening that damn door,*' I thought. About ten minutes later I looked out the window and she was gone but she had left the front gate wide open. That shit scared me. I knew damn well she heard me yelling like that. Were these events a coincidence? I sure didn't think so. Something was going on, but I wasn't sure what.

I finally moved into my new apartment. It was a duplex. It was a cute place, but the neighborhood was a little sketchy. It had been days, and me and Lavender still weren't speaking to each other. I wondered if we would start talking again, but I was stubborn and mean. I wasn't going to start talking to her first. I suddenly came down with the flu. It was really bad. I had been in bed for three days. I could barely move. It was probably the worst flu I ever had.

On January 2, 2006, I had a dream that I was leaving my mother's house and my dad was helping me carry some boxes. It looked like I was moving from her house and going with my dad. I noticed on the back of my left leg I had a tattoo of a pink flower. It was right in the center of my calf. I heard a voice say, "That's a lotus flower." Then I saw an infinity symbol right above it. I then saw a fairy to the right of the flower.

When I woke up, I was definitely confused about what I had just seen. Still feeling under the weather, I jumped up and ran to my computer. '*What the hell is a lodous flower?*' I thought it had a 'd' in it. As I was typing, a beautiful pink flower appeared on the screen. It was the same pink flower I had seen in my dream. My eyes got so big.

It said a lotus flower symbolized purity, enlightenment, self-regeneration, and rebirth. The flower grew in the muddy water and rose above the surface to bloom with remarkable beauty, untouched by the impurity. It also represented long life, health, honor, and good luck. Okay, so I knew what the flower meant, and the infinity symbol meant long life – that I will live forever – but what did the fairy mean? I wondered who told me about the flower. The voice had sounded like a kid's voice to me. It was definitely a very strange but interesting occurrence.

The next day I had enough strength to go outside and check the mail. I noticed there were two young girls walking down my street. It was super cold outside, but the girls seemed to be in a really good mood. I heard one of the girls yell out, "Winter." She said it twice. That caught my attention because when me and Lavender had been on good terms, we had talked about changing my name. She told me why she changed her name to Lavender. That was her spiritual name. So, I decided I wanted a spiritual name too. She thought it was a good idea. I somehow came up with the name Winter. I thought Winter was beautiful. I imagined a winter wonderland. I eventually changed the spelling to Wynturr. I knew that girl was calling my name. How was that even possible?

I went back inside the house and tried to piece together what was going on. I started to think that Lavender sent some kind of spirit or ghost to bother me.

Lavender and I eventually started talking again. I was so excited; I missed her. I asked her if she sent me some kind of ghost or something. "Girl, no! Why would you think that?" she said.

I explained to her all of the things I was experiencing.

"I wrote you a letter," she said. "I was just going to leave it here for you to read. I'll read it to you now." She read the letter out loud to me. The letter pretty much said that she wanted to continue being friends with me. If I chose not to, she was fine with that decision, and she wished me the best. Of course, I wanted to be friends with her again. I felt like she was my soulmate, and she felt the same way.

"Sisters forever," we said to each other.

We were inseparable. We continued to have fun together, sharing stories and talking about spiritual things. We met all the football players and other celebrities that stayed at the hotel. I even tried finding her a boyfriend. I hooked her up with another co-worker. They were getting along pretty well. "How did you know?" she asked.

"I don't know," I said. She was referring to how I knew they would be good together. She thought he was a good match for her.

A week after that, the guy came up to me and said, "Why didn't you tell me she was a man? I'm not into men."

*'What the fuck is he talking about?'* I thought. My curiosity grew. I needed to see why everybody was calling her a man. So, I asked her if she got her period.

She got an attitude and said, "Do I get my period."

I could tell I annoyed her. I didn't mean to be disrespectful in any way, but I didn't just want to come out and ask her. She never answered the question though. So I refrained from asking anymore.

I had just got home from work and Lavender called me while she was riding the bus home. She finally came out to me. "I'm a man," she said.

I was surprised but not surprised. I didn't know how to respond. I had never met someone like that before or even saw one. She told me everything. She was taking hormones to change her body. She told me she was homeless. I didn't want to judge her; after all she was my friend. I didn't act funny towards her after that. How could I be so naïve? I was the only one who didn't catch on. I was curious about how a man becomes a woman. At work I noticed there were light colored spots on her legs from the hormones. "They're just spots," she said softly.

I could tell she was a little embarrassed that she had them. She brought up the homeless situation again. She asked if she could live with me. She was currently bouncing around from house to house. I honestly didn't get along with people; living with someone was out of the question. I liked having my own space. I just told her I didn't think it was a good idea.

Lavender started getting into it with the people at work. I wasn't sure if she was starting trouble or if people were attacking her. I just knew people were starting not to like her. I was caught in the middle. She got into it with one of our co-workers – it was really bad. They were cool at first, but I was talking to Lavender on the phone, and we were both talking shit about the co-worker; she put me on speaker phone. She did that so the other girl could hear what I was saying.

I was pissed. I asked her why she did that. I felt like she was trying to get me involved in the chaos and I didn't want any part of that shit. I decided to distance myself from her again, but I wanted to get her back for doing that. I didn't want a friendship with her anymore. She was causing too many problems. Everybody was trying to get her fired. She was getting so many complaints.

There was this guy who she said was gay behind his back, so I decided to tell him to get back at Lavender. She thought everyone was gay really. She called him gay all the time. He was really angry at her. He must have gone off on her when she was at work. As soon as I walked in the door, she asked, "What did you tell that guy?"

"I didn't tell him nothing." I played it off.

"You must have told him something," she insisted.

"What did he say?" I asked. She wouldn't tell me.

We argued for a bit longer, then she stood in front of me so I couldn't walk past. "Go ahead and make me move," she said.

I couldn't believe someone who called me their friend would come towards me in such a threatening manner. I just wanted her to leave. So, I called our boss and told him everything that was going on. He spoke with her as well. I got back on the phone with my boss, and I gave him an ultimatum. It was either me or her: somebody had to go.

He said, "I'm in the process of getting rid of her. She's been getting too many complaints."

I was so relieved. Apparently, everybody was fed up with her bullshit. She called me later that day being very demanding. She said,

"No, you're not going to stop being my friend," but at that point, I was done.

I changed my number and cut off all contact with her. Too much was going on. I wanted things to get back to the way they were.

Soon after, she was gone. She got fired. She threatened to file a discrimination lawsuit. She said the whole fuckin hotel would fall down because of her. She was very upset. I was glad she was leaving and so was everyone else. I saw the joy on people's faces. I was like, *'Damn, what exactly was she doing to get so many people riled up?'*

Things finally got back to normal. I saw her several months later. She ran right up to me and said, "Hey, girl."

I honestly wished I hadn't seen her. She was telling me how she didn't believe in God anymore and the powers we have are from ourselves. I thought she had lost her mind. Me being a Christian, I was not feeling that. I knew I had to get the hell away from her. I thought something was wrong with her. She tried to come to my house with me. I made some excuse up. I told her my neighborhood was bad. I most certainly did not want her in my home. It just seemed like conflict followed her. I did give her my number but when she called me, I changed it again.

Souls, I never saw her after that. Now looking back on this situation, I feel like she got rejected a lot and was just looking for someone to accept her for who she was. I'm sorry I wasn't a better friend to her, but I appreciate everything she taught me.

# Chapter 2:
# One Who is Awake

Things went back to normal after Lavender left. I began to grow spiritually. My dreams became more vivid and more intense. I started being able to see spirits and angels. I saw a ball of light in my bathroom. I was just standing there, and it flew right past me. I didn't know what it was at first. I found out it was an orb. I also bought a ring with a cross on it. I swear I saw sparkles of light bounce off of it when I put it on. I heard a magical sound like you would hear in a movie. Then at work, I took a picture of myself because I was bored, and a ghost's face appeared over mine. In the picture, my eyes were closed but you could see that the ghost's eyes were open. I showed a lot of people that photo and it would scare them. My best friend stared at the photo. "I swear to God, Brandi, that is not you." I knew it wasn't me but who the hell was it?

At that time, Souls, I still wasn't sure what was going on with me. It was like I just didn't know other people who could see the things I could see. There weren't really any groups that I knew of. Even my family was unsure. I didn't talk a lot about it to my parents because they weren't really open to the topic. My dad didn't believe in spirits or ghosts, and my mom... I'm not sure. She was just so damn rude and nasty that I couldn't talk to her about anything. I think she did believe in them but just didn't want to talk about it. She swept a lot of shit under the rug. My sisters were a bit spiritual. One sister had dreams like I did, and my other sister decoded the dreams.

I had a dream that it was windy and rainy outside. I saw a priest standing in front of me. I asked him if the world was going to end, and he said, "Yes."

When I woke up, I was terrified. I had always had a fear that the world was going to end when I was a child. I guess it was from reading the Bible; it made me always on the lookout for Jesus. I would wake up out of my sleep if I heard a loud noise, all paranoid and shit. I asked my sister what the dream meant. She said effortlessly, "The world is not going to end. Your world is going to end."

"That's my sister," I yelled. She hit it right on the nose. Then the dream made sense.

When my sister announced that she had gone to see a psychic, I knew I had to go. Weird things were happening, but I needed confirmation. She was telling me how accurate the psychic was. I didn't hesitate to make an appointment. I was on that shit the next day.

It was my very first time ever going to a psychic. She was located inside of a bar not far from downtown. She looked a bit scary, to be honest. She was an older white woman with big round spooky eyes. "Come sit down," she said. I was so nervous yet excited. She did psychic readings three days a week and she only charged $20.00. She didn't use any tarot cards or psychic tools. She didn't ask for my birth date or zodiac sign. She just told people what she saw, and she wrote it down. She was the real fuckin deal.

I sat there with anticipation. "You take everything to heart in this life," she said. That was most certainly true. I took everything way too seriously. "You don't like people," she said. I didn't like people at all. I had always felt different from them. I had a hard time understanding them and they had a hard time understanding me. The difference was, I didn't give a fuck if they did or not.

Around the 11th grade, I had changed. I became more introverted for some reason. I would only spend time with a certain group of friends.

After all, I was a Leo sun and Scorpio moon, but I'll get into the zodiac aspect later.

She said I would meet two men and I would have to choose one. She said one of them was Mexican or Puerto Rican, and the other was Eastern European – Czech, and they were both older than me. She said I would get married twice.

I was so excited because my love life sucked. It was nonexistent. I always pictured myself getting married only one time, but I couldn't wait to meet the guys, whoever they were. "Do you know where I will meet them," I asked?

She said I would meet the white man at a country-western bar. She said she saw me moving. "Texas?" she asked.

'*How did she know that*?' I thought. I had been wanting to move to Texas for most of my life. I had family down there on my dad's side. I felt really connected to Texas. I felt like I lived there in a past life, like I was a Mexican woman that had a lot of children back when Texas was a part of Mexico. Well, that's what I thought and felt but who knows if it was actually true. I told her I wanted to move after I finished college. I mean that was the smart thing to do. Right?

"September," she said. September wasn't that far away. That was absolutely out of the question. She nodded her head and said, "Okay."

I told her I could see angels, but they didn't talk to me. She said, "Well, you don't talk to them either."

I started to laugh. I didn't talk to them. I would just stare at them, and they would stare back at me. Fair enough, I guess.

I could see angels in my dreams and inside of other people. I thought of the man that looked like he was wearing a disguise that had come into the gift shop once. He was strange-looking with this brown trench coat and big sunglasses on. I couldn't really see his face, but he walked funny. He came up to me and immediately started talking about angels. His voice was odd too. He said singing voices were a gift from God and they were voices of angels. I never really looked at it that way, but it made perfect sense to me.

The psychic told me there were angels all around me. There were three in particular that were assigned to me, and they were protecting me. They were all women and she told me their names. I can only remember the one name she said, which was Airazaye.

I already knew there were angels protecting me.

When I was in high school, there were two separate occasions where some weird shit happened to me. The first one was when my best friend got into a fight in the lunchroom. I'm not sure why they were fighting, but I watched her walk over to the girl to start the fight. She dragged her off the table and she ended up getting the girl up against the wall. I walked over to them and started punching the girl. Then all of a sudden it got really quiet. Everything and everyone got very still. When I was hitting the girl, I was the only person moving. It happened so fast and then everything went right back to normal. When the fight was over nobody noticed me. Nobody seemed to know I hit the girl, not even the girl.

The second time was when my same friend got into another fight with a different girl. They had been enemies since the 8th grade. The other girl and her best friend were going around school insinuating they were gonna jump my friend. So my friend, of course, gathered some of her friends and family. My crew and I left early the last day of school to meet up with my best friend and her group. We all split up and planned to meet at the school. I wasn't sure what was about to go down, but I wasn't going to miss it. This girl had been harassing my friend for years over some guy.

When we got to the school the other girl wasn't there. We were told that they went to get their people. It was a big ass mess. We started to head down the street and all of a sudden, all of these people started running down the street towards us. The friends I was with were scared but for some reason, I wasn't.

I started telling my friends to take their jackets off so they could fight. They just stood there frozen, their eyes wide with fear. I mean, we were outnumbered: there were people there we had never seen before. "Take your jackets off," I yelled. I proceeded to take their jackets off for them. The group came up to us and everybody started fighting.

Everything began to blur for me. I remember looking for someone to hit so I could help out. I saw the girl who hated my best friend: the one who wanted to fight in the first place. I saw her getting her ass whooped but then she was by herself. I looked at her and saw her face covered in blood. It startled me for a second, but I went and grabbed her by the hair and started punching her in the head making sure none of her blood got on me. As I was punching her, everything and everybody got quiet. Everything became still. Nobody was moving except for me. I felt someone standing beside me, but I couldn't see them. I had no idea who it was. I let go of the girl's hair and things went right back to normal. The sound came back, and everyone continued to move.

The girl looked me right in the face and eventually left. She didn't try to fight me back or nothing. A woman who saw the fight from her car came and picked us up to get away from the fight. I believe someone called the police. I was feeling the rush of it all. "I got her for you," I said to my friend. We all got suspended for fighting. We had to do a mediation meeting before we came back to school. The girl had no idea that I hit her. I told her I did though. I said, "Yeah I hit you too." She said she wanted to fight me one-on-one, but I never jumped her with anyone. I mean she was just standing there by herself. Anyway, she never bothered me after that.

Now that I look back on these situations, Souls, I'm quite sure the angels were protecting me because I was probably going to get my ass whooped. So, they probably came down like, '*Brandi bout to get fucked up.*' I definitely could have gotten seriously hurt in those situations.

I told the psychic about my weird dreams, and she recommended I read the Edgar Cayce books. I had never heard of him. She said he was a sleeping prophet and was insinuating I was too. She also told me I was going to write a book. '*A book*,' I thought, '*I don't want to write a book*.' I hated writing. I mean I was good at it, but it wasn't my favorite thing to do.

I thought overall the psychic reading went really well. She was really accurate. It was a great experience for me.

I had just got home from work around 12:00 midnight. I was so tired that I jumped right into bed. I started dosing off and all of sudden I just woke up. It was quiet and I looked around briefly. Then I heard a noise. Somebody was at my back door. In a panic I flew out of bed and ran to the living room. I grabbed my phone and dialed 911. I could hear the person tearing away at the door. I was so terrified I just told the police my address, put the phone down, and flew out the door. I ran in the bitter cold in my socks and night gown to the police station. I ran so fast my feet barely touched the ground; I flew to that motherfucker. I saw the police cars flying past and I waved one of the cars down. The police officer stopped and told me to stay there. I told him the person was after me, so he let me get in the car. I sat in the car shaking as the police entered my home. '*What the hell is going on*,' I thought.

The officer came out to get me and asked me if I knew anyone who was out to get me. "No," I said.

He asked, "What about a boyfriend?"

I rolled my eyes. "There is no boyfriend." I knew it wasn't a good time to be bitter about not having one but that hit a nerve for me. We walked towards my back door, and I saw that the person was breaking the wood around the glass. I looked the officer right in his eyes and said, "The angels woke me up."

He just stared at me. I was asleep and the angels woke me up because they knew I was in danger. That was the only explanation because usually, I don't wake up right after I've fallen asleep, and I woke up so peaceful and serene. When I was running out of the house, it felt like someone was helping me run.

The police finished up and left, and I went to my aunt's house for the night. I was way too scared to stay at home. When I got to my aunt's house, she called me her angel because she needed me to watch my younger cousin since she was sick. She had never called me that before and that meant a lot to me. That was just another confirmation that angels were around.

Later, I found out it was my landlord's brother who had just gotten out of prison that was trying to break in.

That was my queue: it was time to go.

I looked for another place, but since I was on section 8, it was difficult to find something nice in a good neighborhood. I had been on section 8 since my first apartment. I had moved out of my mom's house because I couldn't stand her, and we didn't get along. My dad had offered to help me with my rent until the section 8 kicked in.

This was my second apartment, and I was already looking for my third one. I had only been at this place for about three months, but with that incident happening, I didn't feel comfortable staying any longer.

Things were okay after that incident until the new neighbors moved the fuck in.

I started having issues with them; we didn't get along. There was a lady and her fifteen-year-old son who lived above me. Her son made a lot of noise. He would jump around and stomp on the floor and shit. Definitely not normal behavior for a teenager.

I told the landlord about it, but the problems continued. I know he was doing it mostly to piss me off. It was pretty clear that something was mentally wrong with him. I thought maybe he had ADHD but after a while I got sick of that shit. So I called the police. I felt like I didn't have a choice. Of course, that upset the mother, but I didn't give a fuck. I was only concerned with my peace.

The lady also had an abusive boyfriend. I would listen to them fight all the time. I didn't even bother to call the cops when they fought because I knew she would stay with him. I was watching TV one night and I heard them threatening to kill each other. It was really scary. I prayed that God would never put me in a situation like that. That lady was a hot fuckin mess. One night I heard her and her boyfriend coming home, and she was upset with me. She started to bang on my door.

Boom! Boom! Boom!

I heard her screaming and hollering. I guessed she was upset because I called the police on her and had been complaining to the landlord. I was used to quiet environments, and she caused a lot of noise. I called the police again. There was no way I was going to open my door at night while two strangers were out there. Her boyfriend kept asking her what was wrong with her. Maybe she was drinking or something. Who knows. The police came and didn't do shit. They just told her to leave me alone.

I had a dream I was walking down a path, and the ground was made of stones and I saw these beautiful pink roses inside a row of bushes. I got to the end of the road and saw a river. The water started to rise up and cover the land. Then a big storm appeared out of nowhere. I ran and tried to go into the houses that were nearby, but the doors were locked. I then got swept into the water, but I held onto a railing. I remember flipping over three times and then letting go. I could feel the water on my face and the sounds were blurred like when you're underwater. I started to drown but then my dream cut to me being in the back of a limo with an angel watching me drown on a laptop. The angel was a white woman dressed in all white. I was telling her what happened and then she said, "He saved you," and then I woke up. I knew she was talking about God. He was saving me from that lady. Maybe she was going to try to harm me in some way.

After that whole situation, I finally found another apartment. I moved to a duplex in a better neighborhood. The street was quiet. It was very peaceful. I was on the top floor, so I didn't have to worry about someone breaking in. It was small, but it was perfect for me. I was ready to get away from that crazy-ass bitch that had been upstairs in my last apartment.

My mom and sister helped me move. "How many times are you going to move, Brandi? We are not going to keep helping you."

I had moved around a lot growing up. My mom and dad lived together when they'd had me. My mom already had my two older sisters. When I was three, my dad left my mom and got his own place. I wasn't exactly sure what happened between them. I just know they both hated each other. My mom hated him more. I was told my mom got pregnant by accident and wanted to get an abortion because she couldn't afford me. She was already on welfare with two other kids. My dad begged her to keep me. My mom said she was really sick and wasn't able to take care of me. She was diagnosed with Crohn's Disease. So after my dad left, my mom made him come get me. I was told many stories, but I lived with my dad as a baby. Then I moved to another town because my dad got married when I was in the 5th grade. From there, I moved to my aunt's house when I was in the 8th grade. Afterward, I went to live with my mom when I was in the 9th grade. I bounced from my dad's to my mom's to my aunt's – back and forth.

It was nice having my own place for a change and not being told what to do.

# Chapter 3:
# Nun Existent Love Life

I spent most of my time alone. I wasn't good at making new friends. I barely went anywhere unless it was to school or work. I didn't really like bars or clubs. I was already twenty-four, and you would think I would have had a boyfriend by then. Nobody I was interested in romantically paid me any attention. I was mostly into white guys, but they weren't really interested in me except a few ugly ones. I was rarely into black men unless they were really attractive. I was really picky, and I only wanted to talk to attractive, older, manly men.

There was this guy I was in college with, and he looked just like the football player I was in love with. I wasn't pleased though. I felt like God was trying to send me a knock-off version because I couldn't have the real thing. He was really tall, and he looked bi-racial. I think he was just black though. He always sat behind me in class. I never truly noticed him until he stood up one day and his face had this glow to it, like a light shining over it. I guess God did that so he would get my attention.

I saw him the next day on the bus. I decided to sit with him, and I tried to spark a conversation. He was nice and seemed to be focused on school. I tried to get something started with him because that was what I thought God wanted me to do. So, I gave him my number. He sure took his time to contact me. I was starting to lose interest, but he finally reached out. We talked for a bit.

Then the next day at school he started acting funny. He was happy to see me at first, but after class, he was acting strange. I tried to make a conversation, but he was blowing me off. I didn't do anything to him for him to be like that. I just moved on. It wasn't that serious.

It seemed like I was not going to have sex any time soon. I had been waiting patiently for a husband. I had been doing everything the Bible said. I had prayed and prayed and still nothing. It didn't make any sense. I even went to a county western bar since the psychic told me I would meet my lover there. I looked like a damn fool in that bar. I couldn't wait anymore; I needed to have sex.

I honestly thought masturbation was a bad thing to do; I couldn't resist the urges anymore. So I said, '*Fuck it,*' and tried it. I put my middle finger inside my vagina. It hurt a little but felt good at the same time. I wasn't able to have an orgasm. Back then, I would be really disappointed when I wasn't able to, and I would get in a bad mood. So, I started practicing more. I started imagining I was having sex with guys I liked, and eventually, I was able to reach an orgasm. It felt like a wave of sensations all over my body. I felt like I was doing something naughty, but I also felt like I had no choice.

I've always had issues in my love life. Most of my friends had boyfriends but I never had one. I wasn't even allowed to date until I was eighteen. My parents were strict about that. There had been a guy I really liked as a teenager. I would go over to his house after school. He had been planning to take my virginity, but there was always some kind of interference when he was on his way to my house. He had a lot of things going on in his personal life, so we ended up going our separate ways. I found out he died two years afterward in a car accident.

The gift shop where I was working was being remodeled and a bunch of men came in from all over. I had a crush on one of them. He was a white, older man with grey hair. It was the first time I was really interested in someone who showed interest back, oddly enough. We flirted and I would always see him checking me out. He came into the gift shop one afternoon. I was so excited. He was looking around the store, so I asked him a few questions. He was looking for a sweatshirt, but we didn't have his size. "You have a lot of big sizes," he said.

"Well, there are a lot of big people in this area," I said.

"You're not big, you look nice," he said.

A smile spread across my face. Little did he know I had been a lot bigger, especially in high school. I looked down and saw that he had a tattoo of a wedding ring on his finger. "Are you married?"

"No," he said, looking unsettled. He gave me a bit of an attitude. "I used to be." Shortly after that, he left.

I really liked him. I couldn't wait to see him again.

A whole week passed. I didn't see him. I was pissed; I wanted to tell him I was interested in him. I was so angry because of my history of men disappearing right when I'm about to tell them I like them. Every guy I liked would fuckin vanish and either I wouldn't see them again or I would see them a while later when I was no longer interested. It only happened when I liked the person.

My love life fuckin sucked. So, when that guy at work disappeared for a week, I was done. I was done with funky-ass Pennsylvania. I knew I couldn't find love there. So, I made the decision to just get up and leave. I wanted to go to Texas. I had always said I would move but never did it. I figured this was the perfect opportunity.

I randomly started talking about doing some kind of transformation with my life. I had no idea what I was talking about. The transformation consisted of me eating healthy and doing fasts. I wanted to cut everybody off and focus on God. I felt really close to God. A woman once told me that God had his hand wrapped around me. She was right, he did. I always felt protected but maybe a little too protected.

Souls, not only was I a Christian but a hardcore Christian.

I went and bought some stones and a white candle. I had this beautiful picture of Jesus I got from a nun when I was thinking about doing volunteer work. I loved me some Jesus. I made a circle with the stones, and I put a picture of Jesus in the middle and lit the candle and prayed. I had no idea what I was doing. I guess it was some kind of ritual to get closer to Jesus.

I kept having dreams that I was alone, but I had a dog with me. It was pouring down raining. I kept seeing a clock tower and I kept crying. I'm not sure if the dream meant I was running out of time. It kind of felt like I was the only person left on earth.

I knew it was time for me to go. I called my aunt in Texas to see if I could stay with her. She lived in a suburb outside of Dallas. I asked her if I could move in with her, but she suggested I stay with my cousin. So, I called my cousin up to see if it was okay. She agreed.

I had dreamed about moving to Texas most of my life and finally, it was happening. It only took me a week to get things in order. I quit my job. I sold my furniture and my car. I quit school. I asked to transfer my section 8 to the Dallas area. The housing authority was fine with it, but I needed to get out of my lease with my current landlord. I dropped everything so I could get the hell out of Pennsylvania. I thought I was making a good decision, and that I would be much happier down in Texas. My dad wasn't happy about me going, but he knew I would be with family. My mom didn't really care.

I was too scared to fly so I bought a bus ticket. I was ready to go.

One night before I left, I had a dream that I was asking somebody about having a boyfriend. I really wanted one. After all, one of the reasons for leaving was to find a boyfriend. The lady was a spirit and she told me not to focus on that right now.

I asked her, "What will happen in the next month?"

She said, "Hero," and she showed me the tarot card: the hermit[1].

I had no idea what that card was, but I looked it up.

Souls, the hermit card in tarot is associated with the hero's journey. The hero's journey is the common template of stories that involve a hero who goes on an adventure, is victorious in a decisive crisis and comes home transformed. This led me to the book *The Hero with a Thousand Faces* by Joseph Campbell, which explained the hero's journey. I started to notice my life was following this pattern.

There are twelve stages in the hero's journey. The first stage is the ordinary world. This is where the hero starts out in their normal life, in the mundane world, before the journey begins. So that was me in the beginning, working at the gift shop. I was just living a regular life.

The next stage is a call to adventure. This is when the hero is faced with something that makes them begin their journey. I would say this happened when I met Lavender.

The third stage is the refusal of the call. I think this was when all that strange spiritual stuff was happening to me. There were some things that were happening to me I didn't want to believe.

The fourth stage is the meeting with the mentor. This is when the hero encounters someone who can give advice and prepare them for the journey ahead. That was definitely Lavender. She was a mentor to me. I didn't know it at the time, but she was. She started the process for me.

# Chapter 4:
# Savages in the South

It was Labor Day, September 7, 2009. I had finally made it to the "Promised Land." It seemed like the psychic was right. I was so excited to finally move to Texas! I had high hopes for my future. I was ready to start a new beginning.

I was greeted by my cousin, Helaina. She smiled and gave me a hug. She was very pretty and was around the same age as me. We looked similar; people thought we were sisters. She had been my favorite cousin when I was younger. When I visited, we always spent time together. I had missed her because it had been a while since I had seen her. She was married with a baby. Her husband was out of town for work. "Let's go," she said. I got inside her huge truck and put my seatbelt on. I couldn't believe this was happening. It felt so surreal.

We stopped to get McDonald's for breakfast and then headed to her apartment. Texas was a lot different from Pennsylvania. The whole vibe was different, and I loved it. Helaina said, "I gotta go to work. Do you want to stay here and relax? I'm takin' the baby to Aunt Lucy's house."

I was too excited to relax so I decided to go with them. I couldn't wait to see my Aunt Lucy! She was one of my favorite aunties from Texas. She was a mean woman but was very sweet to the people of her choosing. She greeted me with a kiss and hug. She still looked the same. She was a beautiful woman with beautiful skin. She still treated me like a baby, even though I was twenty-four at the time. Her name was Lucille Furr.

She lived with her boyfriend of many years and her son. Her son was the same age as me. She stayed home most of the time because she was very sick. She was really close with my dad. I could tell she loved him so much. Her kitchen was always stocked with the best food. I would go in there and just eat my life away. "Eat whatever you want," she would say. They were all happy to see me. She offered for me to use her car to go grocery shopping and other places I needed to go. Later that day, I went back to Helaina's house and finished getting settled in.

Gretchen was Helaina's mother. She stayed next door to her and helped with the baby while Helaina went to work. Helaina was married and worked most of the time. She had been with her husband for a long time. He was not the best-looking fella, but he was cool. I could tell my aunt was truly in love with him. She was also one of my favorite aunts. I remember as a child staying at her home when we came to visit. She and Helaina looked nothing alike. Gretchen had more of a round physique. They had a rocky relationship just like I had with my mom.

There was a guy who also lived in the same apartment complex. He was a local drug dealer and stayed with his girlfriend and their children. He had a crush on Helaina, but that came to a halt when he met me. He would always speak when I saw him. I wasn't interested in him at all. I didn't find him attractive. He had a very nice body though. You would think he worked out at the gym with the muscles he had.

I started seeing him more and more. I wasn't working so I didn't have much to do. Helaina had a gathering at her house and invited him. I put a cute little dress on, nothing too fancy. Her friends started to arrive. I wasn't much of a company person. I rarely had people in my home. I wanted to try new things and be more open though. One of Helaina's friends from childhood showed up. He was a makeup artist. "She's pretty," he said to Helaina. She lifted her head with a hint of jealousy in her eyes. She didn't say a word. I told her friend, "Thank you," and tried my best to be social. Then her neighbor showed up. From the moment he walked in and the rest of the night, he was staring at me. He and I were making more of a connection than he had with Helaina. At first, he was on Helaina heavy, but then he got smitten with me. Perhaps I was developing a crush on him, and he was developing one on me. We joked about him coming over to the house while I was watching the baby and him spending time with me. We also joked about me and him having sex. He said I wouldn't be able to handle him, and he was right. I was too shy and inexperienced, and I was too focused on finding a job and a place to stay. Plus, he had a girlfriend, and I was definitely not the type to mess around with somebody's man.

He did end up coming over one day while I was babysitting. He didn't stay long. He said he was just coming to check on me. I tried out my psychic abilities with him. I made some predictions for him, and he seemed to be impressed. He listened to everything I had to say. He even confirmed some things.

Sometime later, I started to get really depressed because I was worried about my section 8 getting transferred. My previous landlord did not want to break my lease. I wasn't sure what I was going to do if I didn't get it. I wanted to cry; I knew I had made a rash decision moving to Texas and I was paying for it. I offered my landlord to keep my furniture and the rest of the things that were left in the apartment. She still wouldn't budge. I prayed so hard to get out of that situation.

Then one morning, I got a voicemail that said my landlord agreed to break my lease. I couldn't fuckin believe it! It was a miracle! I knew God had helped me. I was able to transfer my section 8 to Texas. It was a relief. I could finally go looking for another place and get out of my cousin's house. I was ready.

After that, I started to see a change in my family's behavior towards me. They started treating me funny for some reason. They wouldn't take me anywhere and I was stuck inside all day. When I asked, they made up an excuse. I could tell there were things being said behind my back. I had a dream in which Helaina said I did something that was not true. I couldn't hear what it was, but I knew the dream was a sign.

I reached out to my other cousins who lived about forty minutes away and I told them what was going on. I told them about the dream I had about Helaina. "That sounds like her," my cousin said.

A few days later I was taking a nap and woke up. I pretended to stay asleep because I heard Gretchen talking to my other aunt. They were on their way to Walmart. My aunt said, "Let's wake up Brandi and see if she wants to go."

Gretchen said, "No."

Helaina said something but I couldn't hear the rest. I knew then that she was making up lies about me. My dream had been right.

I started to feel uncomfortable around them. I wanted to know what was being said but more importantly, I wanted to get the fuck out of there. I felt helpless. I stayed in the room as much as could. I noticed Gretchen was bringing dinner over for Helaina and not me. Before, she would bring both of us something.

Aunt Lucy was acting funny too. She came over to the house and was getting ready to go out with Aunt Gretchen. I asked them if I could go with them. They said, "Yes," but when I finished getting dressed, they had already left. I was so angry. That was fucked up! *'What the fuck is going on,'* I thought.

Helaina was having another gathering and even the neighbor was acting funny. He seemed to be ignoring me. He barely said a word to me. Somebody made a comment that I was being so quiet. I was because something was up. Helaina said, "You seem like you're mad. Why ain't you talkin' to the neighbor?"

The neighbor said, "She mad cause I'm not stuntin' her no more."

"What?!" I said. I had no idea what he was talking about. "That's not why," I said.

As days went on, I started to notice the neighbor was just talking to

Helaina. It was weird. I knew I had to leave immediately. I called my other cousins and asked them if I could stay with them until I got a place. They agreed. I had money saved up and I offered to help out with the bills. They were glad I was leaving Helaina's house.

I happily packed up all my shit. I told Helaina I was going back home to PA. I wasn't telling her shit. It was none of her business. I don't think she believed me though. "What time does your flight come," she asked.

"Oh don't worry, I have a ride," I said.

"Well, I'm sorry you decided this wasn't working out for you," she said. "That's okay," I said. She honestly didn't even seem like she cared that I was leaving.

"Do you want a cookie?" she asked.

'*No, I don't want no fucking cookie you fucking Bitch,*' was what I really wanted to tell her ass but I kept quiet. I declined the cookie and went to sleep.

The next morning, one of my cousins came and picked me up. I didn't say shit to Helaina. I just left. She didn't say bye either.

I know what you're thinking, Souls. What the fuck was going on? I thought that too. I was confused and I felt outcast by my family. This was some bullshit.

I was relieved to be out the house and away from them. My other cousins were all living together temporarily. We had a conversation about what was happening at Helaina's house. I learned that they did fucked up shit to the family. This was their normal routine. They didn't fuck with them either. They started drama with everyone. I had no idea. I mean I had lived in another state, so I wasn't aware of everything that was going on with my family in Texas. So basically, any family member that stayed with them they treated like shit. But why? I didn't understand the intent behind it. I found out that before I came down to stay, one of my other cousins stayed with Helaina and she kicked him out. It seemed like a lot of unnecessary drama. I wanted nothing to do with any of that shit. My family in PA didn't do shit like that so I wasn't used to it. All I knew so far was that Helaina made up a lie about me. She possibly told many lies. My cousins told me she was known to lie for no reason.

Memories started to fill my head. I remembered years before there was speculation she had lied about one of my really close cousins. This was insane to me. Who does shit like that? The only reason I could think of for her to get angry with me was because the neighbor guy liked me. I didn't do anything to her. I gave her money for the rent, which she refused to take, but I made her take it. I cleaned the house and watched her child. This was beyond me. I mean she was also a Scorpio. Souls, Scorpios are known to be big liars, but we will get into that later.

I needed a break from all that shit. My cousins and I decided to get some pizza up the street.

I finally had my section 8 voucher, but I just needed to find a place to live. My older cousin decided he wanted his girlfriend and her two kids to move in with us. I'm not sure why, but I'm sure it was to his benefit. It was already crowded. Once my cousin's girlfriend moved in, things just got worse. There were arguments, of course, but there were too many people for the small space. I didn't have a choice but to stick it out. They all had their own lives. They seemed to be disconnected from each other. I tried my best to stay out of their way. Then the rent was due, and I guess nobody wanted to pay it. I wasn't sure what was happening, I just knew we had to move out. Here I was once again moving.

We went out looking for places. I prayed we would find something soon. I went outside and I looked at the sky and asked God to help us. Maybe an hour later we drove past these really nice townhouses in a nice area. We looked at two different ones but one of them had mold in it. We decided to stay in one townhouse all together. I mean, I was going to be leaving shortly, so it didn't matter to me. My cousins gave the property manger the money so we could move in right away. We were excited. The townhouse was much bigger and there was room for all of us.

We headed back to the old apartment to get our stuff, then we moved into the townhouse and got settled and things seemed to be okay for the moment.

I started feeling like I was making things happen. It was some kind of magic. I could cause good things to happen but also bad things. If someone was mean to me, bad things would happen to them. It reminded me of years before when my supervisor at Home Depot poked me in the back.

Souls, let me tell you what happened.

I was at work one day and a customer asked how much a door was. I think I made some kind of mistake. I can't recall what it was, but I do remember my supervisor getting very angry with me. She got so angry with me that she poked me in the back. I know what you're thinking, Souls, you would have knocked her ass out right? I hear you, but she was an older woman. I was at work and, of course, I didn't want to get fired. I couldn't believe this woman had the fuckin audacity to poke me in my back. She stood behind me and said, "I need to talk to you," and then she poked me. I got so angry that I started to cry. *'I'm gonna kill this bitch,'* I thought. I had a line of people so I couldn't just leave. I checked them out and cried the whole time. A woman in line tried to console me, but I was livid. When I was done, I went looking for that bitch. I was screaming and hollering and didn't give a fuck who heard me.

I quickly called my dad. "That fuckin bitch poked me in my back," I told him. I had never cussed in front of my dad before, but I was mad. I continued to look for her. I wanted to knock her fuckin head off. I didn't see her; I believed she had already gone home. My dad tried to calm me down.

The next day I reported her and filed an incident report for harassment. That bitch was way out of line. Three days later I found out she was in the hospital because she had an aneurism and she wasn't coming back to work. I really didn't care; I was still mad at her. I knew that happened because of what she did to me. When I got angry at people, bad things happened to them. I was glad she was gone.

Then there was the time I worked at Bob Evans. My supervisor went off on me because I didn't seat a guest fast enough. I was a hostess at the time and I hated it. I got in trouble all the time for not smiling but I wasn't a smiling kind of person nor did I care for people I didn't know. He called me into the office and yelled at me. I did not like that very much; I almost wanted to cry. I was furious and I completely ignored him. Three days later he announced he was being transferred to another Bob Evans. I heard he actually got fired, but who knows. He said to me, "I know you're mad at me, but I'm leaving."

I honestly didn't care, but I acted concerned. "What happened?" I asked.

"I'm being transferred to another restaurant."

"Why?" I asked, "Was it because of me?"

"No," he said. He gave me some excuse, but I knew it was because of me in a spiritual sense. He got kicked to the curb for treating me like that. '*Farewell motherfucker,*' I thought.

There were incidents like these that happened all the time. I knew I had some kind of power but wasn't sure exactly what it was.

I hadn't spoken to Helaina in a while, but she texted me asking about her mail. I guess when I stopped my mail it stopped hers too. I told her I would take care of it. The post office must have been giving her a hard time so she called me back several days later leaving a rude message.

'*Oh, hell no!*' I was not with that shit. I wasn't above fighting a family member. I wasn't that much of a fighter, but I would defend myself. I called my dad and told him what was going on.

My dad had been in the loop the whole time. He couldn't do much because he was far away. He was getting fed up with how they were treating me. He must have called and talked to them because the next day, Helaina was being all buddy-buddy with me. Somehow, we got fake cool again. I was pretending because I held on to grudges for dear life. I didn't forgive anybody. She was definitely on my shit-list, and I knew I was on hers.

I heard there was something going on with her and that neighbor guy. I wasn't sure how true this was until we went to her house on Thanksgiving. I put a cute little dress on just to be a smart-ass. I was looking good too, because somebody at the store was saying how fine I was.

When I got to her house, she and that neighbor guy were there inside her bedroom. "Oooooooolllll," I said out loud. So that's what it was. Helaina and that neighbor guy started messing around. She got jealous because he started to show more interest in me. So, she decided to fuck him. I didn't even want the guy and I didn't know it was that serious. I mean, she was married. She didn't think we were coming over so early and her ass got caught. My nosey ass took a look around the room, and I noticed the song "Half on a Baby" by R. Kelly was on the computer screen. They were in there fucking to music. "Those motherfuckin bitches," I said to myself. And I didn't hide my feelings of disgust. I made it known how I felt about that shit. All of this over some nigga I didn't even like.

I remember several of the family members telling me that Helaina was jealous of me. I didn't believe it. I couldn't understand why. I mean, I was pretty, but so was she. She was married and had a family and I didn't have any of those things. This bitch was hatin' on me the whole time. I started to recollect the times she was actin' shady. Like when her friend gave me a compliment or when anyone gave me a compliment. She would have this look on her face. I was getting a lot of attention, but it was because I was new in town.

I wanted to go to a club, and she agreed to go until I pulled out this cute little top and then she quickly changed her mind. It was like she didn't want me to get more attention than her.

Well at least I found out what was going on behind my back. It was Helaina's birthday, so we all went over there. They were going out to some club. I didn't want to go; I hated clubs. I never enjoyed them. I didn't drink either so there was no point. The neighbor guy was there with all his friends. Helaina sat on the couch and the neighbor guy sat next to her and started to put his arm around her like it was okay. Obviously, everybody knew about it. I was not okay with that shit and the fact that he did that shit in front of my face pissed me off. I was like, *'Okay, y'all wanna play with me.'* So I pulled out my phone and started taking pictures. He quickly moved away. He practically lived with her then. I guess he was there all the time at that point. I heard one of his guy friends ask him if he was going somewhere with them and he said, "No, you know Helaina ain't going to let me go." Helaina was salty as fuck I took those pictures. I didn't give a flying fuck. She was wrong for what she was doing. She did me dirty, and she was cheating on her husband.

Meanwhile, back at the townhouse, my cousin's girlfriend said there was some money missing. She was insinuating that everyone thought I took it. I definitely wasn't a thief. I had my own fuckin' money. I kept money because my dad taught me how to save. All I knew was I didn't take any money. When I got home, I went straight to my other cousin. "What's going on?" I asked.

"Shhhh," he said and closed the bathroom door. He said, "There is money missing."

"What money?" I asked.

He said he had a stash of money in the house, and he thought his girlfriend took it.

I told him I felt like I was being accused.

"No, nobody is accusing you," he said.

"That's not what the girlfriend said to me."

He promised this wasn't about me. Something just wasn't right. There were too many weird things going on and too many people around. Shit, my cousin probably took the money and said somebody else took it. I knew he had issues with money. They all did. I wasn't sure, but it just seemed real shady. I was upset about that shit because I didn't want people looking at me crazy for no reason.

Suddenly a string of unfortunate events started happening. My older cousin lost his job. He didn't want to tell anyone, but he had no choice. He was at that job for years and it was strange that they fired him. Then my other cousin's car broke down. My cousin got into this big argument with his girlfriend. It was one thing after another. Things started getting out of control. It was a big-ass mess. I knew this was happening because of how I was being treated. Somebody lied about me, so karma started kicking in.

I sat on my bed and took everything in that was going on. I noticed nothing bad was happening to me because I did nothing wrong. My cousin started catching on because I told him about these patterns that happen to me. He came into the room and looked at me.

"Devil," he said. Then he walked out.

That really hurt my feelings because I didn't do anything to them. People had to learn how to treat me. They weren't being very nice to me. They were talking behind my back and acting funny, but why? I knew it was time for me to leave. I think some of them wanted me to leave and that was fine with me.

Around the same time, I started having dreams about lions attacking me. The dream started out as me being terrified of a lion. I kept going inside the same house and the lion would just be there. The lion would lay on me. I would move its arm off of me so I could get up, but it would put it back on me to hold me down. In other dreams, the lion would roar at me. The very last dream I had about this lion, I was sitting on a living room floor and two lions came in and sat behind me. I was scared shitless. I didn't even turn around to look at them. I started to pray, and I said, "Help me, Jesus." Then all of a sudden, I pulled out a knife and started fighting the lions. I cut the tongue out of one of the lions' mouths. I killed them; somebody was helping me. I couldn't see who it was. Maybe it was another spirit or something that was part of me. I finally defeated that lion and never saw it again afterward. That dream let me know I was stronger than I thought and I could overcome obstacles.

I got word that the guy neighbor was driving Helaina's car on their way to see our other family members in another town. They made his ass drive. It seemed like they turned him into their little bitch. They got pulled over by the police because he was speeding. The car was in her husband's name, so they had to tell him who was driving. I wondered what lie she told to cover herself.

I saw karma was still making its rounds and I was loving it. "That's what the fuck they get," I said to myself.

A few weeks later, I found an apartment. It was in the same apartment complex as my Aunt Lucy. I was so excited to move. Finally, my own place. I really didn't want to live by Lucy, but I had no choice. The place was so nice. It was the nicest apartment I ever lived in. It had a pool, and I had my own balcony. I had my own washer and dryer and a walk-in closet. Nobody seemed to care I was leaving but I was happy to get my life started.

I had already moved three times in just a couple of months since going to Texas. I didn't have any furniture. Somebody gave me an old futon to sleep on and some of the other family gave me a few things, but it was still quite empty. I still needed to find a job and try to get into school.

So in reflection, Souls, I had crossed the first threshold into stage number five. That's when the hero leaves the ordinary world for the first time and crosses into adventure. This was when I left for Texas. Stage six is Test, Allies, and Enemies. This is the stage where the hero meets friends and foes. My family were the foes and they definitely tested me.

# Chapter 5:
# Malediction

I spent most of my time in the house alone. I was basically down there by myself. Nothing really changed from when I had lived in PA. I watched a lot of movies. Movies made me happy because they were an escape from the real world. I probably watched every movie you can imagine.

I got a job working with Aunt Lucy's son, my cousin, at a seafood restaurant. It was very upscale, right by the lake, and not too far from my home. There were busses nearby so I could go back and forth to work. I was a hostess and I really liked it at first.

My first day at work, I was looking forward to earning some money. My coworkers were mostly white, and they were very welcoming. The manager was super nice. The job was pretty easy. It was part-time though since I went to school full-time.

The people who worked there were all friends. They had already formed their cliques. I didn't try to blend in. I kept mostly to myself until they started talking to me. I still felt like an outsider. They all tried to gang up on me.

One time they were acting funny towards me because I got into an argument with our other coworker after he tried to show off in front of his girlfriend. A guest wanted to sit on the patio, and he just told me not to seat him because his girlfriend was there. The guest requested to sit out there so I had no choice. I took the guest to their seat and my coworker got in my face and said, "I thought I told you not to seat there," in a very angry voice.

"They wanted to sit there," I replied.

He walked away in a hurry. I followed right behind him because I didn't like how he was talking to me. I also didn't like how he yelled at me in front of the guest. "Who the fuck do this motherfucker think he is?" I said to myself. I walked in the kitchen with a scowl. "Don't ever talk to me like that again," I said to him.

"Oh, here she comes acting all high and mighty," he said.

"What are you talking about?" I said.

We began to argue, and shit went down. Things quickly escalated. All I remember him saying is, "I don't give a shit about you." Not that I thought he did. I'm not sure why he even said that.

"I don't give a shit about you, you motherfuckin bitch," I yelled. As soon as I said that, everyone got quiet like I did something wrong.

My boss soon walked in and said, "Hey, what's going on in here?"

"You better get her," my coworker said.

"No, you better get him," I said. I felt like everyone was against me because I called him a bitch. He had cussed at me first.

Another time, one of my coworkers called me Queen Latifah. I looked nothing like Queen Latifah. I'm not sure if it was because I wore big hoop earrings, but I felt like he was being racist towards me. I had problems with him often. He would talk smart to me and say inappropriate shit to me all the time. That Queen Latifah comment was the last fuckin straw.

I told my mom about it and all she could say was, "Well, dang, Brandi, how big did you get?"

Yes, I had gained some weight, but I wasn't that big. Her lack of empathy for him calling me names was starting to piss me off. I mean, she had weight on her.

So I decided I was going to report that asshole because I was getting tired of his shit. I told Human Resources what happened, but I added in a few things. I said he said I looked like a fat pig, as an example. I had to add in some flavor, to make it good enough for him to get in trouble. He got called into the office and he sure did get in trouble. They were about to fire his ass. After that, I didn't have any more problems with him or the other coworkers. They all tried to be nice to me, but I wasn't with it.

I remember getting complimented because they were all socializing while I was paying attention and helping a guest. I ended up leaving that job and collecting unemployment after that.

One cool thing is that I met Joe Jackson while working there. I found out we had the same birthday which was very interesting.

I stayed focused on finishing my degree. I was still planning to do social work. Everything seemed like it was coming together.

I hadn't heard from my cousins since I moved in. I really needed rides to the store, and I didn't want to ask Aunt Lucy. She was still acting funny toward me. All of the cousins were acting funny too. I called to see if anybody could take me grocery shopping, but I got no answer. I decided to start riding the bus to the store. I mean, what choice did I have? It was just up the street, but I still had to carry all my groceries. My sister ended up buying me a shopping cart and sending it to me in the mail. That helped me a lot.

It took me two buses to get to school. The first bus was almost an hour long. Imagine traveling almost two hours both ways. It was definitely tiring. I was able to get a work-study job helping students with their financial aid. I made a lot of new friends; it was nice to meet people from all walks of life. '*This is amazing,*' I thought. My social work classes were awesome, and I loved my teachers. I had really great ones.

I also started to get more spiritual. I began seeing number sequences. It started with 111. I was seeing it everywhere. Then my dreams started to change. I had a dream in which I went into this house where there were other people and they were practicing how to use their powers. In the dream, I got an upgrade in my powers.

Then I saw 111 on a TV.

I had another dream where I saw a set of footprints in the sand with 1111 over it and I jumped right into the footprints. I didn't know what that meant. I looked up the information online and it looked like I was having some kind of awakening.

I also started seeing 444 and other number sequences. It just came out of nowhere. I read a book called Starseed 101. A lot of what the book was saying resonated with me. I was a starseed. It made a lot of sense. I wasn't sure what was going on, but I knew I was changing.

I had a dream I was sitting in my living room in the dark. There were dark figures standing in there with me, all lined up in a row. I was pregnant and leaning on a woman for support. She said, "It's not time yet." Then smoke filled the room, and I couldn't hear anything else she said.

Then out of nowhere, I started liking children. Everybody who knew me knew I didn't like kids. Well, it wasn't that exactly, but I just didn't want to be bothered with them. I thought babies were cute to look at, but I didn't want to take care of one.

I think it had come from me babysitting my nephews. I watched my nephew when I was in high school, even when I didn't want to. He had ADHD so he was really hard to deal with. Even though my sister would pay me, I felt like I missed out on my younger years because I was stuck babysitting. Then when she had her second child, it was just too much. He was much easier to handle but there were still two kids to look after. One time, my mom got mad at me because I didn't want to watch them. I didn't want that responsibility on me.

Anyway, I started to like children for some reason. I started having dreams about these dark-skinned men and some of them had dreadlocks and wore black suits. They looked like they were from the islands. I dreamed one of those men in a black suit was sitting on the couch at my mom's house. He never looked at me, he just looked straight ahead and there were kids all around him. He didn't say anything, he just sat there. This man, or men that looked similar to him, kept showing up in my dreams. They were always surrounded by children.

There was a guy who lived across from me in the same apartments. His name was Judas. He stayed there with his mother. He was friends with another guy I had met previously in the neighborhood. I would see them hanging out together outside. He had a crush on me, but I wasn't really interested. He was a few years younger than me, and I wasn't into younger guys. We started hanging out together outside. We mostly just walked around the apartments and walked to the store. He mentioned he was a Scorpio.

Judas and I were walking around one night, and we saw a white owl fly in the sky and then it disappeared. I had never seen a white owl before, and I wondered where it went.

He had a girlfriend. She came to his place quite often. She always gave me the side eye and I could tell she wasn't interested in being cool with me. I completely understood.

I started spending more time with Aunt Lucy since my other cousins completely abandoned me. I would go to visit her just to check on her. She seemed to be warming up to me more. I think it was because of my dad. I would go and watch TV with her and go to the store with her. She let me use her car a few times. She seemed to always be in a bad mood and always angry at something. Since she had health issues, she spent most of her time in bed. I could tell she was really evil. I watched her body language and her facial expressions. One minute she would look regular and the next her whole face would turn demonic. Her eyes would look pitch black. I could tell I wasn't one of her favorites like I used to be. I still loved my Aunt Lucy, but I felt like she was against me. It was probably because of some lie Helaina made up.

One night I went over to the house, and I showed her this website that had pictures of dead people on it. It was really disturbing, but I was kind of fascinated with it. Lucy was too. We looked at the pictures together. I noticed the smoke from Lucy's cigarette was coming out of the cigarette, but it wasn't moving. It was like it was trapped in the air. The smoke was standing still. It reminded me of when the angels came and stood beside me when I was in those fights at school. I stared at the smoke for a while. '*Why isn't it moving?*' I thought. How was that even possible?

I went home for the night. I couldn't go to sleep. I kept tossing and turning. It felt like something was on my back and I couldn't get it off. I started to feel nauseous. I got up and felt really dizzy and fell to the floor. I closed my eyes and yelled, "God, help me!" several times. I wasn't sure what was going on, but after I prayed to God, it came off. I started feeling normal again and went back to bed. I came to the conclusion that some kind of spirit had attacked me, maybe a demon. That would explain the smoke – and we had been looking at dead people.

I called Judas and told him what had happened. "I don't know if you believe in that kind of stuff, but I do," I said.

He said he believed in demons as well. As we continued the conversation, somebody was calling my other line.

"I'll call you back," I said.

"No," he said aggressively. "Don't hang up."

I said, "No, I'll call you right back." I clicked over to answer the other call.

A few minutes later, Judas called back. "I'm going to kill you," he said.

I wasn't sure if he was playing around or not, but the way he said it was very creepy.

Then Judas began to get possessive over me. He asked me one time if I wanted to be his girlfriend. I said no because he already had a girlfriend. Plus, I already had a crush on a guy at my college named

Jerimiah.

Jerimiah had walked into my work-study job, and I had noticed a shiny light flashing over his face. It was the same one I saw over the guy's face back home. He was cute, tall with brown skin and dimples that just made him even cuter. He had left and I had wanted to know who he was.

I had started looking for him, trying to figure out what department he was from. I figured he was doing a work-study as well. I looked all over but couldn't find him. That made me get very angry. De ja vu hit me all over again. *'Why does this always happen to me?'* I thought. I wanted to cry but I had to keep my composure at school. Every time I would find a guy I was interested in, he would disappear!

I gave up the search and a couple of days after that, we went on a school break, and I forgot about him.

When we got back from the school break, I ended up seeing Jerimiah in the office on the floor above me. "That's him," I said under my breath. I was so excited to see him! I had finally found him. I wanted to go in and talk to him, but I didn't even know if I was allowed in the office where he was. I stood in the hallway for a second hoping he would see me. I mean, what would I even say? I ran downstairs and tried to find some information on him. Who was this guy?

Later that day, I got on the bus to go home from school, and I saw him again. He was already on the bus. He sat there waiting patiently with his books in his hands. I had never seen him on the bus before. *'This has to be meant to be,'* I thought. I started talking to him right away and getting to know him. I caught the bus with him every day after school and we sat together every time. I felt like God wanted me to help him in some way. He was more laid back than I was. He seemed to be really quiet most of the time.

I asked him if he was a virgin because I got that energy from him. "That's a bold question, but yes," he said. He was in his early twenties and that was rare. I told him I was one too. It was odd. There weren't too many people like us left out there. The fact that he was inexperienced turned me off though. I didn't like shy inexperienced men. It gave me little boy vibes.

I asked him if he had ever seen an angel before.

"Yes, but it didn't look like what you would think," he said. He described what it looked like to him. I was amazed that someone else had actually seen one.

I became bored with him and upset with God that I had even met Jerimiah. He was moving too slow for me. I wondered why he hadn't asked me for my number yet. I couldn't tell if he was interested in me or not. He would come to my job and visit me, and we sat together every day on the bus but something wasn't connecting. I thought maybe he was gay. I started to get frustrated.

"You're boring," I said one day.

"Why did you say that?" he asked.

I could see his insecurity in his body language. I guess I expected him to be more exciting. Like maybe wanting to have sex like I did. He basically just went to school and to work.

He told me the next day that I was being mean. I honestly wasn't trying to, but he was just disappointing me. He tried his best to be more exciting, but he just didn't have it in him. He was who he was. I told him it was probably a good idea if we separated. I didn't see the point in continuing anything with him.

I started to sit in the back of the bus instead of up front with him. He came to sit in the back with me. "Is it okay to sit back here?" he asked.

"I guess," I said.

He wanted to reconcile, and he finally asked me for my number. We got cool again but the energy was still stagnant. I could tell he was losing interest in me as well. I called him one evening and said, "What is the problem?"

"Can't I just take my time to get to know you?" he asked.

I could tell he had been getting advice from someone else, perhaps a female. I was a bold and up-front person, and I didn't have any time for games. This poor guy didn't stand a chance. He was too soft, and I was too strong.

I stopped talking to him several times and eventually, he backed off completely. He stopped catching the bus and I didn't see him much after that anymore. I did see him a while later talking to some Hispanic chick but that was it. I was kind of jealous that he found someone else to talk to, but he was definitely not for me.

I was still on okay terms with my Aunt Lucy, until she told me she and Helaina and Gretchen were going to Houston to visit our other family members. There was a crisis going on with the family and I wanted to go and support. I told Lucy I wanted to go but they left without me. I was so fucking pissed off. They did that on purpose, but what did I expect? They had been doing me fucking dirty since I had gotten down this bitch.

When they got back from the trip, Lucy had the fucking nerve to come to my house and show me pictures. She knocked on the door and I slowly opened it but not all the way. I stood in the doorway so she couldn't come in. "Yeah?" I asked with an attitude.

She looked at me crazy. She pulled out her phone and started showing me pictures they had taken on their trip. She must have seen the frown on my face. "What's the problem?" she asked.

"You knew I wanted to go to Houston and y'all left me," I said.

"I didn't know you wanted to go," she said. She lied right to my face.

"I told you I wanted to go," I yelled. At that point, I didn't give a fuck if she was my aunt or not. "Then you gonna come over here and show me some damn pictures?"

Lucy was surprised I had spoken to her like that. Usually, I was very respectful toward my aunts, but I had had it with their bullshit. "See, that's why I don't come over here," she said, and she stormed down the stairs.

"Good and don't come back neither," I said. I had started to argue because, while I was usually a quiet person, when I got mad shit went left. I used my words as weapons because I wasn't a physical fighter. I was only five feet tall, and I knew I was too small to beat people up. I knew exactly what to say to hurt people though. I probably got that from my mom. When I got mad, I would say all kinds of shit and then pretend to completely forget everything I said. "You're a sorry-ass aunt," I yelled.

That must have hit a nerve with her because she came charging in my direction. "You bitch," she yelled.

"You're a bitch," I said.

"You're not going to keep calling me a bitch," she said. She was on her way up the stairs when one of my guy friends came and grabbed her.

I didn't really want to fight my aunt, but I had to defend myself. I didn't care if she was sick. I was so fucking tired of them and their thinking they can treat me any way they like. I didn't serve that. I went into the house and closed the door.

Outside she was screaming, "I'll kill you, Hoe."

That really hurt my feelings. The fact that she said she would kill me let me know I meant nothing to her. I only got called a hoe once before that in my life. I was in high school, and some guy called me a dick-sucking hoe for no reason. The title didn't even fit me since I was still a virgin and nowhere near a hoe.

I decided to call the police on her for making threats and to piss her off. I called my dad and told him what happened. He was already angry with them from a few weeks before.

He had called and cussed Lucy out because of how they were treating me. My dad and I were very close. He had my back all the time. He was ready to come down and fight all of them.

After all that, I stayed away from her and all my cousins. My family ended up being a very bad influence on me. I started being like them. I was dishonest about things. It would be small things, but when I was in PA, I rarely told a lie. I was a Christian, so I knew lying was wrong. When I went to Texas, I had to lie. Not all the time, but I definitely felt the need to tell lies because my family was telling them. They weren't big serious lies like the ones Helaina would tell. She told lies that would get someone killed. I was always caught up in some drama with them. I was never like that before.

I got into another argument with Helaina. We were talking about some bracelet she had gotten for Christmas. I was still mad about the situation with her, so I brought up that conversation to be a smart-ass. "Oh, what about that bracelet he bought you? Do your husband know about that?"

She immediately got upset, which was what my intentions had been. I wasn't jealous she was talking to the guy. I was mad about how she treated me because of him. She started to yell and scream. She usually kept her composure. She hid who she really was: a fucking snake. *'How could someone so beautiful be so ugly,'* I thought. We argued for a bit then she did some foul fucked-up shit.

"What did you just say?" she said. "Why are you talking about our family like that?" She was with our other family members during our argument and the sorry-ass bitch made up a fucking lie right when I was on the phone with her. I said nothing about the family, but she made it seem like I did.

"You're a liar," I shouted.

"I will stomp your fucking ass," she said.

"Come on then," I screamed. One thing I didn't like was being threatened. I would fight then. She said she was on her way, so I waited by my door. I had my baseball bat just in case the motherfuckers tried to jump me. Some time passed, and I texted her. *"Where u at you comin or what..."*

*"I'm on my way,"* she texted back.

The bitch never showed up. She was just mad because she was cheating on her husband, and I said something about it.

My dad was livid. After that, I stopped talking to all of them and things started to calm down.

Judas had a younger brother who came home from college for the summer. I thought he was cute. He had chocolate skin, and he was tall with long hair. I asked Judas about him, and I turned my head and smiled. "I saw you smile," Judas said. I wanted to know all about his brother.

Meanwhile, Judas' girlfriend and I started hanging out for some reason. She just started talking to me. So, we all decided we were going to go out on a double date. I hadn't ever been out on a date before, and I was twenty-six at that point. Judas got some free movie tickets, so we decided to go to the movies. The movie was pretty good. We watched *Limitless* with Bradley Cooper. I loved movies.

When the movie was over, we decided to go to McDonald's. I started to realize the brother was kind of strange. I asked Judas if his brother was a virgin and he said, "Yeah."

Why the fuck did I keep running into these guys who were virgins? I thought that was weird and he seemed to be very antisocial and awkward around people. He was similar to me, but I just didn't find that attractive. I was over it and ready to go home.

After we got back, Judas' girlfriend asked me if I wanted to go to her house. Later, we met the guys at Walmart, which was where Judas worked. I was also talking to this other guy who worked with him. I was trying not to make anything awkward. I was ignoring Judas' brother, and I was meeting the other guy for the first time.

I walked right past him, and he looked really weird. I remember him having light skin, pink lips, and a scar on his chest. I walked outside of Walmart, and he followed me. We sat on the benches out front. He decided to tell me his whole life story. He stared at me in a creepy way. I looked at his scar and it looked perfect. Like it was placed there and it wasn't real. He didn't seem real, like he was just placed there for right then. I thought he was some kind of extraterrestrial. Judas and his girlfriend got into an argument. It was time for me to go.

When I got home, I told Judas I couldn't hang out with his brother anymore. His brother annoyed the fuck out of me for some reason. I asked Judas if he was mad and he said, "No, I'm just not fucking with you no more." I didn't care anyway. It was my decision, and I was over the whole thing.

Since Judas wasn't talking to me, I decided to hang out with his girlfriend more. "We broke up," she said.

"Why?" I asked.

The reason why? They got into an argument because she wasn't wearing underwear. She had pajama pants on, so I wasn't sure how he knew but that was no reason to break up with someone. "Well forget him," I said.

She came to my house a couple of times, and we had fun doing girl stuff. Suddenly, she just stopped coming over. She stopped answering my phone calls. I didn't hear from any of them anymore.

I started seeing Judas' girlfriend go back over to his house again. I figured they got back together. It kind of sucked that I didn't have anyone to hang out with anymore. Everyone was mad at me. I just kept to myself and stayed in the house. My bathroom sink was stopped up, so I took the drain out. I noticed flies were everywhere. I wasn't sure where they were coming from, but I thought it was from the sink. Even though they were everywhere, I could barely see them. I was curious about what kind of flies they were, so I looked them up online. They were called 'no see ums' because they were invisible. I hadn't ever heard of no shit like that before. They started biting me too. I had to sleep with a sweatshirt on with the hood over my head. I could barely sleep. I was afraid to.

The next morning, I woke up with a damn crook in my neck. I could not turn my head. It was stuck turned to the right. I got out of bed slowly. I was afraid I wouldn't be able to walk properly. I knew I needed to go to the hospital but how the fuck was I going to get there?

It was a very awkward position. I waited a couple of hours and finally, I was able to turn my head again. I was glad I didn't have to call a taxi. I would have been so embarrassed.

Somebody told me to get some bug spray. I decided to go to Home Depot. There was a Hispanic guy who worked there. He kept staring at me. I asked some of the workers where the bug spray was and that guy yelled, "I'll help her!" I thought he was really cute. He showed me where everything was, and we talked for a moment. He was really flirty. I wasn't a flirty person, but I was definitely interested. He asked for my number, and I gave it to him. Then I asked for his, but his coworker called him to do something. Still, I was really excited.

When I got home, I sprayed my house. I got really sick from all the fumes. It took them a week to leave. I texted a mutual friend of Judas' and told him there were flies in my house. I wanted to see if he was having that problem too. I wanted to know if it was a Texas thing. He never responded. Judas had gotten to him too and gotten him not to talk to me. I saw the mutual friend a week later and his eyes got huge. He looked like he was scared or something. He turned his head and didn't look at me.

I waited for the guy from Home Depot to call me and he never did. *'That's strange,'* I thought. I was interested in him. I rarely got attractive guys to talk to me, so I went down there to see what went wrong. I hopped on the bus and headed back to the store. Something just wasn't right. My mind was racing, and I was so nervous. I didn't want to look desperate. I was though. My love life fucking sucked and I was tired of the bullshit.

When I arrived, the guy ignored me. I was totally confused. What the hell happened from a week before? He was helping a customer and I just stood there waiting for him to get finished. The customer said something to the guy in Spanish and the guy responded. They both looked at me and started laughing. I was so embarrassed. I left the store and was very disappointed. I didn't understand why that was happening.

Things got even weirder after that. I was going to the bathroom, and I saw a dark shadow go under the closet door in the hallway. I second-guessed if I had seen it, but I really did. Then I came home and found a nude gecko jumping around in my bathroom. I didn't know what the fuck it was, though. I screamed and jumped back. It looked like something clear was jumping around. I sprayed it with bug spray, and it died. A week later, I found another one in the tub. I had never seen a gecko in person before, but the occurrences kept happening.

I began to get really sick. I started itching badly. I was having allergic reactions and rashes that were forming. I thought maybe I had bed bugs. Bed bugs were a big thing down there. I did find dead bed bugs in the futon I had, so I stopped sleeping on it. It didn't matter where I slept – the bed, the couch, the futon – it was very uncomfortable, and I still itched badly. I didn't find bed bugs anywhere else. I cried because I couldn't sleep anywhere after I found the bed bugs. Where was I going to sleep? I couldn't sleep on the floor: there could be bugs in the carpet.

I decided to buy an air mattress and when I went to fill it up, an orange dust came flying out and got all over my face. I was walking around with an orange-ass face for the rest of the day. I went to lay down on the air mattress and it started burning my skin, even through the sheets I put over it. I started sleeping on my dining room table. It was a big hard wooden table. It was beautiful but not for sleeping. I tried sleeping on top of the table at first, but it was too hard. So, I sat in a chair and put my feet up in another chair. I barely got any rest. The mornings were awful. I was in so much pain. My hips and ankles started to swell up. Tears were falling. I didn't know what else to do; I didn't have anywhere else to go. I was constantly washing blankets in fear that a bug might be on it. I started to get a chemical taste in my mouth. I knew I needed to see a doctor.

I went to the hospital seven times in two weeks. They thought I was crazy. They didn't find anything wrong with me. All my blood tests came back normal. My last visit to the ER, a social worker came to see me. She said, "Honey, there's nothing wrong with you. Do you have a friend or family member you can trust?"

I honestly didn't. I didn't have anyone. The doctors said there was nothing wrong as they always did when I went to the ER, but I knew something was wrong.

I reached out to a psychic and tarot card reader in Dallas, but she didn't get back to me until about three weeks later. I made an appointment with her. As I walked up to the door, I knocked a couple of times; nobody answered. I tried to open it, but it was locked. I was just about to leave when a woman opened the door. "I can't believe the door was locked. That's odd," she said.

I walked in and it was a little dark. The room she did her readings in was awesome. There were lots of cool metaphysical and voodoo things in there. She allowed me to use a tape recorder. I had my questions ready as she requested. She started off with my birth chart and she told me I was a triple Leo and a triple Scorpio. "This means you're very intense," she said. "You're gonna be taking things on in a big way."

I asked her about my neighbor. "I think I got something on me," I said.

"Yeah, I could tell you had something on you when you came in and I was wondering why you didn't know how to get it off of you," she said.

"I fucking knew it," I said.

She told me Judas and his girlfriend created some kind of energy together in the spiritual realm. "They just put shit on people like it's a game," she said. She told me he didn't do a spell. It wasn't like he got a chicken and cut its head off. That would be too much work. They had a natural ability to do it. "Maybe he just had evil thoughts about you." She said Judas was out to get me.

I wasn't sure why he was attacking me. Was it just because I said I didn't want to hang out with his brother anymore? That just seemed a bit extreme. I just wanted to know how to get the shit off of me. She gave me a spiritual bath to do and instructions. She assured me that having a curse or whatever was on me didn't happen often and that I should be able to remove it and continue on with my life.

I asked about my love life. She saw the same two guys the other psychic had seen. I was so excited. I was ready to have a boyfriend. "They won't be able to see you and you won't be able to see them until you take that bath," she said. "It creates a wall. It's like walking around with shit all over you. Nobody will want to come near you." That was a serious problem.

I asked about my grandfather. I felt I had a connection with him. He died shortly after I was born. She told me he wanted me to finish school and to stop messing around. I had been trying to get finished, but since I transferred to Texas, they were making me take a lot more classes. I told her I had trouble making friends. She said with my Scorpio moon I came off very intense and that scared people. She was right. People were scared of me, and I didn't know why. I rarely made threats to anyone, and I never got into physical fights besides the two in high school. I barely even talked to people.

She told me I was going to write a book, which was the same thing the other psychic said. I really didn't want to write a book, but I did think about writing a children's book. "You've been through so much in your life. You could write about that," she said.

We went over my past lives. She pulled out six cards. I was a man in three of them and a woman in the other three. She said my last life was a high-profile one. "You were a princess or a duchess and either your husband died, or you couldn't find a husband, so you got sent to a nunnery."

That made sense to me because I was still a virgin. She said in that life I was a nun, and I ran off with a man. She said she wasn't sure who the man was, but she said maybe it was someone like the gardener. She said it was a huge scandal and everybody had known about it.

In another life, I was a farmer who didn't like people, only animals. There was one life where I had a bunch of kids and my husband died and I started a business. She said that business was still out today. Maybe that was the life where I was Hispanic.

In another life, I was a lawyer and I'd had a drinking problem. I didn't drink at all, but I argued a lot and wanted justice for unfair situations. It seemed like all my past lives were present in this one. All of them resonated with me.

I told her I felt like I had magical abilities. "I can make things happen. Like a form of manifestation." She did confirm that I have a gift. She said my ancestors practiced this as well but most of them kept it a secret. I knew psychic abilities ran on my mom's side of the family. I had psychic dreams and so did one of my sisters. My older sister decoded the dreams for us, but she was still intuitive. I found out one of my mom's sisters had psychic dreams too. Who knew what other abilities they had that they didn't talk about.

The psychic told me that with the gift I had, only I could make happen what I'm going to do in the future. I asked her if this was my last life on earth. She said, "No, you're going to keep coming back because there is so much you want to do." I didn't believe that. I hated living on Earth. I felt it in my bones that this is my last life. We finished up the session and overall, I really enjoyed it.

I got all the ingredients I needed for the spiritual bath. I was scared as hell. I stayed in touch with the psychic lady who did my reading. She said she would stick around until I removed whatever was on me. "Do I have to do it right away?" I asked.

"Well how uncomfortable are you?" she said.

She was right. I needed to take action immediately. I felt very sick and tired. I ran my bath with warm water and put the ingredients in. I got naked and got in the water. I lit the candles and said the prayer that I was instructed to say. Then I immersed myself under the water. As I was coming out, the water splashed and one of the candles went out. I told the reader what happened, and she told me to try again.

So I tried the bath again and this time the drain stopper wasn't working. As I was filling the tub, it was draining at the same time. "What the fuck!" I yelled. Fear set upon me like a ton of bricks. What was I going to do?

The psychic reader recommended that I make a bucket with the bath in it and then pour it over my head. I did as I was told, and this time salt got in my eye and it started burning. The water put the candle out once again. I dried off and sobbed quietly.

The psychic reader said, "Wow you got something really nasty on you."

I was terrified.

She told me to try doing the bath at someone else's house. I didn't want my family in my business, so I went to my deceased aunt's husband's house. He agreed to let me do the bath. It finally seemed to come off, but I asked God to send me a sign that it really had.

Then all of a sudden, a friend from school texted me. I hadn't heard from him in a while. I called him my brother. He was a very sweet guy, and he was very intuitive like me. We had gotten closer when we had gone on a class trip. I ended up sitting next to him on the bus. I had no idea he was into the spiritual things I was. We talked about seeing all these number sequences and as we were talking, we started seeing them. 111, 333, 444 – it was insane. He had told me when he was younger, he would get rid of demons, but he couldn't do it anymore. I was telling him about the dream I had when I first became psychic. The one with the tattoo on the back of my leg with the lotus flower and infinity symbol and the fairy. I told him I knew what the lotus and infinity symbol meant, but not what the fairy meant. He said, "It means you have magical powers."

"Yes!" I said, "You are right." We felt a deep connection with each other from a past life.

"How did you know to contact me at this time?" I asked when he texted me.

"I don't know," he said.

That was my confirmation. I told him what was going on and he decided to come to my house to help me. Once he got there, he looked around the entire apartment. He looked inside my closets and put his arm out like he was showing any evil spirits he was in charge. I giggled a little out of nervousness. I couldn't believe this was actually happening to me. Then he grabbed me and picked me up. I guess he thought that would get all the evil off of me. He gave me a necklace with a wooden cross and Jesus on it. "There, use this for protection," he said. I thanked him as he left. I thought I was in the clear and everything was okay.

I moved on to the next thing the psychic reader told me to do which was a spiritual house cleaning. This called for a cap full of ammonia and a few other things. I cleaned up my house from top to bottom and put all the ingredients in a bucket of water. I already had an allergy to a lot of cleaning products, especially bleach. I couldn't even use bleach to wash my clothes. My skin would start burning. So I wasn't too sure about the ammonia but I thought it was okay since it was just a small amount. I mixed everything up and put the water in a spray bottle. I began to spray my home with it. I sprayed the walls, the floor, my furniture, everything. This was supposed to help remove any evil spirits in the house.

When it was done, my eyes felt funny. My vision started to change. Then my eyes started to burn, and it got worse when I would look at the walls. I opened all the windows and turned the fan on to air everything out. After hours went by, my eyes still hurt. I looked around and noticed there were burn marks on the wall and the carpet. Maybe I didn't do something right; something was wrong. I started feeling sick all over again and I could barely breathe. The ammonia fumes were burning my nose, face, and eyes.

I called my mom and told her what was going on. She immediately started yelling at me. That was her form of communication. She yelled all the time for no reason. "I knew I felt sick for some reason," she said.

Apparently, while all that was happening to me, she had felt it.

I got off the phone with her and tried to clean everything again with soapy water. That didn't help at all. I didn't know what to do. I had nowhere to go. I went to sleep that night by my open window praying to God for help.

The next day wasn't any better. I felt like I was dying. I knew I needed to go to the hospital again, but I didn't have any energy to even move. I tried to stick it out as I lay on the floor. I thought, *'Is this how I'm going to go out?'* I knew my family would miss me if I died. My breathing started to slow even more. I thought about hanging myself with a chord just to get some relief. I called my friend, the guy I called my brother. "I'm dying," I said.

"Go to the hospital right now, sister," he said.

"I can't move," I said. I didn't want to call the ambulance, so I told him to come and take me.

"I don't have my van right now," he said.

I told him it was okay.

"Go right now, sister," he said.

I found the strength to get up. I was so nauseous I could barely put my clothes on. I called a taxi to pick me up. I went to the ER doctors, and they said the same thing: nothing was wrong. No chemicals were detected in my body.

I dreaded going back home. That place was fucked up. The house started to get a little better; it was tolerable. Obviously, I was still getting attacked spiritually. I got the shit off but it must have come back on somehow. I was having eye pain. Bright lights hurt my eyes. So did the computer. I went to the eye doctor, and he found nothing wrong with my eyes. I was unable to complete my classwork online. I had to drop out of all my classes. My computer was completely off-limits.

I was having a string of bad luck. One thing after another, it just kept going. My health was bad, my sinuses were messed up, and my eyes were ruined. At one point my garbage can lid was swinging by itself. The oven timer went off, but I hadn't turned it on.

On top of that, I began to get roaches. I heard the man downstairs had them. They were huge too. I was so scared to go in the kitchen. One of the roaches was so fucking big it peeked its head from behind the wall. As soon as I pulled out the Raid can, that motherfucker ran. It was like the roach seen it before and knew what it did. The exterminators came many times; it was so hard to get rid of them. I had never had roaches in any of my apartments before.

On my way back to the store, I saw Judas, his girlfriend, and his friend sitting by the steps of my house. I walked right past them. I didn't say a word to them or even looked at them. I felt like they were ganging up on me. I heard them laughing as I walked away. What had I even done to them? It was still a mystery to me. I didn't want to be anywhere around them.

I contacted a man that specialized in hexes and curses. I found him on a root worker website. He did a reading on me. He said that Judas was trying to harm me, and I was in real danger. He said he was really evil and had done this to other people. He said he could help me, but it cost too much. I was running out of money.

Weeks later I walked to the mailbox to pick up my mail and I saw Judas standing on his balcony. "Hi," he said.

I just ignored him and kept walking.

"I said hi," he yelled.

It startled me. That wasn't the guy I used to hang out with. I would look at his Facebook sometimes and when I did, I would get attacked again. I didn't even know how that was possible. I completely blocked his page. I started losing a lot of weight as well. I could barely eat anything. I looked at my thin frame in the mirror. I felt like I was wasting away.

After speaking with another psychic, I knew it was time for me to go back to PA. I didn't want to go back home. I hated it there. I didn't have a job in Texas, and I was getting my ass kicked. If I stayed there, it was possible I could be killed. I had to leave and get away from Judas.

I put my furniture on Craigslist. I just bought that shit and now I had to sell it. I sold pretty much everything and gave the rest to a guy I met. All my friends and family wanted me to move back. My dad said I could stay with him until I got back on my feet. I was getting the fuck out of that place. I tried to get out of my lease, and they wouldn't let me so I just left and lost my section 8.

# Chapter 6:
# All Bitter No Sweet

I was actually happy to get back home. Everybody there seemed to be happy I was back as well. I wasn't too happy about moving back in with my dad, especially with his girlfriend and her daughters. I didn't really know them. It took me some time to adjust to that place. It was a small drug town. Everybody looked like zombies. The people there were missing teeth, and a lot of people were balding.

My dad's girlfriend name was Mouse. They called her Mouse because she was quiet and sneaky. She looked like a mouse too. You wouldn't even know she was in the house she was so quiet. She shoplifted for a living. She would walk out with a hand full of clothes and she would never get caught. She had not one tooth in her mouth and her hair was really thin. She was in her late thirties. She was one of the ugliest white women I had ever seen in person. I wondered what my dad saw in her. She came across as not being very smart, but it was probably because she smoked weed all day. When she smoked, she barely responded to anything. If I asked her a question she would just look at me.

It seemed like my dad was just using her and she pretty much did everything he said. She was a "yes bitch". She was all up his ass. She followed him around like a lost little puppy. I thought it was pathetic and I hoped I would never end up in a relationship like that. I knew he cheated on her a lot. I heard many stories, but I didn't understand why she put up with it.

My dad said she set my room up for me. My room was nice and neat. A new sheet set and comforter was laid down, and it was purple – my favorite color.

I know my dad was excited to have me closer to him. "Relax," he said. I needed to relax after what I had just gone through. It seemed like the curse had lifted and things were getting better.

My dad sold drugs so there were people in and out of the house. I hated that shit. He was good at it though and made a decent amount of money. My dad was a good businessman.

Mouse and her nieces got us tickets to go to this male strip show that was coming to town. At first, I really didn't want to go. I didn't like stuff like that. I mean I really didn't like anything, but strippers were too advanced for me. I did want to try something new though. I was always in hermit mode; I needed to let loose. The night of, we were all excited to go.

When we got there the place was full of women. I wanted to relax and have a good time. I started dancing my ass off. One of the guys from the show noticed me and came over to me. He told me to make sure I sat in the front.

It was time for the show to start and the first guy came out. He did a little routine and then he took all his clothes off. I mean everything, even his underwear. I had no idea they were going to be completely naked. I was shocked but pleasantly surprised. That guy had a nice sized penis too. He called me up to the stage and I was like, "Who me? Oh hell naw."

Then he stood there and waited for me. I was so nervous. I got up there and he flipped me around. He pulled my legs up and started grinding on me. I was so embarrassed because I knew I looked awkward. I was still a virgin. I didn't know how to thrust and move my body around. That shit was crazy and exciting at the same time. That was the most dick I had ever had in my life. *'Hey, I'll take it,'* I thought. The whole event was awesome. I got called up a few more times. It was definitely one of the most fun times I've ever had in my life. When we got home, we couldn't stop talking about it.

I kept hearing about this man who owned a barbershop in his home. I heard he was fine as hell. I doubted he was that attractive. I found most people to be unattractive, especially in that area. PA had some of the ugliest men. I usually wouldn't give a fuck what anybody looked like but because I was nosey as fuck, I just had to see who they were talking about.

My dad made an appointment to get his hair cut so I went along with him. Mouse's niece was downstairs visiting. She was pretty with long hair that went down her back. She looked nothing like Mouse or her daughters. She carried herself a little differently than her family. She had a sister who was complete trash. I didn't really like her. She was always in some bullshit and was a big-ass liar. She never took care of her kids. Mouse's niece needed a ride up the street. "Where y'all going?" she asked.

"We are going to Duke's. I gotta go get my haircut," my dad said.

"Ohh that's why you're going," she said. "You're going to go see Duke." Then she laughed.

I wasn't sure why she said it like that. She said it like I had a crush on him. I had never even seen him before. It wasn't like I had anything else to do. I did want to see what he looked like, but it wasn't that serious. We dropped her off and we got to Duke's house. I walked in and was pleasantly surprised. He was actually really attractive. He had a 90's R&B vibe but he also reminded me of Duke Ellington. He was definitely different from the other cats out there. He was in his early 40's, married with kids. He was a smooth talker. I tried not to stare while my dad got shaped up. I sat there quietly. He kept staring at me and asking me questions.

"She's trying to get her degree in social work," my dad said.

"Oh yeah?" he said. "Well let me know when you graduate. I can help you find a job." I could tell he was showing off. He was talking loudly and making sure he got my attention. My dad was all finished and we left.

A couple of weeks later, Mouse's daughter asked me if I wanted to go to church with them. I agreed to go because I needed some peace after what happened to me in Texas. We went to a Jehovah's Witness church. Mouse's daughter was dating a guy who was a Jehovah's Witness. We all drove down there together. I had never been to a church like that before, but I figured I'd try it out. We sat down in the seats right next to Duke. Duke was Mouse's daughter's boyfriend's stepdad. I had not been expecting him to be there. He greeted us with a smile. He looked at me and waved. I immediately put my head down. I started to freeze up and get tense. I thought about my hair. I didn't like how I did my hair that day and if I had known he would be there, I would have done it differently. I waited for the service to be over. It was boring as fuck.

Everyone got up and began talking to each other. I sat there waiting for Mouse's daughter to tell me we were leaving. I saw Duke talking to other people, but I could tell he couldn't wait to come talk to me. He didn't want to make it obvious. "Hey," he came over in a hurry.

"Hi," I said.

"It's nice that you could come join us."

I barely looked him in his eyes. I couldn't; he made me blush. I felt like a little girl who had a crush on an older man.

Souls, did you ever see the movie *Memoirs of a Geisha*? Remember when Sanyuri met that older man when she was a kid, and he became her love interest when she got older? He bought her that snow cone. Yep, that's how I felt at that moment. We were ready to leave, and Duke was the star of the show. He had a lot of personality. He was cracking jokes with me to make me laugh. The jokes were corny, but I laughed anyway.

When I got home, I masturbated to relieve all the sexual tension. I wondered if God would let me have sex with him. '*I doubt it*,' I thought. Mouse's daughter asked if I wanted to go to church again with them. "Sure," I said. This time, I was gonna dress up and look real nice. I had a cute black and white dress that I hardly wore. I never really went anywhere so I didn't care about clothes. I usually dressed really boring and comfortable. I wore black most of the time and not on purpose. I was just drawn to darker colors, I guess. I had a really cute weave ponytail that I only wore on special occasions.

We got to church, and we sat down next to Duke and his family. His wife sat right beside him. I didn't look at her very much. After service, his wife asked if I wanted to come over to their house for lunch. I didn't even know those people or her. I wondered why she would invite me to their house. I thought it was okay because Mouse's daughter knew them pretty well. I started talking to Duke and he was being his usual self. He was being really flirty and in front of his wife too. She just stood there and watched.

Another woman came in between us and tried to distract me. She pulled me away and asked me if I was thinking about joining the church. I honestly wasn't sure what I wanted to do. We all got into the car. "What do you want from Wendy's, Bran?" Duke asked.

Omg, he called me Bran. Only people who really knew me called me that. "I'm a vegetarian, so no meat," I said.

"Okay, I will get you a salad, then."

We got to their house, and I sat down next to Mouse's daughter.

"Here's your salad, Bran," Duke said.

"Thank you," I said.

He and his wife began to talk about some drama they were having with other people. After everyone ate, I stood in the kitchen and Duke stood by the basement door. He waved for me to come with him. I ran after him. I saw his wife just stare at me. We went into the basement where his barbershop was. He told me to sit in the chair. He trimmed my eyebrows for me. When he was done, he looked at me and smiled.

"How much is it?" I asked.

"It's free," he said.

I thanked him and then hopped out of the chair.

Duke's wife had asked Mouse's daughter if I wanted to do bible study classes with them. I agreed. I mean I wasn't doing anything else. The next day, we walked to their house which was right up the street. Mouse's daughter walked ahead of me. Duke was standing on the porch. "Where's Bran?" he asked.

"She's coming up the hill," she said.

I spoke to Duke as I was walking in. I could tell he had been waiting for me. We went into the living room and started the lessons. It was a pretty good session. The wife was very kind and knowledgeable. Duke kept walking past the living room. I honestly just wanted to see him. It was like an adrenaline rush but on the other hand, I had no idea what was going on. I'm not sure why I felt a connection to him. It was weird. It was weird that every time we were in the same room, it seemed like we were the only two people there. Duke walked by the living room again and we made eye contact. He looked at me with this creepy look. I started to feel a little uncomfortable. I thought, '*What am I doing here? I got to get out of this man's house.*' I was in no position to start anything romantic with this grown-ass man. I had no type of experience, sexual or relationship-wise. Plus, he was married. It was just in a flirty phase, but it felt like it would have continued to go further if I stuck around.

The following Sunday, I went to church with them again. This time I wore a short jean skirt and a white top. The top had a button missing so I used this rose pin I had to close it. I didn't really have any church clothes to wear, and it was summertime. I knew it wasn't church attire, but I wasn't a member, so I thought it was fine. When we got to church, I noticed people were looking at me and I started feeling uncomfortable. A man got on stage and started talking about the dress code and I knew they were talking about me. I can't recall everything he said, but I was so fuckin embarrassed. *'How dare these motherfuckers put me on blast like that,'* I thought.

When service was over, I was livid. My heart was pounding, I had never been more humiliated in my life. Duke's stepdaughter looked at me and said, "Are you ok? You look like you're about to cry." She said it with a half-smile. I knew she was trying to be a smart-ass. I didn't say a word. I was about to blackout from anger. It was about to go the fuck down in that church. I wanted to tell that stepdaughter bitch off so bad, *'No I'm not about to cry; I'm about to blow this church up with everybody in it.'* That's what I was thinking, and I was fuckin serious. I was in Carrie-mode.

Souls, remember the movie, *Carrie*? Yeah, shit was about to go down. I was hoping I could catch something on fire with my mind. I looked for Duke. When I saw him, he tried to run away. "Duke," I yelled. "They were talking about me, about the dress code."

"No, they weren't," he said.

I watched his wife and stepdaughter stare at us from afar. Then the stepdaughter snuck her way up on me and stood very close to me, I guess to hear what we were talking about.

"Come with me so we can talk," Duke said, and we went to a separate area. "Brandi, calm down," he said. He looked surprised that I was so angry. He promised they weren't talking about me, but I know damn well they were.

I left there still pissed off and was never going to return again. I was even mad at Mouse's daughter. "Well, I told you you had to wear certain clothes," she said.

"When? You never told me that," I said. She never said anything about the dress code. I knew it was church, but like I said, I wasn't a member. That was the end of that and any communication with that family. Mouse's daughter ended up telling me Duke was a big-ass player and he was always cheating on his wife. She said the wife found pictures of him and other women in his phone. I wasn't surprised.

After a few weeks, I became angry. I was getting tired of not being able to have a boyfriend or have sex. I was mad at Duke because after the church incident, I felt like he kicked me to the curb. The whole family did really, even Mouse's daughter. I didn't think I did anything wrong. I decided to do a love spell on him. I ordered a kit online. I was supposed to burn a candle each night for seven days.

On the last night, while I was burning the candle, Mouse's nieces asked me to come out. It was one of their birthdays. I put the candle out and got dressed. We went to some club. I started itching around my mouth.

The next morning, I woke up to find I had a rash under my nose and right above my top lip. It was nasty as fuck. I start freaking out. It looked like a herpes outbreak. I was still a virgin, but it can still get passed through skin contact from what I had read. I went to the ER to see where the fuck the rash came from. Even the doctor was backing away from me. She didn't want to come near me. At that time, I was taking an antibiotic for a sinus infection and thought maybe it was from that. The doctor said, "No, antibiotics don't cause that." I asked her if she thought it was from herpes. "Are you having sex?" she asked.

"No," I said.

"Did you kiss anyone?" she asked.

"No," I said.

She gave me a prescription for medication for herpes. I took the medicine, and it took about a week for the rash to go away. The love spell never worked. I never heard from that man again. I realized I made some errors when I did the spell, and I wasn't supposed to put the flame out in the candle. Also, I got tested for herpes and I was negative, so I think the rash was from the antibiotic.

My dad was friends with a guy from New York Aquarius. He was ugly as hell, but he dressed nice and was smart. He was into music and had his own radio station which I thought was cool. I never really paid him any attention but for some reason things started to change. He was married with kids. I remember talking to him at my dad's birthday party and his wife was looking at me all crazy. He would come over to bring Mouse some weed. He also made CDs and we would buy them often. I got used to him coming around and would talk for a while.

He came over one morning. I was still in my pajamas. I ran downstairs and gave him a hug. He instantly started humping me and moaned a little bit. I was confused. *'Why is he doing that?'* I thought. I stepped away from him. Then I hugged him again.

"What you up to," he said.

I said, "Nothing, just in my room."

He gave Mouse the weed and left. He came back a little later and I hollered down the steps asking him what his zodiac sign was. He said Leo. Great, we were both Leos. He was very similar to me. This made me feel connected to him. Everybody thought he was a clown, but I felt like I understood him. I mean he was loud and obnoxious, but I was too sometimes. I could tell people really didn't like him, but they didn't like me either.

My dad yelled, "Bran, go in your room," like I was a little-ass kid. I went in my room pissed. I waited for my dad to come up. "Don't let that big girl get ahold of you." He was referring to Aquarius's wife.

"Why? I didn't do anything," I said.

"I see you flirting with him," he said.

"I don't think I was flirting with him," I said.

"Yeah, and you always asking questions about him." Apparently, my dad was catching on to the connection.

We did have sexual energy towards each other, and it just kept increasing. I wanted to have sex with him so badly it was driving me crazy. I wondered where all this sexual energy was coming from. It had to be from him.

He came over one day with his brother-in-law. I was in the living room watching TV. He came up to me and asked me for a hug. I stood up on the couch and hugged him. I had a nightgown on, and he started rubbing on my legs and on my butt. He then started raising my gown up. I let go of him. I looked at his brother-in-law and he just stared at me. We then went to the kitchen and sat down. My dad came down and was getting something for him. My dad had his back turned to us.

Aquarius grabbed my hand and started rubbing it. My dad handed him his shit and he went upstairs. Aquarius started telling me about his radio station and how I should listen to it. At this point his brother-in-law went back to the car; he didn't say one word while he was in there. I felt the sexual tension. I was hoping he would just slide my panties off and have sex with me there in the kitchen. We started to lean in towards each other. I heard my dad coming back downstairs. We quickly backed away from each other.

"You still here?" my dad said to Aquarius. I could hear the annoyance in his voice.

He said, "Yeah, I was just showing her my radio station."

"Bran, when he leave, make sure he don't let the dog out the gate."

"Okay, Dad," I said.

Aquarius then got up to leave and I walked with him towards the door. He then turned around and leaned against the wall. I leaned in closer to him and then he kissed me. He kissed me like an insecure little boy. I didn't even know how to kiss. I had my first kiss in the 8th grade. I'd never been kissed after that. On his way out the door, he said he wanted to kiss me again. So, I leaned over and kissed him again. Then the dog got out. I came back in the house with a smile on my face. I was so happy. I looked in the mirror and I was glowing. I was surprised God let me kiss anyone.

My dad yelled down the steps, "How did the dog get out?"

"He just ran out," I said.

Aquarius would come over to get weed and to see me. He came over dressed up one night. He was about to go out to a party, and we were talking. He wanted to make out again, so he pulled me closer to him and started rubbing on my body. Then my dad came down the steps and I ran and sat on the couch. Aquarius quickly turned around and pretended to wait in the hallway. As he was leaving, he said something along the lines of, "You're twenty-seven years old and you're not acting like it."

Well shit. First of all, he was married. Second of all, my dad would have went off if he found out. I was trying to avoid any type of drama.

He called me the next day and referred to me as juicy booty and it pissed me off. I felt he was disrespecting me, so we stopped talking for a couple of days.

Then we started up again. I told him I was into witchcraft. He said he believed in that stuff but that his wife was into it too. "She has an altar and everything," he said.

"Wow," I said, "Maybe she can give me some tips." I was still fairly new.

He was having a get together at his home. I told him I wanted him to make me a CD and to bring it over. When he got to my house, he was drunk. I could smell it on his breath. It turned me all the way off. He handed me the CD and I started talking about how I was virgin. I was definitely considering letting him take my virginity.

"Wait a minute," he said, "Why are we talking about your sex life?" He seemed to be annoyed. He was acting more rudely than usual because of the alcohol, which was why I didn't like alcohol.

"I was trying to tell you I'm a virgin," I said.

"Can I take your virginity?" he said in low tone.

Right when he said that, my dad came galloping down the steps.

"Why are you still here?" he said to Aquarius. He said it really rudely that time.

Aquarius said, "Because I was talking to her." His tone was rude back and I didn't want no part of that shit.

My dad yelled, "I don't like this shit," and threw both of his arms down. He stomped upstairs. "And call next time before you come over," said my dad.

Aquarius got very angry, and they began to argue. That was exactly what I wanted to avoid. My dad made it seem like he was mad because he didn't call when he came over when really, he didn't want me to talk to him. My dad was straight-up cock blocking. Aquarius said, "I don't have to come over here and buy weed."

My dad came down the steps and they were in each other's faces. I was so scared. I didn't know what to do. I was so worried for Aquarius because I didn't want him to get knocked the fuck out. It was about to be curtains for his ass.

My dad was a good fighter, he was known to be. I heard stories from when he was younger, when he would whoop people's asses. He never fought in front of me though. I would hear him arguing with people but that's it. When I was a kid, I would watch him about to fuck somebody up, but then he would look at me and calm down. It used to scare me when he got into it with people. Even as an adult he was careful. I still would hear about him fighting at a bar or something. He broke his finger once and tried to lie and say the air conditioner fell on it. I wasn't falling for the shit. He ended up telling me he knocked somebody out. Then one time there was dry blood on the ceiling. Mouse told me he beat somebody up in the kitchen and there was blood everywhere. He was also very protective of me. He would be ready to fight any man or woman over me. That's just the kind of dad he was.

Maybe he thought he was protecting me from Aquarius. He probably knew what kind of guy he was. As they were both arguing in each other's faces, I grabbed my dad's arm. "What," he shouted. I shook my head no. They continued to argue, and my dad told Aquarius to leave.

Aquarius was not trying to leave. He was just digging a hole for himself. He finally left untouched and quite honestly, I was surprised. I felt so bad about the situation, so I called Aquarius to apologize for what happened. You could tell he was still upset about it. He stopped coming over at after that. Then he and I stopped talking. Whelp, there went my chance of getting some dick.

I got a job at a call center for a phone company. It was in a town nearby. My dad let me drive his car. It was full-time and paid pretty good. I had to go through a month of training first. I was nervous when I first got there. I was quiet and didn't bother anyone. I ended up making friends with a guy who didn't live too far from me. Then after just a week, people started dropping out of training for odd reasons. One guy had kidney stones, so he left. This one girl's dad died. Each week we were losing people due to a health issue or a death. This one guy had two deaths in his family while he was there. It was very concerning to me. I was trying to figure out what the hell was going on. They were dropping like flies; each week something new came up.

I had a dream about a guy in my training class. I never really interacted with him. I dreamed he was buying carpet at a store. I told him about it, and he said he was getting new carpet put in his home. We started to get closer after that. He also noticed the bizarre things that were happening to the people who were in our class. We wondered who was next. After getting to know everyone, I found out most of them could see number sequences like I did. Everyone seemed to be strange like I was. I felt like I was in some time warp or a portal.

We started out with seventeen of us and at the end of the class, there were only eight. I was one of the eight. We survived whatever that was. Soon it was time for us to go out on the floor. Training was over. I did pretty well at that job, but it became boring. Talking on the phone for  hours didn't fit me. I only lasted there for two months.

I stopped working so I was home a lot more. I didn't like my dad and his girlfriend's way of life. I felt like they were okay doing nothing with their life. They definitely didn't resonate with me. I felt like I was stuck. It was very depressing.

I spent most of my time in my room. I stayed away from all that weed smoke and drinking they had going on. Meanwhile, I was getting my ass whooped by demons. I would constantly stare at the walls and ceiling and see demonic faces. I took a picture of myself, and I saw a dark figure over my face that looked like a demon[2].

I went to the library often. It was peaceful and I loved books. I didn't really like reading books, but I liked books because they held information. I liked old, used books: the ones with dust all over them. This town had a very little library with a nice selection. I would select some books and just sit down and look though them. I was mostly drawn to the metaphysical section. I read through some of the Silvia Browne books. I also read some books about aliens. This stuff intrigued me and made me happy. It also gave me a place to go when I was pretending to go to work. I never told my dad I quit. I just told him they cut my hours.

I came across a book on how to read tarot cards. When I went to check it out, the clerk went to the back and grabbed a deck of tarot cards. The book came with them. It was a used deck. I remembered what had happened the last time I had them. I was so attracted to these cards for some reason. I figured if the cards made me feel uncomfortable, I could just bring them back.

I left the library and was on my way to get my hair and nails done. On my way there, I began to feel very tired for some reason. I kept hearing that song *I Only Have Eyes For You*: the song I heard when I got my first tarot deck in California. While I was at the nail shop, I wanted to get a design on my toes. I showed the girl a picture of the Egyptian eye of Horus. I just wanted it on one toe at first but decided to get it on both.

She did a very good job, but the eyes looked weird to me. I immediately started thinking of that song again. It was like the song was trying to tell me some spirits were watching me, and they actually influenced me to get these eyes on my toes. I thought, *'This is weird as fuck.'* Then it reminded me of the dream I had not too long ago about King Tut. I remember seeing him and then the dream zoomed up on his eye and then his eye was inside a triangle.

I then went to my hair appointment. I noticed while I was getting my hair done, I saw a Sponge Bob cap with these big-ass eyes on it. *'There go those eyes again,'* I thought. By the time I got home, I was completely exhausted. I realized the cards were draining my energy.

Souls, you're not supposed to use a deck of cards that belonged to anyone else or cards that have been used. I mean this deck was from the library, so no telling how many people used them and mishandled them.

Later that day, I felt something on my back hanging on to me, just like when I was in Texas and I had looked at that website. *'Awwwww shit, I got a demon on me.'* I hurried to grab a Bible and put it right next to the cards. I noticed the energies calmed down. I tried to cleanse the cards by putting them in a container of salt, but I still felt uneasy. I knew I had to get rid of them. It was too late to take them back then, so I went to bed.

As soon as I woke up, I was out the door. I dropped those cards off so fast. I wanted to leave a note on them that said, 'Do not lend these cards out.' I was just glad they were away from me. Maybe cards weren't for me. I could not tolerate the energies coming from them.

It was my dad's birthday, and I was throwing him a surprise party. I did it a couple of weeks before his actual birthday so he wouldn't suspect anything. I got up early and started cooking. I went out to the stores and grabbed a few things. Mouse helped as well. When I got home, I decorated, and my dad came downstairs looking around. "What's going on?" I told him it was a party for one of the kids. He came in the kitchen and noticed I made taco dip. "Taco dip for a kid's party?" he asked. I felt like he was starting to catch on, but I had to finish getting things set up.

Around 3pm, I told him to get dressed. "For what?" he said.

"Just get dressed," I said. I had been holding in the secret for a while. I usually told my dad everything, so it was very hard to do. I waited for everyone to arrive. I was proud of myself. I invited everyone, did all the decorations, cooked some of the food, bought some food, and I got him a cake made with a glass of beer on it from Dairy Queen. We had a lot of fun. My dad was so happy. We took pictures and people who weren't even invited came. The guests mostly drank and danced to music. I socialized as much as I could. It was definitely a time to remember.

The next morning, I went downstairs and there was a white balloon in the corner of the wall. I went into the kitchen, and I heard a noise so I turned around and the same white balloon was behind me at eye level. I quickly backed the fuck up. I wondered how the balloon got down there so fast. A part of me wanted to ask, '*Is this motherfucka following me*?' I went back upstairs and couldn't go back to sleep. I went back downstairs a few more times and noticed the white balloon had floated upstairs in the hallway but when though? The last time I had seen it, it was still downstairs. Everyone in the house was asleep. I laid back down in my bed. I was laying facing the wall. I then heard a tiny noise. I slowly turned my head around like an actor would in any suspense or horror scene. I saw that same damn balloon on the floor. My eyes became so big. "What the fuck?" I said out loud. The balloon was placed on the ground as if someone put it there. Something was holding the ribbon down so it would stay in place. Somebody put that balloon in my room, and it wasn't me. That balloon did not float up there on its own. I got up and touched it. It was just a normal balloon, nothing different about it.

After everything that happened, my eyes finally had gotten better and went back to normal, but then they messed up again. I'm not sure why; maybe because of the fumes from cleaning products. I wanted my eyes to be okay before I started my new job at the resort. I went to a job fair and got hired on the spot. I was going to be on the computer all day making reservations. I went to see a specialist. He was a younger guy, and I could tell he wasn't sure what he was doing. He didn't see anything wrong with my eyes. He gave me some antibiotic eye drops. They didn't work.

When I started my job, I was in so much pain on the computer. It was so hard and painful to keep going. The resort was beautiful, and I liked my position, but I had to quit after a week. I couldn't take it anymore.

After I took the antibiotic drops, my eyes were permanently fucked up. They never went back to normal after that. I wanted to sue those motherfuckers. I had to sit in my room with no lights on. Even the glare from the TV would hurt sometimes and the glare from the windows. I had to get dark curtains to shut the natural light out. The sunlight was horrible. I always had to have sunglasses on. I was constantly in pain. I couldn't use the computer at all at that point. The pain would get so bad that I would get nauseous and dizzy. The only thing I could do was lay down and close my eyes. No medicine would work for me.

Then to top it off, my sinuses were also ruined from the incident in Texas. I started having really bad sinus infections that made me vomit. I had to get an antibiotic from the doctor and the first one they gave me made me vomit even more. It was a mess. I laid face down on the floor after vomiting. It was the only thing that would help with the uneasiness in my stomach. The dog came in to check on me because he knew I was super sick. He lay right beside me. Then my dad came to check on me. "Bran," he said. I could barely talk. "I'm just checking on you," he said.

A few weeks later I got a job at a daycare. I had to work where I didn't have to be on a computer all day. I watched a group of two-year-olds. I really loved kids, but working at a daycare drained my energy. I was so bored and unfulfilled. I didn't have a choice at that point. It was going well until I saw a worker pull a little girl by her hair. I was feeding the kids lunch and I looked out the door. My coworker wanted one of the children to get to the back of the line and she wouldn't move. So she grabbed the girl by her braid and pulled her to the back of the line. I was devastated. What did I just see? I put the kids down for nap time and I started to cry. I had to tell someone. This was child abuse. I told my supervisor and then I reported the woman to CPS. I felt like it was the right thing to do. After that, shit got weird at work. I felt like everybody was against me. I knew it was time for me to leave. I didn't stay long at any job, and I was getting restless.

For some reason, I got the urge to be a nun. I felt very pure and holy all the time. Even though I was into tarot cards and magic, I still loved Jesus. I also found a nunnery right up the street from me. I had no idea it was there.

It was beautiful. I had never seen anything like it. In fact, I was so amazed, it felt like home to me. It was so peaceful. The place was huge. The landscape and the statues were all amazing. This was it! This was my life's calling: to be a nun. I contacted them and tried to get in, but they never responded to me. The area I lived in had mostly white people in it. Maybe it was because I was black. Have you ever seen a black nun before? I never have in person. The only one I'd seen was on the movie *Sister Act*.

I also applied to a nunnery in California. I had a conversation with one of the women there. "Why do you want to be a nun?" she asked.

"Because I love God, and I feel like that's what I'm supposed to do." I told her how old I was, and it seemed she felt I was too old to be a nun. "You know, in this day and age, people don't want to be a nun anymore." I felt like I wasn't doing anything else with my life, so maybe that was the direction I should go. But they never got back to me either.

I got a reading by a psychic who lived close to my area. She told me I was a nun in my past life. It all started to make sense. That's why I was a virgin. That's why I was so religious growing up. That's why I stayed in the house most of time, and wasn't around many people. "You're not still wearing black all the time are you?" she asked.

"Yes, I am."

"You can stop wearing black now. You're not a nun anymore. It's okay to have sex." When she said that I was relieved, and I wanted to cry at the same time. I knew it was okay to have sex but just hearing that from her made it seem like I was given permission. It was like a child who was on punishment and the parents gave permission to go outside and play. I wanted to have sex, but I wasn't meeting anybody who wanted a relationship with me. That's what I really wanted. I wanted to get married.

I told the psychic about me trying to be a nun in this life. She said, "You already were a nun in your past life. You can't be one in this life." She told me I was going to read cards like she was doing. "It will be like a side business," she said.

"I tried to read them, but they are not resonating with me. Spirits attach themselves to me," I said.

"It's not your time to read yet," she said. She also told me this was my last life on Earth. I didn't even ask her that. I knew it. I had known it for a long time. There was no way in hell I was coming back to Earth. She told me this was her last life here as well. She was a very accurate reader.

I started having problems with Mouse. She really irritated the fuck out of me. For one, she did nothing during the day but smoke weed and watch TV. She worked all weekend and was home Monday through Friday. The people in that neighborhood had no drive. They sat around and did drugs. That was too much of a low vibration for me to the point it started making me sick.

Mouse's older daughter didn't do drugs. She pretty much had her shit together. Her youngest daughter was a piece of shit. Well Mouse was a piece of shit. They would smoke weed together all the time. The daughter was a thief too. She would steal regularly, even from the house, and they all knew about it. I was confused. Why the fuck was she allowed to keep coming to the house? She never stole anything of mine, but I also had a lock on my door. I wasn't with that shit.

Mouse would smoke nonstop all day. It didn't bother me at first, but it started to mess with my sinuses. Everything bothered my sinuses, really, but the weed was fucking horrible. Since she smoked it all day, I became allergic to it. I mean I already had seasonal allergies, and weed is a plant. My nose would get all stuffed up and my eyes would feel swollen. I complained all the time. *'Like damn can we breathe regular air,'* I thought. I understood it was her house, but this was bullshit. The weed she smoked was strong; it would burn my nose. I started putting a towel under my door to keep the smoke out of my room. I tried using a fan to blow the smell away as well.

My dad would always get mad at her because she would spend all her money on weed. She would get her check from work, pay her bills and then be broke until next pay. She was definitely addicted. She would have to borrow money off my dad until next pay. I felt like he was dumb for doing that. He had his own addiction. He loved him some beer. He drank beer every single night. I knew to stay away from him when he was drinking. He was the type to start arguments and shit. He would wake people up in the middle of the night to start drama. He didn't do that to me at first but then he started to. So I would lock my door. I never liked alcohol. I couldn't tolerate it; it made me feel sick. I didn't like being around alcoholics or drug addicts because of their behavior.

Mouse always sat in the living room on the couch. She always looked out of touch with reality, which bothered me. I wanted to watch TV sometimes in the living room. If she wasn't home, I would go down and watch TV. She would be okay with it sometimes, but other times she would whine to my dad about it. Yes, I was being petty, but so was she. I didn't want to be in my room all the time and I didn't want to sit down there with her either. Especially with all that fuckin smoke. One day my dad kicked me out of the living room so she could watch TV. That pissed me the fuck off. So one day I loosened one of the chords on the cable box and she could not figure out why the TV wouldn't come on. They assumed I did something, but I didn't give a fuck. I was tired of fighting over the living room.

I bought some stinky-ass spray online to spray in the house. If I had to smell weed all day, they were gonna smell shit all day. I thought it was only fair. I sprayed it in the bathroom and in the kitchen where she was. Then I would spray some down the vents. I could barely tolerate the smell.

Mouse would tell on me to my dad. Like what the fuck was he going to do? I was an adult. I was tired of her bullshit. She tried to act like she was innocent. I wanted to fight her so many times, but I was worried my dad would kick me out. I didn't really think my dad would kick me out, but this was her house too, so I wasn't sure.

One time I heard Mouse talking shit behind my back, so I confronted her. I didn't care if I got kicked out at that point. She told me I thought I was better than everybody. I didn't think that. I just had goals and nobody over there did. "So I think I'm better because I want to go to college?"

As we were arguing my dad came out of the bathroom and said, "She's going back with her mom." He took her side.

I stomped up the stairs and went to my room. He started threatening for me to leave. He claimed when I came that all this drama started but there was drama before I got there.

I was still pretty new to spell work, but I decided to do a spell on Mouse to get her to leave the house. I knew I would feel much better when she was gone. I did a spell to remove her from my life.

The next day I went to Walmart and as I was parking the car, I looked down for a second and two cars crashed in front of me. Like how do two cars crash head on in a parking lot? One of the women asked me if I saw the accident but I didn't. I was looking at my phone. I knew that spell had thrown the energy off.

Later that day, Mouse was complaining about her back hurting. She said, "I gotta sleep with one eye open." I had no idea what she was talking about. I had forgotten all about the spell I did. I then found a spell to make someone move. I sprinkled the mixture in her slippers – no one could see anything. A couple of days later she stopped wearing them. Then a week later, Mouse left the house without saying why. My dad said she just packed her stuff and left. I was so happy she was gone. The spell had worked, but then the bitch came back.

# Chapter 7:
# College Woes

I was waiting patiently to get a decision in the mail. I wasn't that worried, but I knew I had to get the fuck out of my dad's house. The letter finally came: I got accepted. It was definitely a relief. I was gonna be staying on campus in the dorms. Hey, that was better than living with my dad or my mom. I really didn't want to go back to college, but I didn't have a choice; I needed somewhere to live. I was excited because this was a four-year college, a real university. I never thought I would actually go to a university.

I decided to go stay with my mom the night before I moved in. My dad was acting funny, and I didn't want him taking me up there. I asked one of my cousins to drive me and help me move in. My mom seemed like she could care less what I was doing. She wasn't a big fan of me doing anything positive. She was negative about everything. I think she was secretly jealous that I was going to college. She would say negative shit like, "You been in school how many years?" or, "You been in school a long time."

"So what?" I would tell her. "At least I kept going." I didn't have much further to go. I might as well go ahead and complete my degree so I could get a real job. I was tired of living with other people. I needed to support myself.

I wanted to get baptized before I started school. I wanted to start a whole new life and I was hoping that I would stop getting attacked by demons. I didn't want to take that shit to school with me. So I went to my old church. I loved that church and loved the pastor. He was the best pastor I ever came across. He was really good. He was well known from all over. He was a tiny man with a strong voice. I used to have a crush on him when I was younger. I probably still did; he was that powerful.

I went to Sunday service. I asked one of the church members if I could talk to the pastor. That church was big, so I had to go through some people to talk to him. He was kind of like a celebrity. "What do you need to talk to him about?" they asked.

"I want to get baptized before I start college." They sent me to talk to a woman who was in charge of scheduling the baptisms. "Why do you want to get baptized?" she asked.

"I'm being attacked by demons, and I'm about to start school," I said.

She looked at me in a strange way. I told her how everything started in Texas with Judas. "Do you still speak to him?" she asked.

I said, "No." This woman seemed to be against me getting baptized. She tried to talk me out of doing it, but I was very determined. She kept talking and I zoned her out and saw the pastor. I got up and the woman said, "Where are you going?"

I said, "I'll be right back."

She said, "No, don't go over there."

I went over there anyway; fuck that lady. I sat right by the pastor and told him what was going on. I noticed the lady got up and sat closer to us with her ear turned our way so she could listen to our conversation. I looked in her direction with a frown on my face. She looked strange and unhuman-like to me. The pastor had grey and white hair and it looked so nice on him. I had never gotten this close to him. I always wanted to talk to him; I even pictured being in choir. I also thought about having sex with him, but I felt bad because it was wrong to do that. He was a married man.

I told him I had psychic dreams. He then grabbed his bible then started reading. He read the part that said psychics were evil and their gift was not from God. I tried to explain more to him, but he was like, "I gotta go." He said, "Get this woman baptized before she goes to school."

The men of the church agreed. They said I would receive a call about the day they were going to do it. As I was leaving, the lady that was against me getting baptized said, "You're not getting baptized."

I turned around and looked at her like, '*Bitch, who the fuck do you think you're talking to.*' I most certainly didn't say that, but I thought it. I had a smart-ass mouth, and I would cuss anybody the fuck out. I didn't give a fuck, but because I really wanted to get baptized, I just looked at her.

"Not here, you're not," she said.

I left the church because I didn't want to go off on that hoe. As I was leaving, I wondered why the lady didn't want me to get baptized. I've never heard of no shit like that. Then I realized that lady was a demon.

Souls, that's the first time I witnessed a demon in a church. Days passed and I didn't get a call from them. So I went the fuck back up there. This was not a game, folks. All the doors were locked, and nobody was answering the phone. I went around to the side and saw a cracked door open and slid in. I saw a woman in her office and told her about the situation. She sent me into another room, and I waited. Two men came in and started talking to me. I told them why I was there. "I know exactly what you're talking about," one of the men said. They understood everything I was saying. They believed me. "Us talking to you was meant to be. We weren't even supposed to be here today." One of them asked me how old I was.

"I'm twenty-nine, sir," I said.

They both looked at each other. "You are a very special person. God's gotta have something planned for you with you looking so young like that and being the age you are," he said.

I always looked younger than my age. I worried that I had some kind of disorder or something. I asked my dad once if there was something wrong with me. I would look at my classmates and wonder why I wasn't aging like them. It started to turn into an insecurity because I wasn't understanding why I wasn't aging. Everyone said it was a good thing, but I didn't see it that way. It made me stand out, and people didn't respect me. They thought I was a kid, so they would talk smart to me or overlook look me. Nobody took me seriously. I did use it to my advantage sometimes to get away with shit or act like I didn't know anything.

The men told me to go upstairs to meet with another guy. He was nice and welcoming. He told me he and the pastor had a conversation about me and they decided I wasn't ready to get baptized.

"What?" I said. Since when did churches deny people to get baptized? I knew that demon bitch convinced the pastor to change his mind.

"We think you should take classes first," he said.

"I don't have time. I'm going to school."

He said the demon lady said she already called me to let me know. I said, "No, she didn't." That old-ass bitch lied. I left that church very disappointed. I texted that demon lady and asked her why she lied and told them she contacted me. I also let her know that I was gonna get baptized regardless and she couldn't stop me. I wanted to cry. Those demons were blocking me from getting baptized and I would have to go to school with whatever shit I had on me.

A couple of days later, I was sleeping on the couch and I had a dream I was out in the woods and saw all these kids running. They were yelling, "Wolf-man!" Then I saw a man with a wolf head. All the kids were scared of him so I ran in a house and told all the kids to come inside. I woke up and was terrified. I felt like in the dream he was trying to rape the children. I then went back to sleep and had another dream. I dreamed I was sitting in the living room on the couch and a psychic medium was sitting across from me. She looked very scary. She said, "It's hot as Hell," and she spelled the word hell out. Her voice then turned demonic and I told her, "You're scaring me," and then I woke up. I felt like demons didn't want me to start college. I also looked up who the wolf-man was, and he was a man who killed children back in the day. Demons started harassing me in my dreams after that.

My cousin came early to pick me up. We drove all the way to my dad's house so I could get my stuff. I got all my things and happily left. My dad acted like he was glad I was leaving, but I knew that was a front.

I moved into my dorm and was ready to meet my roommate. I hoped that we would get along and that she wasn't a bitch. She came in very friendly but very shy. She had long, flowing hair and wore glasses. "Hi," she said.

"Hi," I responded.

She came in with her whole family. This was her second semester. She wanted to do forensic work. We had the same interests. She liked weird, creepy shit like me. We got along really well. She was the perfect roommate. I got lucky.

The college I went to was small and I liked that. It was easy for me to get around. I really liked my classes. Even though I was twenty-nine, I still looked young so I blended in. I was nervous to tell my roommate my age, but I told her. She stared at me, and her eyes got so big. "Wow," she said. "You look so young." She said she was cool with it, and she hung with older people anyway.

I had a dream I was sleeping in my bed like I was in real life and a woman with long red hair came into my room and stood over me. She said if I didn't protect myself, the devil was going to get me and then she left my room. "Don't let him win," she said.

I was having up to six dreams a night. I would have headaches when I woke up. They were all nightmares. I went to a museum in Washington DC on a college trip and bought an authentic dream catcher. I put it over my bed, but I couldn't go to sleep. It felt like there was pressure on my head, like the dreams were fighting against it. I felt weird so I took the dream catcher down. I needed to do something about these dreams. It was not normal, and they were terrifying.

At that point, I was afraid to go to sleep. I dreaded nighttime. I slept with the TV on so that when I would wake up from a dream there was some light on. I told my roommate about it, and she said she used to have nightmares too. She said Freddy Cougar kept harassing her and then finally one day she stood up to him. She said she cussed him the fuck out, like, "Look, you're not going to keep harassing me," and she said, "Oh, he didn't like that very much."

I was getting harassed every night and I was scared as shit.

My eyes were still a problem. I tried to sign up with the disabilities office they had on campus, but they needed a letter from a doctor. I was having problems with lighting in the classrooms. I was afraid I was going to have to drop out of school. I made an appointment to see another eye care specialist. I was hoping somebody could find out what was wrong with my eyes. I had seen several eye doctors.

I waited patiently in the waiting room. A man came out and said to me, "Dr. Whitman is a good doctor. If you have him, he's a good doctor."

That was my doctor, and I took that as a sign that he could help me. They had the intern students look at my eyes first. They didn't see anything wrong. They said my eyes looked healthy and they didn't understand why I was having problems. Dr. Whitman came in and took a look. "Oh, you have photophobia. My wife has it, that's how I know. Guys, next time you find something neat like this come get me," he said to the interns.

'Well, I wouldn't consider this cool,' I thought. "Photophobia," I said.

"Yes, it's when your eyes are sensitive to light. There is no cure for it."

"Oh no," I said.

"I can give you some eye drops to help with the pain. We also have these rose-colored glasses that help with the light." It was a rare disorder. I was so relieved that I finally got a diagnosis: idiopathic photophobia. Idiopathic means the cause is unknown.

I knew what caused it. It was from that house cleansing I was trying to do in Texas. The ammonia I sprayed on the wall did it, even though it went back to normal after that. Those eye drops the other eye doctor gave me made it permanent. In a spiritual sense, demons did that to my eyes to attack me.

I ordered my glasses and got my eye drops. I got a note to give to the disabilities office. The disabilities office was really helpful. They made accommodations for me. I took all my tests in a separate room instead of on the computer. I had a separate room in the library to use. They gave me extended time to get my work done. I was able to use the computer but for a short period of time. When I did use the computer, it was in a room with the lights out. The rose-colored glasses worked at first but then they stopped working for some reason. The eye drops helped but they were just a band-aid for my eyes.

I was able to get all my work done and still continue college. I had been really worried I wouldn't be able to continue. "Somebody must really want you to stay in school," a woman said.

I knew it was God. He was definitely helping me. I met a woman who worked in the disabilities office who wanted to change the settings on my computer. She wanted the screen to be more comfortable for me. It took her two seconds, and she changed the background of the screen to black and the words became purple. "Here try this," she said.

"Omg!" I said. "I'm not having any pain at all." That continued to work for me. I was able to tolerate the computer. It was definitely a blessing. I had to wear sunglasses every time I went outside, and a black cap to block the light. As I left from school, I heard a guy say, "Is it sunny out here?"

It was a very gloomy day, and he was teasing me for wearing

sunglasses. I didn't think that shit was funny. People started to refer to me as the girl with the sunglasses. I sat in class with my sunglasses too. It was tough. Thank God most classrooms had two different light settings. I would ask the teachers to put the lights on the lowest level. I would sit in the corners of the rooms away from the light fixtures.

I was looking at other colleges and I found this one college had one of the best social work programs in the country. I felt like if I was going to go to a university, I needed to go to the best one. I filled out the application and turned everything in they required. I was so impatient and I kept calling to see what the results were. It seemed like it took forever. I was in my dorm room and my dad called me. "I got the letter from that school."

"What does it say, Papa?"

"You better tell your roommate she gotta find another roomate."

"I got in?"

"Yep!"

"Yessss," I said. I couldn't fucking believe it. That school was hard to get into – especially the social work program. I thought maybe whatever evil that had been on me was gone. It felt like I was having good luck for a change.

When the semester was over, my dad helped me move out and back home with him. I had to find somewhere to live that was closer to my new college. The school was way more expensive, and, with all my loans, I couldn't afford to stay in the dorms. I started looking for apartments in that area. I found a girl online who needed a roommate. I didn't really want a roommate, but I was running out of options. It was much cheaper too.

The house was near campus. I was lucky to find something that close. It was a very old building and very historic looking. I got a U-Haul and moved all my stuff in by myself. Nobody wanted to help me move because I moved around so much. The shit was heavy. I was so embarrassed moving my bed by myself, but it had to be done. My roommate was nice. She was very busy and never really home. We went to Starbucks together to get some studying done.

I started class at my new college. I was so excited; it was a fresh new start. It was a serious school so I had to make sure I was on top of shit. The school was huge. There were a lot more people than at my last school. It kind of made me uncomfortable. I wasn't used to big-ass classrooms with 100 people in them. The good thing about that school was that the rooms were a lot bigger, so I didn't have many problems with lighting. The workload was a lot. We had to read a lot of books and do so many assignments. I wasn't used to that. I tried to keep up as much as could. I was kind of lazy when it came to school. I was used to not having to study and still get passing grades. Not there; I couldn't slack at all and they didn't give a damn about my eye disorder. Everything was so fast paced.

I noticed people started acting funny toward me. I was cool with some of my classmates but some of them were very unfriendly. I understood I was a black woman at a school where I was a minority. In one of my classes, we had to partner up. I hated group work. I liked working by myself. Plus, nobody ever wanted to partner up with me. I was always the person without a partner. I didn't know why – I was always really quiet and barely said anything. I would be lying if I said it didn't hurt my feelings, but there was nothing I could do about it.

Once again, I was without a partner. There was this guy that was in the bathroom, so he missed the part about having a partner. "Brandi doesn't have a partner," the teacher said. "You can work with her." I stayed in my seat and continued to work by myself.

I heard the guy talking to another classmate. "Who is your partner?" she said to him.

In a sad, unwanted tone I heard him say, "I have to work with *her*." Then he put his head down.

"Who?" she said.

"Her," and then he gestured his head towards me.

I immediately got very angry. I thought me and him were cool. He was in some of my other classes. I never had a problem with him. I went up to him and said, "If you don't want to be my partner, that's fine."

He tried to act like there was no problem, but I knew there was. I was so upset I could barely contain myself. I sat down in my seat to calm down. He came over to me and said, "I don't have a problem with you. Let's just get started on the assignment."

"No," I yelled. I began to grow even angrier. I wanted to scream and blow his fucking head off. *'How dare this bitch,'* I thought.

He asked me to come out in the hallway to talk to him.

I stormed out of the room. I was on the verge of crying but not from sadness; it was because of rejection. "What's the problem?" he asked.

"You act like you don't want to work with me."

"I never said that," he said.

"You got an attitude when you were talking to your friend like you didn't want to."

"I do want to work with you," he said.

I felt a little bad for going off on him, but he was lying. "I'm working by myself," I yelled.

"Okay," he said.

I walked back into the room and told the teacher I was working by myself, and she was okay with that.

Another time I was in class and a guy was looking for somewhere to sit. The class was full but there was one seat next to me. I told him he could sit there. He looked at me and said no with attitude like he was insulted that I even recommended he sit by me. Then there was the time a guy in my class dropped something and I picked it up and gave it to him and he looked at me with disgust.

There was definitely some weird shit going on. I knew I had to be getting attacked. Whatever curse that was put on me in Texas never came off. It had to be making people not like me. It was bad enough I already had issues with people, but this made it worse. I felt like I was out there walking around with spiritual shit on me, and I didn't know how to get it off.

See, that's why I needed to get baptized. I needed to find another church quickly.

I was at home sitting on my bed, and I saw a flag with a skull and cross bones on it across the street from me. I didn't really pay any attention to it. I do remember when I had a dream while I was in Texas about the skull and cross bones on a card.

Three days later, shit hit the fan and things blew the fuck up. Me and my roommate started not getting along. I'm not sure how it started. She was paying for the cable in the living room. She decided to turn it off because she was upset with me, and I didn't care because I barely watched it. She kept doing little shit to pick on me. Since I was petty, I picked back. I was the master at getting people back. I did not like to get fucked with. We went back and forth with each other.

Then things started to escalate. I texted her and asked her a question about the house and she got smart with me. She then went on to say that she is never home because she has a lot of friends, as if to insinuate she had more friends than me. So what? I was almost thirty years old. I said, "Oh I thought you weren't home a lot because you were out sucking those football players' dicks." I could tell I pissed her off. The conversation went on, so I told her I was going to get a ghost to haunt her and she sent me articles about having a mental disorder. I was dead-ass serious too. She thought sending me mental health articles made me feel some type of way but nope. She tried to act like she didn't believe in ghosts, but I know she did.

I was in class, and she texted me talking about how she went into my room and took the lamp out. I was fuckin livid. I did not like people going in my room without permission. She crossed the line. I told my teacher I had to leave, and I stormed out of class. All I kept thinking was '*I'm probably going to go to jail*,' and I was okay with that. That bitch was testing my gangsta. I already decided in my head that I was going to spit on her. I didn't give a fuck anymore.

I called my mom yelling and told her what happened. She started yelling too. She was the wrong person to call. "Don't get yourself in trouble," she said. I hung up on her like I always did when she started to irritate me. When I got home, I slammed the front door and headed to my room to put my books down. I angrily headed to her bedroom and kicked the door open. I went off on her. I asked why the fuck she was in my room.

She said, "I just went in there to get my lamp."

It wasn't even her lamp. It came with the room. Technically, it was mine because I was renting it. I knew she was doing it to piss me off. I told her we already had this conversation about going into each other's rooms and respecting each other's boundaries. I didn't have a lock on my door so I couldn't lock it. She stood there while I yelled in her face and she acted like it didn't phase her. While I was yelling, I was collecting saliva in my mouth. I finally built up enough and spit right on the bitch's forehead.

She started talking shit and she tried to outsmart me by saying stuff to piss me off while she was calling the police. I didn't know she had called them until they pulled up. I saw them park right in front of the house. I panicked so I quickly destroyed my room. I threw stuff and tossed garbage everywhere to make it look like she tore my room up. The police came in and she still had the spit on her face. She never wiped it off. They were like, "She's saying you spit on her."

I was like, "No I didn't."

They said, "Well she had spit on her face."

I was like, "That's not my problem." I told them she came in my room and messed it up and money was missing. I felt like I had to make some shit up to get out of trouble. The police said there was no proof that she came into my room and took any money. I said, "Well there is no proof I spit on her."

Then he said, "She said you were trying to scare her, talking about how you were gonna get a ghost to haunt her."

I started laughing. "I was just playing with her." I most certainly wasn't. I was going to do it.

The officer said, "Stop doing that, you're scaring her."

I thought, '*How the fuck you gonna tell the police on me about ghosts like they gonna do something about it?*'

They said she didn't want to press charges and left.

Yeah, I bet she didn't because she started the shit. Things calmed down a bit after that. My roommate tried to get the landlord to get me to move but he said that it was on us. He didn't want to get involved. He just wanted the rent money. I offered to pay for next month's rent. "No," she said and started shaking her head.

I really didn't have anywhere else to go and I had just started school. I was out of luck. I had only been there for three months, and I had to move again.

# Chapter 8:
# Sorceress Vixen

I got lucky and found another apartment not too far from the old one. It was even closer to the college. The room was really small, but I had the whole downstairs to myself. There was a living room area with a little kitchen attached to it. There was another bedroom next to me, but it was empty, and I was very happy about that. There were two girls who occupied the two bedrooms upstairs. They claimed they were cousins, but I think they were just best friends. They told me the girl who was in my room had just moved out. There seemed to be some conflict between them.

My dad helped me move in. I felt bad that I kept moving and my dad had to help me. My dad had a bad back and I didn't want him to get hurt. I was happy to get settled in. Hopefully, I wouldn't have any problems. School was burdensome enough.

I started working at my old job again: part-time at the hotel gift shop. The name of the business had changed and there was a new supervisor. He was very nice and friendly and had no problem rehiring me. I wasn't at the same hotel either; the old one was being remolded, so they put me at the hotel by the river. I didn't really like that one; I had worked there a few times before when someone called off. There was a Starbucks across the hall. A lady named Mahogany worked over there Monday through Friday. I would talk to her briefly while she made my hot chocolate. Sometimes she would give them to me for free.

I was falling behind in my schoolwork. I tried to study at work, but I couldn't focus. I was on my phone most of the time because it wasn't that busy throughout the week. I just felt school wasn't going well.

I found a priest who did exorcisms locally. He was in a news article that said he was one of the best in town. I figured he could help me. I needed a real professional. I called the church where he was located and made an appointment to meet. That same day, I got on the bus to meet him. I couldn't believe I was actually going to see a real priest. When I was on the bus, I saw a skull and cross bones on the back of this guy's jacket. *'Oh shit,'* I thought. *'I'm bout to get fucked up again.'* I got off the bus and walked up the hill. I walked in and the receptionist told me to wait in the room. I was very nervous. I wondered what he would think about me. I was a black woman complaining about demons attacking her and not too many black folks did that. He came in and sat down. He had a fatherly energy to him. He was happy to see me. I told him what was going on with me.

"You have what we call demonic oppression," he said.

Souls, demonic oppression is when demons have been given permission or access to harass you but aren't inside of you possessing you. So, they can taunt you, mess with you, give you nightmares, and wreak havoc around you. Some people think they're experiencing a haunting, but it's actually demonic oppression and attacks.

I had never heard of that, but it didn't sound good and it scared me. The priest said it like it was normal. He gave me some prayers to say and some holy oil. "Say this every night before you go to sleep and get rid of any ghost or black magic stuff you have." I agreed to do everything he said. I threw all of my ghost pictures and anything witchy away.

More problems arose when I heard one of the roommates having sex with some guy. It woke me up and I was not with that shit and I didn't want to hear it. I thought it was disgusting.

The next day, I told her about it and how disrespectful it was and when I left, the bitch started laughing about it. So that kicked the shit off. There was tension in the air.

I was still looking to get baptized, and I found a church I really liked. I started taking bible lessons there, which I enjoyed. The church was very welcoming and that's what I liked about them. I signed up to get baptized. I got a phone call from the man who was going to do it. He asked me why I wanted to get baptized. I said because it was something I wanted to do. "Your reason is not good enough," he said.

I said to myself, *"Oh hell no. I'm getting baptized."* I was being blocked again! Out loud to the man I asked, "What do you mean my reason wasn't good enough?"

"I don't feel like your reason is good enough. I don't think you're ready," he said.

I went off on his mothafuckin ass. "How are you going to tell somebody they ain't ready to get baptized?" I argued. "Since when is a person denied a baptism?"

The man raised his voice and argued with me back. I couldn't believe this shit. "I am not approving you to get baptized."

I wouldn't take no for an answer. Who the fuck did he think he was talking to? I called the church the next day and reported that man. They apologized and told me I couldn't get baptized until I spoke with one of the members because that's how the rules were set up. Another man ended up calling me and I had no problem with him. I was all scheduled and was ready to go.

My roommates had stopped talking to me, which I didn't give a fuck. Then the one girl asked for her cable box back that she let me use. "No problem," I said. These bitches wanted to play, and I was ready.

One night, I was asleep in my bed and a guy knocked on my bedroom door saying, "Hello." It scared me because it woke me up. I didn't know who it was, so I didn't open the door, of course. I immediately called my dad and told him what was going on. Apparently, those two bitch roommates sent one of their guy friends down there to scare me. He sounded like he was drunk. He went back upstairs, and I could hear all of them talking. There was another guy upstairs too, perhaps the guy my other roommate was fucking.

"Put one of them on the phone," my dad said. My dad was drunk as well. It was his usual beer time.

"No," I yelled. I didn't know those men.

"No?" he said. "Let me talk to one of them so I can see if there is a problem."

I didn't want to go up there. I was worried they would all try to attack me. My dad started to argue with me, so I hung up with him and stayed in my room. I could hear the guys upstairs saying they had been through this before and that they always have problems with roommates. They eventually left.

I woke up in the morning fucking pissed. I started going off saying I was going to get someone down here to beat those guys up. I heard one of the roommates running erratically to the other roommate's room. I knew it was the heavier roommate thumping around with her fat ass. I slammed the fucking door and left. Once again, I had to deal with some roommate bullshit. I left to attend my baptism.

At the baptism, they gave us a white gown to put on. I was so happy but nervous. The other people who were getting baptized were excited as well. We all stood in line, and they called us one by one. It was my turn. I stepped up on the stage and was so ready. I smiled and I looked at the crowd of people staring at me. I stepped into the pool of water. They leaned me backward and dipped me in the water. I felt different; at least I thought I did. I went home and started to feel sick like I had a cold or something. '*Oh this can't be good,*' I thought.

I told Mahogany I just got baptized and wanted to start a new life with new people. She was very nice and very positive. "Congratulations," she said with a smile on her face. I wanted to hang out with her, but I wasn't sure what to do. What did women in their early thirties enjoy doing? I was so nervous for some reason to ask her. I figured she'd say no because she had children and didn't have time. I also felt nervous because it felt like I was asking her out on a date. "Do you want to go to casino?" I asked. She paused. "I know you're busy with your children," I added.

Without making any eye contact with me, she said, "Yeah. I have to find time to do things." So we exchanged numbers.

I showed up to the casino very excited to spend time with my new friend. After all, I didn't really have any friends. She came in with a turban wrapped around her head. She had a unique sense of style, but I liked it. We greeted each other. "Hey, girl!" she said. We headed upstairs to the buffet. We talked about many different things. I ended up telling her I see ghosts. I told her I didn't want to scare her. "Oh girl, you ain't gonna scare me." She told me about her ability to hear ghosts talking when she was a child. We shared our weird experiences and then went downstairs to gamble.

"This earth is not real," I said.

"I know," she said.

I asked her if she knew about that group of black men that used to come in my dreams.

"I heard of them," she said.

We had a good time and connected really well.

Everything seemed all good and dandy until I got home. My roommates and I got into an argument. I got out my book with prayers against demons that I had bought online and started reading it out loud. I knew I was under attack. I walked back and forth. I also grabbed the holy oil the priest gave me and put some on my door and sprinkled it around the room. It seemed like getting baptized had pissed off those demons. I felt it. I knew something was going on with my roommates. It seemed like demons started attacking me through people instead of my dreams now. Instead of getting rid of the demons, they just started attacking me in a different way. I couldn't get rid of these mothafuckas. I was scared because I was in this house by myself with two other people with demons using their bodies to fuck with me.

I called the priest again and he told me to keep saying my prayers. I didn't want to stay there at the moment with those bitches, so I decided to go on a church retreat. I had started going to church service on Sundays. They were having something called a staycation. Basically, we would stay at the church for one week and do charity work. It cost but it was used for food and other things we needed. The preacher was a young guy, but I connected with him and I felt comfortable. I told him what was going on and he tried to help me as well. He thought the staycation would be good for me.

There were a bunch of college kids there. I put all my things inside the church on the floor; I felt so relieved. We all had to sleep on the floor. Let me tell you that floor was so comfortable. The floor was hard but comfortable to me. I was knocked the fuck out on that floor. I felt safe there.

Our first assignment was to see how it was to be homeless, so they wanted us to stay the night in an abandoned building. It was winter and cold as fuck outside. First, we went to this place where they gave us a background on homeless people. The abandoned building was right next to it. They told us to dress warm and we were allowed to bring a piece of cardboard to sleep on. I didn't like that idea at all. When we got to the place, they showed us around. We went upstairs where they had clothes for the homeless people. They talked to us about being homeless and what they go through. Then they showed us a video. "All right guys, you will be spending the whole night in the abandoned building." I was afraid and thinking of ways to get out of it. There was no way I could stay a whole night in an abandoned building. It was like twenty degrees outside, and we only had our coats and a blanket to sleep with.

The building was gutted out. There were no walls or windows, just steps to the upstairs. It was dark, cold, and creepy. We headed to the top floor. I couldn't believe that shit. We all laid out our pieces of cardboard on the dirty ground. I was so cold I couldn't sleep. Some of the students were knocked out; I could hear the snores. It got really quiet, and I thought how hard it was to be homeless. I couldn't imagine that lifestyle. I couldn't take it. I wanted to cry. I wondered what was so bad I had done in my life to have to experience this.

The man said we weren't allowed back in the house and there were cameras and he could see if we were downstairs. I was like, '*Fuck it, I will take my ass home.*' I left out the back and went to the bathroom. It felt so good to feel warm again. I took my time in there too. I left and hesitated to go back into the abandoned building. '*God, please help me!*' I screamed in my head. I went back in and went back to my sleeping spot. Everyone was sound asleep or pretending to be. I laid back down on the cold dirty floor. My feet started to freeze. It didn't feel right so I got up again for the second time and left. On my way out, the young preacher asked the person next to him where I was going like he would know. I told him I was going to the bathroom, but I was trying to see how I was going to get home.

I stood outside thinking, '*How am I gonna get the fuck out of here?*' It was too late to catch a bus. I didn't even know exactly where I was. I knew it would be hard for someone to come and pick me up.

I went back into the building again and sat down. I said to myself, "If that man sees me, oh well." I sat downstairs on the couch for hours recovering from the cold. My feet were numb. I wanted to take my shoes and socks off and warm them up. I heard that man walking around upstairs hoping that he didn't see or hear me. Eventually, the students started coming back in. They were all shaking. I wasn't sure how they made it out there for that long.

The next day there was a homeless man that was given a house and it was our job to paint it. I really didn't want to be there. I had too much going on. While we were painting the man's house, one of the girls in the group told me not to paint the bathroom door, but she said it rudely. I asked her if she was telling me or asking me. She said, "I'm telling you."

I said, "I'll do what I want." I didn't realize the primer wasn't dry yet, and I painted over the door. The door I was painting was fucked up. I was upset that I messed this man's bathroom door up. I was irritated with that girl and the door, so I decided to leave. I just wanted to cry.

I told the young preacher I needed to go back to my house. I caught the bus back to the church. I was thinking about how I always got into conflict with other people. I rarely got along with anyone. I couldn't live with anyone because there was always a problem. I realized I couldn't deal with roommates; I needed my own space.

While I was still at the church the group came back. "You're still here?" the preacher said with an irritated tone.

"Yeah," I said.

"I thought you needed to go home."

"I do," I said, "I just didn't leave yet."

He then went off on me telling me it wasn't okay for me to leave because for the staycation, we had to do volunteer work, and that he was responsible for me.

I didn't like his tone, and he was talking to me like I was a child. I got real sassy with his ass, and I told him that I was an adult and not to talk to me like that. I mean I understood where he was coming from, but I didn't give a fuck. I also spoke up about the other girl getting smart with me. I must have went hard because everybody got really quiet. The girl laid down and went to sleep; she didn't want any problems.

I went home to see what the fuck was going on at the house with my roommates. When I got home, it was really quiet. I thought those hoes left so I decided to put holy oil on their doors so they would calm down. I occupied the downstairs, but the stove was upstairs, so I pretended I needed to cook and grabbed a pack of chicken. I nervously walked up the steps and tried my best to tip toe. I placed the chicken on the table and pulled the holy oil out of my pocket. I put a dab on my finger and went to put a cross on one of the girl's rooms.

All of a sudden, the other roommate opened her door. I stood there startled. "What are you doing?" said one of the roommates. They were both in the room.

I said, "I was just about to cook some chicken. I thought you guys weren't home."

She said, "Well, we are here. We're always here, and we don't want you up here." Her mouth was too fuckin smart for me, but I had to be careful because these were demons in human bodies.

I said, "Fine, and don't come down here either."

Then she said, "And don't sit on my couch down there either."

I said, "I won't sit on your stanky-ass couch." I went downstairs and soon left back out to finish the staycation. We were on a winter break from school, so we didn't have any classes at the time.

Another girl moved into the fourth bedroom downstairs with me. She was tall with wavy blonde hair. She looked just like the other roommates. She was friendly at first, but then she started acting funny because I didn't get along with those bitches upstairs. That really pissed me off. She just started to ignore me. She spent most of her time up there with them.

What made me mad was that she was ignoring me but using my microwave. I was like, '*Oh hell no, that's not okay. How are you going to use my microwave and you don't even speak to me? You got me fucked up.*' I waited until she came out of her room. I confronted her about it. I told her she couldn't use my stuff: none of my stuff. She said, "No, I'm using it because it's in an open area." She was a smart-ass like me, but I was very protective over my shit. So, we got into an argument.

I walked across the room and got in her face. Then the bitch pushed me. I was shocked. I hadn't gotten pushed since I was a kid. What the hell? So, I pushed her back and told her, "Don't you ever put your fuckin hands on me." I had my finger in her face, and I could tell she was ready to fight. All of a sudden, she backed up. I turned around; the roommates were standing by the steps. This bitch backed away so I could look like the aggressor. I got in her face first, but she pushed me first. She walked over to the roommates and acted like she was in distress. I went into my room and slammed the door. I didn't want to get kicked out, so I called the police just to cover myself. I also contacted the landlord.

When the landlord arrived, I told him exactly how everything happened. He agreed with me; he was on my side. He had everyone come out of their rooms and talk. He said, "I don't like what's going on here." He told the roommate in the room across from me, "If Brandi doesn't want you to use her microwave, then you can't use it."

She said, "It's in a common area."

He then began to yell. "No, that's her stuff and if she says she don't want you using it, then you can't use it."

She then calmed her ass down and started playing the victim role. She stood there with fake tears in her eyes. She stated she was moving upstairs with the other girls.

"Good," the landlord said. "I don't want any more problems with you guys."

The roommate then said, "I'm not trying to cause any problems."

Suddenly the police knocked on the door. I stepped outside and told them what happened. The police went and talked with them. After the police left, I left the house. I received a text from Mahogany that said, "Are you okay? Do I have to come down there?"

I hadn't even told her what happened. I responded, "How did you know?"

She asked me what was going on, and I told her the situation. She suggested we go to the park so I could get a break from the house.

She came and picked me up with her children. I was telling her I was thinking about dropping out of school. Nothing was working out, not with school or my living situation, and I was just tired of getting into conflict with people.

It was very peaceful when I was around Mahogany. We continued to talk and bond with each other. "Maybe you're supposed to help me," I said.

"No, I'm not," she said.

I told her I was seeing a priest and maybe she should see him as well.

"No, he probably would try to burn my witch-ass."

On our way home, her son asked us if we liked each other with a smile on his face. "What do you mean?" Mahogany asked.

"Like girlfriend and boyfriend," he said.

My eyes got so big. *'How did he know*?' I thought.

"Boy, sit back and be quiet," Mahogany said. She looked at me and said, "He just says stuff to be silly."

I did notice I had started to develop a little crush on her, but I just ignored it. I wasn't sure what was going on, but I enjoyed being friends with her. I had a dream that night. I saw a big tree and it was scary looking.

Later that night, I heard someone crying in the living room. It woke me up out of my sleep. I heard my roommates saying, "Come on, we gotta go upstairs."

"No," the other roommate yelled.

*'There is always some shit going on,'* I thought. I really didn't care to open my door, but I wanted to see what was going on. I opened my door in pure fucking annoyance. I saw my roommate face down at the bottom of the steps – she was shaking uncontrollably. I thought maybe she was having a seizure or something. I really didn't give a fuck. I walked right past her and went to the bathroom. I then went back to my room and shut the door. Then I said to myself, "No, I can't do that. I can't just leave

her there." I definitely was not in the mood to call an ambulance for this hoe. So I walked over to her and I touched her on her on her back. "Are you okay," I said.

She got right up and said, "Yeah, I'm fine." She went up the steps like nothing was wrong with her all of sudden.

'*That was strange,*' I thought. I went back to bed hoping whatever was going on with her was over for the night.

The next morning, I said to myself, "That's what that bitch gets for fuckin with me." I knew because she had pushed me; that's why that happened to her. That was her karma for putting her hands on me. She was lucky she didn't die.

As the day went on, I found out that she had vomited all over the front porch. The landlord was livid. He came down there and cussed her ass out. "I've never seen anything like this," he said. "This is unacceptable." He called her parents and everything. Her parents came to get her ass. I guess the roommates had gone out that night and she got super drunk and couldn't hold her liquor. Oh yeah, that was definitely karma for what she did, instant karma.

I guess the landlord had enough and had a talk with my dad. My dad thought I was down there causing trouble. He said after talking with him, he knew it was not me. They decided it was best if I moved out. I had moved 600 times already. I was tired of moving. I was fighting so hard to stay there but it looked like I didn't have a choice. I was so pissed, but I knew that house wasn't a good place for me to be. So, it was back to my dad's house. My dad came down with a U-Haul to get my stuff. I knew he was tired of helping me move. The roommates had a bunch of their friends over, I guess in case I tried to fight with them. Scared-ass bitches. They didn't say one word.

I was not excited to be back at my dad's house. I knew Mouse wasn't enthused either. It was the third time I had moved that year. I didn't even know why I unpacked my clothes. I dropped out of school and decided to take a break. Obviously, I was still under spiritual attack. My dreams started to change but they were still scary.

Like I said before, Souls, the demons stopped coming into my dreams and started attacking me through people, or so I thought. I went to sleep just fine, but it wasn't peaceful sleep. I would wake up feeling so restless. I had no clue what direction I was headed in. I kept my job at the gift shop, but I had to take a bus an hour and a half both ways.

Mahogany was going through her own issues in her relationship with her boyfriend. She broke up with him and deep down I was really excited. I could feel her sadness. I looked into her eyes filled with tears. I had never seen a woman this heartbroken before. I just wanted to support her. I really wanted to tell her I liked her, but that was definitely the wrong time. It was so hard for me to hold it in.

"I have to tell you something," I said.

"What is it?" She looked at me with her sad eyes.

"Never mind, I will tell you later."

"No tell me now. Nothing you can tell me will hurt me anymore than I feel now."

I insisted on telling her later.

She was on her way out, leaving work early. She told me she felt like there was a hole in her heart. I gave her a hug goodbye. As she was leaving, she turned around and looked at me through the glass window in the store. She waved goodbye, and we stared at each other for a while and then she left. I had to build up the courage to say something to her. I was extremely nervous, but I felt I needed to. I finally picked up my phone and texted her. I wrote, "I think I have a crush on you, but I hope everything works out with you and your boyfriend." I waited for her response. I just knew she was going to think I was a weirdo. It seemed like she took forever. I was sweating bullets.

Then she replied, "If it makes you feel any better, I feel the same way."

I couldn't believe my eyes. '*What!*' She wasn't supposed to say that! "Why are you dismissing yourself....lol. Are you serious or just playing around?" I replied. It had to be a joke. I couldn't believe that shit. I couldn't believe what I was reading.

She went on to say that she thought we made a cute couple. She was serious, but none of it made any sense. We didn't make any sense as far as anything romantic. I'd never had a crush on a woman before, and she said the same thing. I'd never really paid any attention to a woman. This was a first for me and a first for her.

Me and Mahogany became really close. We would text each other and talk on the phone all day long. I looked forward to hearing from her when I woke up each day. She made me happy. I finally found a friend that I could connect with on a spiritual level. We spent a lot of time together. She asked me if I wanted to stay the night over at her house and that way it would be easier for me to get to work. I could just ride with her. We both worked the morning shift so it was perfect.

When I first walked into her house, I noticed she had a huge picture in her living room of her aunt who passed away. I immediately picked up on her energy. It was almost felt like she tapped me on the shoulder. I'm pretty sure she did, actually. I wasn't sure what was going on. Her house felt very peaceful, and I wasn't picking up on any bad energies. I felt safe there, and it felt like home. I sat in the living room and saw that Mahogany had a deck of angel cards on her table. '*Aww shit,*' I thought. "Where did you get these?" I asked Mahogany. I had stopped any type of black magic practices like the priest told me to. I was nervous. Then her son came over and asked me if I wanted to read the cards. I told him no. "Your aunt is trying to get me to contact her though those cards."

"Really," she said. "She doesn't talk to me."

'*This is crazy,*' I thought. "Why she want to talk to me?" I said.

"I don't know," Mahogany said.

I didn't understand why the deceased, angels, and demons were contacting me. It reminded me of the times I felt like my grandfather was trying to contact me. I had a dream there was a picture of him in a gold frame and it was floating in the air. I always felt close to my grandfather even though I never met him. I asked her to put the cards away because they made me uncomfortable.

We went upstairs so I could see the rest of the house. She had an altar in her bedroom. She had pictures and personal items of her deceased family members on there. She also showed me other photos of them she had in a photo album. I went to touch one of her aunt's scarves and I got the feeling she didn't want me to touch it. I quickly moved my hand away. "This lady here don't want me touchin her stuff," I said.

"Yeah, she was like that in real life," Mahogany said.

I went to touch her other aunt's stuff and I was able to. "She doesn't mind if I touch her things," I said. I was fascinated. I was fascinated with dead people in general, but also how strong the energy was in her house. It was time for bed, and she gave me the option to sleep in the bed with her or on the couch. Her bed was huge, so I didn't see any problem with it. We both got in the bed and talked for a while and then went to sleep.

At work we texted each other all day. I was putting items away on the shelf and I got a text that said, "I want you to wear your hair up in a bun, and I want you to wear red lipstick. You would look so sexy that way." I stopped what I was doing and instantly felt my vagina getting moist. I really didn't know how to react, so I just said, "Ok." I told her I masturbated to her. She said she masturbated to me as well but then she stopped because she felt like she was making me do something I don't want to do. I wasn't sure what I wanted to do. "There's something about you being a virgin. I find that so sexy," she said. "Really," I replied. The fact I was almost thirty and still a virgin made me insecure. I didn't think that was attractive at all, but she did.

I went back home after a couple of days. I had a dream a guy who was dead got hit by a bus. He was covered in blood and was scaring me. He took me through his whole death. Then he tried to attack me. Somehow, we ended up at my aunt's house. Then he said he was going to get my dad too. "No," I yelled. "Leave my dad alone." I woke up crying. That dream scared the hell out of me.

I called the priest to tell him what happened. When I asked for him, the receptionist sighed like I was calling him too much. He got on the phone, and I immediately started crying again. He also sighed. I told him the dream I had and said I was still getting attacked and didn't know why. "I'm doing everything you told me to do," I said.

He insisted that I keep reading the prayers. He told me to make an appointment to come and see him again. I went in my dad's room and started crying. "What's wrong," he said.

I gave him hug. I said, "I don't want you to get hurt. I want you to be okay."

"I'm okay," he said.

"I had a dream this man was trying to get you," I said.

"It was just a dream, Bran." That's what he always said. That it was just a dream. It wasn't just a dream. I was over getting tortured by demons and dead people and there was nothing I could do about it. Not even the priest could help me. I was doomed. I was so tired of that shit. I just wanted to have a good night's sleep in peace.

Mahogany asked me if I wanted to come back over and stay the night. Of course I did. When I was around her, I wasn't getting attacked by any demons or having any bad dreams. She started a second job, and she asked if I wanted to babysit her children. Mahogany said it wasn't every day that she met a nurturer and she trusted me with her children. I was happy to do it. Her children were so polite and well behaved. I wanted to help her and become a part of the family. We talked about getting a place together. We went looking for places too.

I went back over to Mahogany's house where I felt welcomed and appreciated. Mahogany made us dinner that night. She ate healthy just like I did. Our favorite place to eat was Wholefoods. We would get our food and talk for hours. While we were eating, she sat beside me and started to act really flirty. She was saying she was open to polygamous relationships. "Who knows, I might want a girlfriend one day," she said.

I was more traditional. I just wanted to marry one man. I didn't like doing anything with a group of people; it didn't matter what the situation was. I was faced towards the table, and she turned sideways, facing me, and leaned towards me and started laughing. I knew she was flirting with me. I honestly didn't know how to flirt. I was always really awkward. She then stood up and somehow, we got on the subject of seeing each other's breast. She mentioned how saggy her breasts were. She made it seem like they were out of the ordinary. "I want to see," I said. It wasn't in a sexual way, though. It was more out of curiosity.

"I want to see your breasts too," she said. She looked at me with a smirk on her face.

I got really nervous and said, "Okay," like I didn't care. Shit, my titties were saggy too and it was something I was slightly insecure about. I always stood in the mirror and looked at them just hanging there. "They are supposed to sit up," I would say to myself. "The nipple is supposed to be in the middle, not on the bottom."

We headed upstairs for the night. We both got in the bed. "I usually sleep naked," she said.

I didn't know what to say. I closed my eyes for a while and then I opened them. I caught her staring at me for the second time. The first time I caught her, she hurried to turn her head. The second time, she just stared at me. I wondered if she always stared at me when I wasn't aware. I thought it was a little strange. She then moved her leg and brushed it against mine. I got excited. I thought that was the moment it was going to happen. I thought there was a possibility we were going to have sex. I mean, I didn't even know how to start. She then hurried and turned to the other side.

The next morning, she got up and got into the shower. She came into the room and was completely naked. She stared at me, and I tried not to look at her. I couldn't believe she was naked. She started to walk towards me. I looked at her breasts. She was right: they were very unique and strange looking. She sat on the bed to get dressed. I examined her breasts even more out of curiosity. I almost wanted to touch them but not in a sexual way. "I like them," I said. I didn't want her to feel insecure about them and plus, I didn't want to make this moment more awkward than it was.

"Thank you," she said. It was something she said a lot. She was always very grateful and appreciative. Maybe she wanted me to see her body to see how I was going to react. I'm not sure. I honestly didn't look at it as anything sexual. Maybe that was her way of flirting or just being comfortable. It was definitely a weird situation for me.

We went out as we always did, and while we were in the car she said, "I'm not sure what's going on with me and you, but I know one thing. I'm not eating nobody's coochie."

"Me either," I replied. I wasn't even thinking about eating nobody's coochie nor nobody eating mine. I hadn't even gotten that far in my thinking. I wondered why she said that. Oral sex was way too advanced for me, especially with a woman. I hadn't even sucked dick yet and I wasn't even comfortable with that. I think I had a fear of sucking dick. I always said I didn't want to do it because I didn't want to get lock jaw. Eating pussy was out of the question for me because I thought they were gross. They looked nasty to me and there was wet stuff that came out of it. I didn't want that shit anywhere near me or my mouth.

I wasn't sure what direction me and Mahogany were going into. I wasn't sure what our purpose was, but I honestly wished the sexual tension would go away and we would just be regular friends. I just felt like I was too immature for her anyway. She was mature and had children. She had a lot of responsibilities and there I was just in the way. I wanted to remove myself from her because it felt like our relationship wasn't going anywhere. We were just friends that had a sexual attraction towards each other, but I knew there was more. We were actually sister soulmates. We weren't going to date each other, and it was so hard just to be her friend.

She was a great mother, and I would watch her take on that role. She was so supportive and caring towards her children. It made me admire her even more and I grew more and more attracted to her. At the same time, I wanted to go away. I wanted her to find a husband and get married and be happy. I felt like she was just leading me on when all she had to say was she was not interested in having sex with me. I could tell sometimes she wanted to and then she would change her mind. "I have to ask my ancestors first and see if they would be ok with it," she said. She gave a lot of excuses on why there was a delay. I was confused but very wrapped up in her energy. I just wanted to buy her things and do everything she told me to do. I told her I had a dream that these people dressed in black with black capes asked me if I wanted to join their cult. I told them no because they sacrificed animals. Mahogany found the dream interesting. "I'm about to get into Santeria. I think that's something you might like. You are very powerful," she said. "You have natural raw power. You and me together can become a powerhouse." I listened to everything she said, but I wasn't into that voodoo religion. I was trying to get away from witchcraft.

She was on her way out the door for work and I was watching her kids. I was getting irritated with her at that point. She gave all the kids a kiss goodbye and then asked if I wanted a kiss too. With an attitude, I said no. She quickly stepped away from me and seemed to be upset. She left and slammed the door. She would flirt with me and take no action. Like, what the fuck? I felt like she was playing a little game with me. I didn't understand why she was upset. I just wanted to go back home;

things with her were causing me a lot of anxiety.

Before I headed back, I went to see the priest one last time. I told him about Mahogany. "What are you doing sleeping in her bed?" he asked.

"I knew you were going to say that," I said. We both started laughing. "I don't know. I didn't think it was a big deal."

"You can't sleep anywhere else?" he asked. I knew he wouldn't approve, but I wanted to be honest with him. He suggested I step away from her and I did try.

I stopped talking to her several times, but then I would miss her. I couldn't live my life without her. We told each other we loved each other all the time but I didn't take it too seriously. I told her we should separate for a while, and she said she was okay with it.

Then days later I would apologize and feel bad for doing it. "I'm really sorry," I would say.

"That's okay, I'm still here," she would say.

One time she was at a picnic, and I was upset with her for some reason. I told her I didn't want to be friends anymore. I could tell she was sad about it.

That night I was asleep in my bed. I was at my dad's house. It had to be around 2am. I heard a loud noise downstairs. I got up and asked my dad what that noise was. He looked spooked. A picture had fallen off the kitchen wall, and it happened to have a picture of a picnic table on it. "I don't know what happened," my dad said. "It just fell. I'm not into ghosts, but whatever that was, was evil," he said.

I wondered, '*Did Mahogany do that*?'

I asked her about it and asked if she was upset with me. She assured me she wasn't. It was strange to me she had just been at a picnic and then a picture with a picnic table fell.

I was telling her about demons harassing me in my dreams. "Just don't be afraid of them. Don't let them scare you," she said.

"Okay," I told her.

She told me about a time she and a friend were in a car and a demon was in a car next to them and it kept ramming into their car while they were driving. She never mentioned any incidents she had with demons before, but I could tell it scared her. She told me she wanted to see me, and she wanted to come to my dad's house. "I want to meet your dad," she said.

"Okay," I said. I was excited. With a smile on my face, I told my dad she wanted to meet him.

"Okay," he said. He looked at me like I was acting strange.

I took Mahogany's advice and stopped being afraid of the demons. *'Fuck them niggas,'* I thought. I was so sick of their bullshit. I was driving home to my dad's. It was the month of April and it was snowing outside. I saw a man walking with shorts on. I thought that was strange because it was cold. I stared at him, and I noticed his face started to change. His eyes got really big and dark. It scared the hell out of me. He was right across the street from a catholic church. I ran up the stairs when I got home. "Dad, I just saw a demon."

"No, you didn't," he said.

"Yes, I did. He had shorts on."

My dad didn't believe in that stuff. He needed to see to believe.

I had a dream my deceased grandmother was sitting on my bed. As I got closer to her, her face started to turn demonic. I whispered in her ear and said, "Tell him I'm with God." Then we started fighting. A demon tried to attack me through my grandmother. When I said, 'Tell him I'm with God,' I was talking about the devil. I whooped that demon's ass.

Another dream I had I was sitting next to a nun. Then all of a sudden, the door started to creep open, and I knew it was demons. I tried to run out another door, but it wouldn't open. I yelled, "Jesus!" several times and it still wouldn't open. Usually when I yelled, "Jesus," just once, I got help but the door was not opening. I continued to say it. Then the door finally opened. I ran outside in front of the building. I noticed two demons standing in the window. One of them had a white face. I started to levitate up to where they were and stuck my middle finger up at them and then I woke up.

"Yes!" I said. I was finally starting to gain my power back.

Mahogany asked me to come back over to her house so we could go to an event. Then one night, she made dinner for a guy who was a Yoruba priest. He came to the house after we all ate. I wondered why she was making this nigga dinner. He was a cute guy and kind of chubby. I could tell they liked each other. Their energy was so strong I could taste it. I became so jealous and outraged. That wasn't like me at all. I was rarely a jealous person but for some reason, I became bothered. I was so upset he was there, and I wanted him to leave. I didn't want them to like each other. The attraction was so strong and heavy. I went upstairs and left them downstairs. I waited for her to come upstairs to bed. "Do you like him?" I asked.

With a lil smile on her face she said, "Do I like him? No, but I think he likes me."

"I think he likes you," I said.

She then climbed into bed. We talked for a bit and then I told her to stay still. "I'm gonna attempt to lay beside you," I said. I was trying to see if I felt comfortable lying beside her. I scooched over to her. "Do you feel weird?" I asked.

"No," she replied. "Do you?"

"No," I said, but I did a little bit. It felt weird laying with anyone this close. I barely let anyone get this close to me, especially in a romantic way. I felt her knee blocking me from getting closer and trying anything with her. I wasn't trying to, though; I was too afraid to try something. I wouldn't even know where to start. I just wanted to see if this was something we both were comfortable with.

She got nervous and hurried to hop out of the bed. She blamed it on the fact that she had to fart. I was so confused. This woman was confusing. I wasn't sure why she was acting this way. I was angry and I felt rejected. *'Why is she rejecting me?'* I thought. I couldn't wait to go back home. I told her I was going home, and she asked why. I said, "This is not working out." Again, I felt she was leading me on and playing with my fucking emotions. She always left the door open for me but then wouldn't let me in; though she didn't close it either. This had to be some weird Scorpio shit or something. I just wanted to get away from her and her house.

I was really hurt, so I decided to stay over at my other friend's house until the next morning; then I would go back to my dad's house. I got to my friend's house, and I was happy to see her. I hadn't seen her in a while. We had been friends since the 10th grade. Her ex-girlfriend happened to be at the house too. "What is she doing here?" I asked.

"She wanted to see the house," she said. My friend had just moved into a brand-new house. I didn't like her girlfriend because she was toxic. I could feel her energy. She was negative as fuck. I could tell she caused my friend a lot of pain. I was just hoping she was not dealing with her anymore, but I had my own problems. My friend and I went on the back porch to catch up.

Later that day, I went upstairs to the room I was sleeping in and was texting Mahogany. I was still hurt to the point of tears, but I didn't think it was fair to just completely cut her off. All of a sudden, I heard my friend and her ex-girlfriend arguing. It startled me. It reminded me of when my dad used to argue with his girlfriends back in the day. The way they argued was scary to me. It was so intense I thought they were physically fighting. "Why is she here?" the girlfriend shouted, insinuating that me and my friend had something romantic going on.

I couldn't believe it. I said to myself, "Who, me and her?" Like, damn, I couldn't stay the night at my friend's house? It was insane.

They continued to argue for hours. I heard the girlfriend call me a bitch and everything. '*How am I even in this?*' I thought. I called Mahogany and told her what was going on. She said she could hear them through the phone, and I was way upstairs. I asked her if she could come get me. Obviously, I wasn't welcome there. "I'm on my way," Mahogany said.

My friend's daughter was in the room, and I asked her what was going on. She said, "Everything was fine until you got here."

I went downstairs and I was shaking, but not because I was scared; it was because I was caught off-guard about what this was all about. I shouted for both of them to calm down. "What is the problem?" I asked.

"I don't like you," the ex-girlfriend said.

Now, usually, I would have cussed this bitch out and said, "*Who the fuck are you talking to?*" I simply said, "Okay, is that it? Is that what y'all arguing about."

"You were talking about me," she said.

I said, "Yeah," nonchalantly. Apparently, my friend told her I was saying things about her, and I was, because my friend was telling me the stuff that she was doing to her. I thought I was being a supportive friend, but I guess my friend used what I was saying as a weapon to hurt her. I knew nothing about it. I didn't even talk to my friend that often. I told the girlfriend I was always going to take my friend's side no matter what and her friends would probably do the same for her. I said, "You know what? I'm leaving. I don't have time for this dumb bullshit." My feelings were already hurt. I just wanted to go back to my dad's. Honestly, I felt like the girlfriend should have left. My friend just let me walk out of her house and didn't even ask where I was going or if I needed a ride. I was very upset with her.

Mahogany pulled up. I got in the car with relief. "Thank you for coming to get me," I said.

"No problem," she said. She had a glass bowl with fruit sitting next to her. "I brought this bowl with me just in case I had to hit somebody in the head with it."

I went to sleep that night thinking maybe I was supposed to be around Mahogany. She was my real friend. I rarely had real friends. I was safe with her and safe in her house. She didn't think twice about coming to get me. I think what happened that night was a sign that God didn't want me to be gay. I would never date someone with that type of energy. That was obviously a demonic attack. I would most certainly never date a woman after that experience. That scared me and Mahogany was playing some kind of weird game with me. No thank you.

I went home the next day. I quit my job at the gift shop because my coworkers were getting on my nerves. I was already on edge. I always quit my jobs when people pissed me off. I would just quit and walk off. I never stayed at jobs very long. I texted Mahogany and told her I quit. Even with what happened, I was still angry with her for rejecting me and sent her an angry message.

I knew I had an issue with going off on people and cussing them out when they pissed me off and that I had some real anger issues. It would just come out of nowhere. A lot of people would distance themselves from me because of that. In the text, I told her she shouldn't have me sleeping in her bed if she didn't want to have sex with me. I told her how she was just playing games with me, and I was sick of the shit.

She was upset with me and texted back and said, "Everybody sleeps in my bed." She told me she didn't want any sex with me or any relationship with me. "With your dense ass," was what she replied. Her vocabulary was very broad and mature. More mature than mine. I had to look up the word dense. '*Whelp, she called me dumb,*' I thought. "This is what I get for bringing strays home," she said. She was making it seem like I was some lost animal that she found off the street. She insisted I should get a new religion because the one I was in would not condone me being a lesbian. I didn't consider myself a lesbian. I was trying to have sex with her, but I thought I was supposed to.

At that point, I felt like I had reached the stage in the hero's journey called the meeting with the goddess. It's when the hero meets a powerful female figure with whom he finds unity and bonding of some kind. The goddess represents the female side of the hero, which, if he can join, will make him whole. The hero and the goddess would represent the divine couple or sacred marriage. The hero would gain more power that way. The hero wins the boon of love. Mahogany was definitely the divine goddess. She was my mentor and together we were very powerful. I thought I was being rewarded because she was so kind to me, and she helped me escape the demons for some time.

# Chapter 9:
# Dream Invasion

I was still upset at Mahogany. I looked on her Facebook page and saw that she was calling me a hoe. She never said my name, but she quoted some lyrics to a song that said she was just a hoe.

"I'm not hoe," I said to myself. "Why is she saying that?" I texted her and told her that I wanted all my stuff back.

She replied with an attitude. "You mean the stuff that you gave me? I'm not giving you anything back," she said. "I'm not concerned with you. I am trying to get these grants for my nonprofit. Don't contact me again or I will have to take extreme measures. Check the local dumpster."

I stared at the text messages. I was very hurt by them. I couldn't believe she was talking about killing me. She made it seem like I didn't mean anything to her.

Just like that, she was done with me, and she was serious. I wasn't afraid that she threatened to kill me. I was very hurt that she would say something like that to me. *'Like, you're going to kill me now? For what though*?' I never responded to her.

The next couple of days I was in a somber mood. I had a dream I was flying through the air with a skirt on but no underwear. I saw Grant Hill and then I fell to the ground. When I woke up, my coochie was sore. It felt like somebody had been sticking something in my vagina.

The next night, Mahogany came into my dreams and she was holding her baby. It was dark, but she lit a stick on fire so I could see her. She leaned over and kissed me. It wasn't a pleasant kiss; it was a nasty kiss with her nasty tongue licking me all in my mouth. Then she made me kiss her baby on the mouth in a nasty way.

When I woke up, I was fuckin pissed. Why would she come into my dream with some nasty shit like that? I went into my dad's room yelling. "That girl came in my dreams," I yelled.

"What are you talking about?" my dad said.

"Mahogany. She is bothering me in my dreams."

"Get out of here with that," he said. He then shooed me away. My dad pissed me off. He wasn't open to any of the weird shit that was happening to me.

I had nobody to talk with about it. I stomped back into my room. *'This is bullshit.'*

Over the next few weeks, the dreams continued. She made it clear that she was not interested in me. I had a dream we were at a mall. She was standing by an escalator with a man. I walked over to her, and she turned around with her back facing me. She yelled, "Go!" I got on the escalator and went to the lower-level floor.

I tried to do a spell to stop her from attacking me in my dreams. That night, I had a dream she punched me in the face. I could feel the punch too. I wondered how she was able to harm me and cause real pain in my dream. Where was my protection at?

I decided to do some research on the matter. It was called astral projection. She was using black magic to astral project into my dreams. It was also called dream invasion. I read it could be done by using a person's handwriting. I wondered how she got my handwriting. Then I remembered I wrote on the back of a piece of paper and left it on her dresser.

The article said that certain crystals and herbs could protect me. They also had something called a dream pillow. I tried using herbs at first, but I was allergic to them. The whole side of my face swelled up and became numb. Then I tried the crystals. I placed the crystals under my pillow, and it worked.

A week went by, and I didn't have any dreams of Mahogany. I slept peacefully. I decided I didn't need them anymore, so I removed them from my pillow and put them away. That night, the bitch came back into my dream. How did she even know there were crystals under my pillow? I was so frustrated, and my anxiety was getting out of control. I didn't even know why she was attacking me. I never contacted her after she told me not to. So what was the fucking problem? I tried putting the crystals back under my pillow, but the crystals were no longer working. She was still getting through somehow.

I decided to contact the priest again. I wasn't sure how to handle the situation. He tried his best to help me, but nothing was working.

I started to have strange things happen to me. I ate a sandwich from Subway, and it had banana peppers on it. My tongue began to swell up in my mouth. I had bumps all over my tongue. It was not like I had never eaten banana peppers before. It felt like a weird coincidence that happened, because the other night before that happened, she came into my dream with her cousin. She had started bringing her cousin into my dreams, I guess to train her. In the dream, Mahogany and her cousin were accusing me of talking about them and telling their business. "No," I said. Then the cousin pulled my tongue out of my mouth, and it became enlarged. It was a nasty tongue with bumps all over it.

These attacks turned into months of dream humiliation and bullying. I wasn't even looking at her pictures anymore and I blocked her on Facebook. I started having dreams of having sex with other women and I found it quite disgusting. I would watch other women having sex too.

I had a dream that Mahogany pretended to be nice to me. We were sitting on the bed, and she was doing my hair. She grabbed my hand and pulled me downstairs. I saw all her ancestors sitting in the living room. She then threw my hand away from her and told me to get out of the house. I walked out the front door and more of her family members were outside. I heard someone calling me 'white girl' over and over again. I did some research on Mahogany and I found out she did come from a family of witches. Her last name was the last name of a very famous witch lineage.

I decided to go see a therapist about my nightmares. I made an appointment with a local counseling facility. During the intake, I told the man that a witch was coming into my dreams and harassing me. He looked at me and laughed. It was not a game, but apparently, he thought I was crazy. I met with someone to be put on medication for my nightmares. I was against taking medication. I felt like medications caused more problems than helped. My body was very sensitive, and I always had side effects. I was nervous to try it, but I felt like I had no other choice. They also suggested I try a sleep study. They wanted to see if I had sleep apnea. I was willing to try anything. I wanted these nightmares to stop. I tried the new medication for three days and of course, I started having side effects.

I stopped taking the medication, but something strange started happening. I started seeing visions of aliens. I would see them before I dozed off, before completely falling asleep, and then I would see them after waking up. I thought this would last for a couple of days, but it lasted for two years. How was it possible to have visions of aliens for two years without being on the medication? That's fucking impossible. The medication must have done something to the chemicals in my brain. I didn't fuck with aliens too much. I didn't think they liked me. I had many dreams about them, and they were always mean to me. Well, the Pleiadians were, and they were supposed to be the kind ones. The greys were nice to me though. I'm not sure why.

I dreamed I was watching a video screen. The grey aliens were there: it was three of them. At the bottom of the screen, it said, *"You will meet them."* Then I woke up. That dream scared me. I really didn't want to meet them. I was thinking, '*Meet them for what?*'

I had another dream that I was talking to the grey aliens, and they spoke to me telepathically. They showed me where they hide their spaceships. They asked me if I wanted them to kill all of mankind and I yelled, "No." Then I woke up. I wondered who I was for them to give me such authority.

I found a psychic on YouTube. Her readings were really accurate. I told her about the demon attacks and the dreams. We got on the subject of aliens. "Yeah, what about them?" I asked.

"I fight them all the time," she said.

I told her they kept coming into my dreams and they were mean to me.

"Don't talk to them," she said and then the phone hung up.

'*What just happened?*' I thought.

She called me back. She wasn't sure what happened either. It reminded me of when the phone hung up as I was talking to that other psychic when I went to visit my aunt in California. "Don't talk to them," she said. "They are trying to mess with your mind."

When she told me that, I stopped dreaming about them. I still had visions though.

I went to a sleep specialist and stayed overnight. I was hooked up with all these tubes. It was so peaceful. They told me I didn't have sleep apnea and they didn't see anything abnormal.

With everything going on, I felt miserable. I was still a virgin and sexually frustrated. I didn't have many friends. I was living with my dad in a boring drug town. I was still being attacked by demons and I wasn't getting any peaceful sleep. All of this was happening and not a soul could help me. Where was God? I was being tortured for some reason and I couldn't figure out why. I was trying to decide what religion I wanted to be a part of. Wiccan seemed to resonate with me. I bought books and joined groups. I tried to learn as much as I could. I became a witch, and

I was proud of it. I wore an Archangel Michael medallion. I loved Michael for some reason. Christianity was not working out for me, but I still held on to it a little bit.

I went to see a local psychic. She read playing cards instead of tarot cards. She was a nice lady and very honest. I brought my crucifix with me so I wouldn't get attacked. "Oh, honey, you don't need that. I'm not evil," she said.

"I know," I said. "I get attacked when I get readings done now." I told her I was Wiccan.

"Those are witches," she said.

"I know," I said.

She looked at me like she didn't fuck with witches and like she really didn't want me in there. She said she saw a baby boy.

"I don't want kids," I said.

"Well, only if you want to, there is a child here for you." She said Mouse was jealous of me. "She is jealous of you and your dad's relationship." I couldn't understand why. She also said I would move to West Virginia, and there were a lot of Witches out there.

'*West Virginia? Who the hell wants to live in West Virginia?*' I thought. I brought up the topic of demons.

"They stopped bothering you, didn't they?"

"Yes," I said. I did get a little break from them because I changed my religion thinking it would help. Boy was I wrong.

I started getting attacked again. I went to my mom's house because I was not getting along with my dad and Mouse. I was under serious attack. I couldn't sleep. I tried to sleep with the light on. I lay on the bed with the covers over my face, sweating. I fell asleep briefly.

I dreamed I was laying in my bed, and I got up and walked into the hallway. I looked down the stairs and I saw this clown monster figure standing on the steps. I just stared at him, and he stared at me. Then I heard someone say Alice in Wonderland. He looked like the Mad Hatter.

Then, all of a sudden, I couldn't breathe. I placed my hand on my chest and said out loud, "I can't breathe." Then an angel came to save me. He was a black man with wings. Somehow, I ended up at the bottom of my mom's steps and the angel stood in front of me. I kneeled behind him and hid from the demon. The demon started singing the name Jesus very loudly. Then I woke up.

I could barely breathe because of the covers on my face. I really couldn't breathe in real life. That demon had tried to kill me. I quickly removed the covers from my face. I then heard a voice that sounded like my dad's. "Bran," it said. I knew they were trying to trick me to get me to go into the dark hallway, but I stood still, waiting for morning to come with some daylight when my mom would get home.

When my mother arrived home from work from her overnight job, I got up to get dressed. I was exhausted, but I was glad somebody was there with me. I walked downstairs and noticed she had the news on, and they were talking about a murder. It's like it was magnified. It got my attention. My mom had these African masks on her wall that had belonged to my grandmother. They originally were gold, but my mom had spray-painted them black. I could tell there were demons in them because they kept fuckin with me too. They would make faces at me, and I would make faces back. Every time I would go downstairs, I would look at them with a side eye and say, "Fuck y'all." I wasn't sure why they hid in those masks.

I decided to use the holy oil the priest gave me and put some on them. It only caused me to get attacked even more. The dreams continued. The priest told me I should not have touched the masks with my hands. I was so frustrated. I ended up going back to my dad's.

I was still not getting along with Mouse or her daughters and I stopped talking to everyone completely. Those people were not the kind of people I wanted to be around. I needed to stop bouncing around from house to house. I just wished I had my own place so I wouldn't have to be bothered. I needed to have my own stability.

Not having a boyfriend and not being able to have sex was tough on me. I cried when I was alone because it didn't seem like anything was going to happen with the situation. I was so tired of masturbating. I didn't really get any satisfaction out of it. It reminded me that I didn't have anybody to have sex with. I would masturbate and cry afterwards. It was tough seeing other people in relationships. It wasn't that I was lonely; I was trying to find some form of normalcy. Normal people had sex.

I was so fuckin tired of hearing Mouse and my dad having sex. I thought it was disgusting. It made me so fucking angry that I could hear her in the other room. I would turn the fan on to try to block out the noise. One time, I was getting ready for work, and they started having sex knowing I was up. I yelled out the door, "Really?!" Like, wtf. They could, at least, have waited until after I left. As I got in the car, my dad opened the window and called me a bitch. My dad had never called me that before. That really hurt. I mean, I didn't mind being called a bitch, but not by my dad.

When I was younger, my dad would have all these women over to the house. I would hear them having sex and it would traumatize me. I didn't even know what sex was. I would hear noises. It sounded like the women were being harmed in some kind of way. I would bang on the wall because I couldn't go to sleep. My dad would come in my room like, "What?"

"I'm hearing noises, and I can't go to sleep."

"It's just the TV," he would say, or, "It's the radio."

I wasn't falling for that shit. I would cry when I woke up in the morning and when I went to school. I hated nighttime and I hated when women came over. I would get anxiety.

Mahogany was still sending me nightmares. I dreamed I was sitting on the floor, and somebody told me to close my eyes. I did, but I opened them back up. I saw two women having sex on a screen. They were having rough sex and it didn't look pleasurable. I didn't like that at all, and I thought it was scary. It was like they were having painful sex. Then I had another dream of this big fat woman sitting on me and I could feel the pain. I couldn't breathe. I wondered how long this was going to go on.

One peaceful day, as I was comfortable in my bed watching TV, I heard a noise downstairs. Somebody was screaming. So I went down there and somebody had shot through the doorway. The bullet went through the mirror in the hallway and into the living room. Mouse and her daughter were laying down on the floor in fear. The bullet had landed right beside them. Mouse was freaking out. My dad came downstairs as well. "I'm scared," I said.

"You?" Mouse said. She was terrified. I didn't care because I didn't like the bitch and I saw the situation as some form of karma for how she was treating me. I knew I was safe. I felt comfortable in my room.

There was too much conflict going on at the house though. Mouse's thief-ass daughter was stealing my juice and was hiding the empty bottles under the couch. I wanted to fight that bitch. I know it was just juice but still, buy your own shit. She was such a bum like her mother. They never kept any money and stole shit. I'm glad I was locking my door because she probably would have stolen other shit.

My dad was acting dumb saying, "What do you want me to do about it?"

'Like, why do you keep letting her in the house?' I thought. There was something wrong with the picture. Those motherfuckas were on some other shit.

I needed to get out of the house. The only choice was to go back to college and finish my degree so I would be away from those sorry-ass people. I went up to my old college from before and told them what was going on. My home life was horrible. They had a room available in one of their student apartments. I had just enough money in my account to pay for it. I went home and packed all my shit up and got the hell out.

Souls, in the hero's journey, there is a stage called Woman as Temptress. This is the part of the journey where the hero may meet temptation in female form. She is a test to see if the hero will place gratification over his or her own path. I find it very interesting that the goddess and temptress can be the same person. Mahogany was both. She was kind at first and took me in and showed me unconditional love. Then she attacked me. I guess our sexual chemistry was the temptation and the test for me was if I would really have sex with her. I didn't. I didn't see anything wrong with having sex with her. According to the hero's journey, she was supposed to reject me and obviously, I didn't pass the test. I didn't see how having sex would get me off my path. I was being punished for wanting to have sex with this woman when the sexual energy was placed there. It wasn't natural. I think I was more attracted to her energy than her.

# Chapter 10:
# College Woes Continued

I was ready to be back in college. I was a junior and only had one semester left until I would finally be a senior.

I had yet another roommate. She was very neat and well organized. She always talked about her forty-year-old boyfriend. I thought it was weird she was dating someone that old. Our dorm room was a decent size.

I saw a witch decoration on the dorm room across from us. It was around Halloween, so I didn't really pay it much attention. Shortly after that, my roommate and I stopped getting along. We both started being petty for whatever reason roommates get into it. She would try to get up in the morning and make noise. So I would get right up with her. She would try to play music to annoy me, and I would sing along with every song. I liked all kinds of music. I knew I made her mad as she changed each station and I knew every word.

I told her previously about my nightmare issues. I still couldn't sleep comfortably. She wanted me to turn my night light off. "You're a grown woman sleeping with a night light on. She didn't understand the severity of it, and I didn't expect her to.

"Everyone has nightmares," she yelled one time.

"Not the kind that I have," I said.

She tried to clown me for using it. I needed that light on. I tried to compromise with her.

I came in after class and she and a friend were watching a scary movie. She had the volume up really loud. She was trying to scare me so I would have nightmares. I started slamming shit around and I even poured water on the floor, hoping she would slip and fall. Her friend was terrified. She had no idea what was going on. I wasn't afraid of scary movies. I used to be terrified of them when I was younger. I would get so stressed out watching them, so I stopped watching them. I got to the point where I was comfortable enough to watch them again. The movies were nowhere close to what I was experiencing in my dreams. *'This stupid bitch,'* I thought.

I couldn't take any more of her shit, so I reported her, and apparently, she reported me too around the same time. We had to go to mediation and talk about our differences. The roommate had mentioned the age difference and she believed that was one of the problems. We both agreed to try to get along better.

I joined a paranormal group at school. I found out the school was known to be haunted. I also found an on-campus priest. He was a younger guy and I saw him being very flirty with the female students. I sent him pictures of the ghost I had and asked him what he thought. He was like, "Yeah, I can see them." He told me I could make my own holy water and he showed me how to do it, but it didn't work for me.

I met a lot of psychic and intuitive people at that school. Almost everybody I talked to had some type of psychic ability. It was amazing.

I really began to like the school compared to the other one. I started to feel more comfortable. My social worker teachers were awesome. They were very helpful to me. There were several I bonded with, but there was one in particular who I liked the most. She was in her forties. She was also a preacher on the side. She was very kind to me but stern. She would always cut me a break when I needed one. We talked about other things as well. I would be so excited to have class with her. I started having dreams about her turning into a demon. I would be standing there looking at her in the classroom and her face would morph into a demon. We were standing in the elevator together and I told her about the dreams. She took a step away from me and said, "No demons here." I could tell I made her feel uncomfortable, but I was hoping she could tell me why this was happening. I asked her about this dream I had where I was wearing an ankh and I was being attacked by these dark forces. Somebody was trying to take it away from me. I knew it had something to do with Mahogany.

Me and my roommate started bumping heads again. She started purposely turning the lights on knowing they bothered my eyes. "I need the lights on," she yelled.

I understood it was an inconvenience for her, but I was stuck. At that point, she was doing it to piss me off. A man who worked for the school came up to our room and cussed her out. He said, "She has an eye disorder, and you need to take that seriously."

She started mouthing off and he went off on her ass.

He pretty much told her she would do what he told her to do. After all, turning the lights on knowing I have a disorder was looked at as discrimination. We agreed she would turn the top light on when I was out of the room. Lamps were okay for me, but she wanted the big light on. My first roommate never had a problem with this, but I tried to be understanding from her perspective too.

A couple of days later, a girl came up to me and asked me if I was roommates with her. "How could you live with her?" she asked.

I was like, "Girllll."

She was her previous roommate. She said she had a lot of problems with her too. We both started laughing. She had mentioned that my roommate stole her bracelet.

I started hanging out with that girl and I invited her and her friends to my room just to fuck with my roommate. She was pissed. It was amazing. Karma started to take place on her ass. I didn't have to do anything; it just happened naturally. She went and snitched about the old roommate being there and the girl got kicked out. My roommate ended up leaving for the weekend and went back home. I was so happy she was gone. It was a nice little break.

The semester was almost over, and I was certain I was going to have my own mothafuckin room next semester. I could not handle having roommates. Summer was coming, and there was no way in hell I was going back to my dad's, so I decided to stay on campus for the summer. I moved into the college apartments. I had my own room finally. There were four roommates in that place. Once again, I was moving my shit around like a bag lady. I assumed that all the roommates were leaving for the summer. I thought I was going to have the place to myself. I was sadly mistaken. I watched all the roommates move out with their shit one by one. I noticed the last roommate was still in there. I could tell she was waiting for me to leave too. I was so pissed off. I just wanted to be alone.

I started a work-study job at an academic office. '*This is great,*' I thought. I needed money for the summer. It was an easy job, but I had to get used to it. I wasn't used to office work. My supervisor got irritated with me because I moved so slowly. I didn't get along with her or the other lady that worked there at first, but it got better throughout the summer. I ended up getting really close with her; she was actually a really nice woman who taught me a lot.

I was so thankful my dad helped me pay for my housing over the summer. My new roommate was very quiet, and I barely saw her, which I liked. I didn't talk to her at all. I didn't feel the need to.

Then some shit popped off, of course. She started banging pots around in the kitchen and doing shit to piss me off. She was a psych major, so she started playing these psychological mind games with me. I had never seen anything like it in my life. She would do shit and act like nothing happened. She put some fish odor in the living room; it was so strong and disgusting. It was unbearable. It starting hurting my eyes. I reported it to the school, and when they went in there, they said they didn't smell anything. Apparently, she had removed the odor.

She made me look like the aggressor. The staff would say, "She's not doing anything to you." I couldn't take it anymore. She was driving me crazy, so I was gonna fuck her up the best that I could. I didn't care if I got kicked out of school.

I waited until the bitch got home and I sat with my door open. Shit was about to go down. She came in and I gave her that look like, *'Try me, Bitch.'* I was waiting for her to try some shit. I could tell she felt the tension. She was scared, but she still came out of her room. She pretended like she was changing the temperature on the thermostat, which was in view by my door. She slowly turned her head and looked at me. She then went back to her room. I was waiting for her to say something smart or make some kind of noise. She was quiet the rest of the day, but I knew I had to take matters into my own hands.

I started leaving music and the TV on and turning it up really loud in the mornings. I would leave for the day and lock my door. Apparently, she was reporting it because when I got home, the TV would be off. I could tell I was waking her up in the morning and she had a job too, so she was tired. When I turned my shower on while she was taking a shower, the water would turn cold. So, when she was in the shower I would hop in and it would make her water cold. She wasn't too happy about that. I would see her riding the bus. When we would get off, I played Christian music loudly on my phone and followed her. She got really annoyed and started walking as fast as she could to get away from me. "Where you going, Bitch?" I chuckled to myself.

One time, she was waiting for the bus, and I stood behind her very closely. When she got on the bus, as she sat down, I bumped her leg with my knee really hard. She was pissed. She tried so hard not to let me get to her; she tried not to show any emotion, but I was getting to the bitch.

I decided I wanted to move to yet another room with other roommates. I couldn't do another semester with that bitch. She was gonna get me kicked out of school. The summer semester was finally over. I packed up all my shit, and I thought, *'What can I do to get her back?'* One last hoorah for this bitch.

I went into the kitchen and got a bottle and put pine-sol in it and opened the refrigerator door. I sprayed it all over her food. I didn't place it directly in her food, but on the outside of everything. I honestly didn't give a fuck. I didn't feel like that was enough. So I went into my bathroom and began to trim my pubic hair. I collected the hairs and placed them in my hand. I went into the kitchen and sprinkled it all over. I put it on the floor, the counter, the refrigerator, and the kitchen sink. *'That should do it,'* I thought. I knew it was foul and that was my intent.

Then summer was over and I was finally a senior. I was almost done! My new roommates didn't bother me in the new apartment. I barely saw them. I spent most of my time in my room. I had a dream about Mouse. I was in my room at my dad's house. She was putting her grandkids' toys in my room. It was weird because I could hear the TV in the background like it wasn't a dream – like I was really there. I felt like she was trying to kick me out of my dad's house, but I wasn't even there. I was in college.

I did a spell on her and I used cayenne pepper. After the spell, I started to get heartburn. It got very bothersome, so I decided to remove the spell. *'That's odd,'* I thought. I had used cayenne pepper before with no problem. I did the same spell on my dad without the pepper because he pissed me off. He was always taking Mouse's side. He didn't even like the bitch. He was so fake. I was trying to remove my dad from my life for good because he pissed me off. We got into an argument about where I was going to live when I graduated.

Mahogany was still coming into my dreams with her bullshit. *'This is insane,'* I thought. I would dream we were sitting at the table, and she would make me eat food that I usually didn't eat. Once when I ate seafood she came into my dream and attacked me.

I didn't eat seafood for a whole year as a result.

I got a reading from the lady on YouTube again to see what the fuck was going on. "She keeps doing the same spell on you over and over again. I'm starting to question her mental health," she said.

"Why is she doing this?" I asked.

"Love, because she loved you."

That still didn't make any sense as to why she would still be doing this. The reader offered to do some spell work to help me, but it didn't work.

Meanwhile, I was doing some spell work of my own. I did a love spell I found online. It was a combination of cinnamon and honey.

An hour later, I looked out my window and saw a student from the top floor run down to the first floor. He opened a bedroom window and crawled inside it. He came out minutes later with a game system and some other items. He then went back upstairs. *'What the hell?'* I hadn't ever seen shit like that before: someone breaking into someone's house. I turned back around, and the same guy came back out and went in there again. This time, his roommate was a lookout for him. He came out with more stuff. I ducked down even lower. I was hoping he hadn't seen me. The area had a high crime rate, so I was not trying to get a cap popped in my ass. I didn't know what to do. I saw the girl come home and I saw her upset that someone stole her stuff. She must have had a friend over that unlocked her window. They knew she would be gone that night. It was crazy that people did shit like that.

The police came, and I wondered if I should tell them what I saw. I was so afraid. I wondered if my spell did that. I think it did. My eyes were protected from me seeing a lot of stuff, and maybe the spell removed that shield somehow. Later, some guy asked me to hang out, but he was too young. The spell did not completely work how I wanted it to.

I dreamed I was asleep in my bed, and I watched a hand grab me by my hair and drag me up the wall. I started levitating. It was dark and smoky in my room. The only thing visible was the poster of Jesus on my wall. I tried to lift my head up several times and was unsuccessful. I yelled, "Fuck you!" to the demons and stuck my middle finger up in rotation because I couldn't see, and I didn't know exactly where the demons were at. I finally woke up and I could feel myself trying to lift my head up. I was terrified. I couldn't believe I was levitating like the girl on *The Exorcist*. I would never watch that fuckin movie, but I had seen parts of it. Jesus had saved me once again.

It was my last semester, and it was very tough and stressful. I got an internship at a church right by the school. '*A church*,' I thought. I was excited. It was the first time they had an intern. The pastor was nice, and he looked really young. I had my own office space. My job was to make brochures of the church's services. I had to help with their food program and help search for grants. There was also a thrift shop downstairs they had with donated items. Most of the time, I ran the register, but sometimes I put clothing out. I really enjoyed doing those things. They made me happy.

Soon, conflict started between me and the pastor. I didn't really care for him, and he didn't care for me either. I felt like he was acting funny towards me. When he would leave for the day, he started locking the offices. It made me feel like he didn't trust me or maybe I would try to steal something. That definitely rubbed me the wrong way. Like, what if I needed some supplies out of there? I wanted to go the fuck off on him.

I decided to take down all the fall decorations I had put up. I spent my own money on those decorations. I was trying to make the office look more lively. It was so boring in there. After snatching all my decorations off the wall in rage, I decided to leave the lights on in the church so their bill would be high. I left with all the lights on and went downstairs to the thrift store to get my two hours in. One of the men who worked in the church came to the thrift store and said, "Are you

Brandi?"

"Yeah," I said.

He looked at me with wide eyes. "You know you left the lights on upstairs."

"Yes, I know," I said.

He was looking at me like I was crazy, and he looked scared. I wasn't sure why. Maybe somebody saw me acting a damn fool taking those decorations down. I didn't give a fuck.

The next day, the tension was thick as fuck. I was ready to confront the pastor. I was so angry I was about to explode. I wanted to burst into tears – war tears. "I need to talk to you," I said angrily.

He calmly told me to come sit down.

I plopped down in the chair. "I don't like how you started locking the offices up. You weren't doing that before."

He assured me it had nothing to do with me, but I could tell he was lying. His body language and facial expression had guilt written all over it. He told me if I thought he was being funny about locking the doors, I could give him his key back and leave. I took the key off my keyring and slammed the key on the desk and left. "Toodooloo mufucka," I said to myself. Who did he think he was talking to like that?

I told my advisor, who happened to be the director of the program, what happened. I could tell she was upset with me and so she scheduled a meeting with me. I sat in the waiting room nervously. I wondered if I was going to get in trouble. One of my social work teachers came and walked right past me. She didn't even look at me. They called me into the room. They were pissed. "Brandi, you can't just quit an internship," the director said. "If you're having a problem, you need to talk to us."

I tried to explain myself, but they were not trying to hear my side of the story. I had only been at the church for a month.

"Well, what do you want to do?" she asked.

"I want to find another internship," I said.

"I'll see if I can find you another one, but you may not be able to graduate this semester."

I sat there with disappointment. *'Are you serious*?' I thought. I had come a long way; I had been in school for so many years. There was no way I could do *another* semester. I was so worried. I really fucked up this time. The temper tantrum I wanted to throw wasn't appropriate for this school setting. I was used to just quitting a job if someone pissed me off. I did it all the time. I would just leave and not give a fuck. I bet I would never do that shit again.

I started looking for another internship. I was pressed for time. The director ended up finding me a spot at a counseling facility. It took two buses for me to get there, but at least I found something.

It was my first day, and I was excited. I always wanted to do therapy or some kind of counseling. I felt so comfortable there. I observed therapy sessions and intakes. I also observed drug and alcohol groups and created activities for them. I loved it. It was very interesting hearing other people's problems.

There was one girl who came in every week and was having nightmares about her father. Her dad had passed away. She said she and her family were living with other relatives and her dad got into it with them and the relatives ended up kicking them out on the street. She said her dad was into black magic. She said that all of their relatives started dying one by one. Her dad ended up dying and she'd been having dreams about him with demons and they scared her. That definitely sparked my interest. I wanted to ask her more and try to help her, but I knew I couldn't.

There was a guy I was attracted to in the drug and alcohol program. I don't know why I was attracted to him. He was all dirty looking. I think it had something to do with his red hair. I was attracted to people with red hair for some reason. He wasn't cute at all, but I just kept staring at him. It got to the point where the therapist had to wave her hand in my face. "Hello," she said. I wanted to say, *"What, Bitch. Don't put your motherfuckin hand in my face."*

I noticed every time I saw that guy, I would dream about demons.

In another therapy session, two of the clients got into an argument. The one girl was really religious, and she always talked about Jesus. Her name was Brandi too. The other lady wasn't religious at all. Brandi stood up for herself and stood for what she believed in. The lady said, "I'll shove my foot up Jesus' ass," and started laughing. I felt very uncomfortable, and I charged out of the room. That was bullshit. Even though I wasn't Christian anymore, I still had history with Jesus. Whether others thought Jesus was real or not or whatever the case may be, he had saved me from demons many times.

The other thing that bothered me was the disrespect of another person's religion. I wanted to go in my office and cry my eyes out. It always hurt my feelings when people said mean things about Jesus. I sat in my office and cried for a bit and then I went and spoke with the supervisor. I was so upset. I calmed down and went back in the room. The woman got in trouble for saying that. Apparently, when I left, the two women got into a fight and Brandi was sent home.

When I returned the following week for their session, I learned that Brandi had died from an overdose. It was normal for social workers. I was devastated. I couldn't believe it. She was my age and she had left behind three children.

There was a guy at school who was stalking me. He was a nerdy dude with glasses. He would stare at me in class. Then when I would go certain places, he would come out of nowhere. He never said anything to me, but he was creepy. I started to avoid him.

One day, I was talking to the teacher, and he stood behind me very closely. I was like, *'Alright that's it, I'm gonna cuss this little boy out.'* I saw him in the library, and I told him I wanted to talk to him. We stood in the front of the library. "Is there a problem?" I yelled.

"What are you talking about?" he asked.

"Why do you keep following me?"

"I'm not following you." He looked really pissed off. He got really defensive with me and implied the things he was doing were not stalking.

I told his ass to leave me alone or I was going to report him to the police. I went back inside the library. I asked the workers if they knew his name. They told me he had been harassing another girl and that I should report him. I went to the campus police and told them about him and what he'd been doing. They must have contacted him, because he stopped bothering me after that.

I was in the library and I came out for a break. I ran into one of my dad's friends. "That's crazy what happened to your dad," she said.

"What happened?" I asked.

"He got robbed at gun point."

"What," I panicked for a second. "No, I didn't know that. I haven't talked to my dad in a while, so I had no idea." I was really worried about him, so I contacted him to see what the fuck was going on.

I called my roommate and asked her if she wanted to come with me to go see my dad. We caught the bus over there. When we got to the house, that bitch Mouse was outside with the dog. She put her head down because she was scared. She wasn't sure if me and my roommate were gonna fuck her ugly ass up. She quickly went into the house and hid upstairs in her room.

My dad started telling me what happened. Mouse had left for work that night and my dad usually left the door unlocked while he drank in the kitchen. He said he heard someone come in and thought it was Mouse. He went to check it out; there were two men with guns standing there. They pointed the guns at him and made him go upstairs and give them his money. Now, nobody knew where my dad kept his money except for the people who were inside the house. So obviously, somebody told the men where everything was. He said the whole time they pointed the gun at him, they made him stand to the side while they stole the money. My dad had quickly run to the other bedroom across the hall and locked the door. He hurried to grab a gun from the closet. The men shot through the bedroom door before taking off; my dad shot back through the door. My dad saw them running outside and shot out the window, breaking the window into pieces. He said he thought he shot one of them, but he didn't.

I could tell the event had frightened him. I was, of course, thankful that he was okay, but on the other hand, I thought it was karma from him treating me badly and not taking my side. He didn't listen to anything I had to tell him about those bitches. I also felt like God was trying to tell him to stop selling drugs. I hated that my dad was doing that. I knew one day something bad was going to happen to make him stop.

He had previously gone to jail for almost two years for drugs. He didn't get caught; somebody ratted him out. My dad was too smart to get caught, honestly. When my dad went to jail, I was so mad at him. I was very disappointed in him. I didn't know he was selling drugs at the time because I wasn't around him then. I knew he was doing something to make money, but I never investigated anything. I was too busy living my own life.

After talking to my dad, I went back home, and I had my deck of playing cards in my drawer. I had tried reading playing cards before; I felt called to read them. A couple of summers before then, I had gone to visit my cousin in Arizona and one of her neighbors had a deck of playing cards with cute little puppies on the back. I had wanted to see if reading playing cards was different than using the regular cards, since I had issues with the tarot. I had shuffled the cards and was watching a video on reading them. Each card that the guy in the video pulled from the deck was in my deck. He pulled an ace of clubs; it was the same card I had on top of my deck. Then he pulled eight of hearts and that was also my next card on top my deck. It was incredible. How the fuck did I pull the same cards he was pulling in the video? I stopped trying to read them after that, but after what happened with my dad, I felt it was the perfect opportunity to bring them back out. I wanted to know who robbed my dad.

I asked the cards who was responsible. Three women came out. I saw the queen of hearts, swords, and diamonds. So, three bitches had something to do with it. They were either friends or sisters. I asked several times, and the same three bitches were coming out. I also saw two men and one of them looked like there was a snake around him. In the card, there was no snake, but I had seen a snake.

I called my dad and told him about the three girls. "I think they are sisters, Dad," I said.

He said, "Or three friends." He believed that one of Mouse's daughters got him set up.

"What," I said. I was flabbergasted.

He said he was pretty sure she did it. My dad always called her dumb. Well, obviously she wasn't that dumb if she planned all of this. I knew she and my dad didn't get along. He said he had kicked her out because she was stealing change out of the house.

There was a part of me that was happy that karma came against my dad for not doing anything about her when she stole my juice. I had tried to tell my dad back then those bitches were bad news. So that's what he get. He should have listened to me. He was out in that town letting a young girl undermine him. That had to be embarrassing. I didn't plan to do anything about it, honestly. She didn't set me up to get robbed. I was already on to her thief-ass. Mouse was a thief too. I knew that taught my dad a lesson. I had seen in the cards that the three girls came up with a plan and Mouse's daughter had been the leader. I could even see that they were some ugly bitches and that one was black girl and the other two were white. They were all nasty looking. I got a good description of those hoes.

A couple of months before, I got approved for section 8 again in the same area my dad lived in. I was hoping to find a place so I wouldn't have to live with anyone. I was running out of time and could not find anything. I decided to go look at a place on my own. I waited and waited and the bus never showed up. I called the bus company, and they said the bus came by that stop, but they lied. I tried again to catch the bus to go look at a place. The bus didn't show up again. It was odd that happened twice in a row. I started to cry because my voucher was about to expire. What was I going to do? I didn't have anywhere to live after I would graduate from school.

For some reason, my school decided to go on strike. It was a big mess. Nobody knew what was going on or what was going to happen. We weren't sure how long it was going to last or if we would even graduate that semester. Again, it was another delay. I felt like there were a lot of interferences as far as me graduating school. Somebody did not want me to graduate, I thought.

The strike was over after a week and then we were at the end of the semester. I was so stressed out. I was worried I didn't have enough hours for my internship. All these papers were due, and all these tests were coming up. In one class, there was a twenty-page paper due. Twenty pages? I could barely do a five-page paper. I hated writing papers. I was good at it, but I hated doing it. I just wanted to get done already.

Still, I managed to finish up my internship, write an eighteen-page paper, and pass all my tests. I was finally done. All those years of schooling and going to different colleges, going back and forth, changing roommates, my eye disorder, and going through all those spiritual attacks and I was officially done with school. I didn't even want to go to graduation; I just wanted my degree in my hands.

I got my grades back, and I got all A's and one B. I actually went over the limit of the internship hours I needed, and I qualified for the Master's program. It had been one of the best semesters I ever had in college, grade-wise. I worked long and hard and it had seemed like I wasn't going to make it, but I crossed the finish line.

Afterward, I had no choice but to move back in with my dad. "Why didn't you tell me you needed help looking for a place?" my dad asked.

My dad came and helped me pack and move my stuff. I was so happy I graduated, and he was too. My mom, on the other hand, didn't seem too pleased, but I didn't expect her to be. I felt on top of the world, but I hated that I had to go back to my dad's with those trash-ass bitches. Mouse's daughter was banned from the house, of course, but Mouse was still there.

Souls, this was the Approach stage of the hero's journey for me. This stage is when setbacks occur, causing the hero to try a new approach or form new ideas. This is a lesson for the hero to see how persistent he is, and I was very persistent to graduate. There were many setbacks, with the strike, and me quitting my internship. When I failed, I tried again.

# Chapter 11:
# The Mouse's Trap

**F**eelings of misery set in as I walked through the door at my dad's house once again. I turned my head to the right and, as usual, there was Mouse sitting on the couch doing nothing but smoking weed and watching TV. I couldn't stand her and her wrinkled-ass skin. She looked much older than what she really was, and she was built funny. She was built like a twelve-year-old boy. She wasn't girly at all. She never wore dresses or skirts, she never carried a purse, and she never wore makeup – even though she needed it. Makeup couldn't help her though. She needed a completely new face. She constantly coughed like an old man and had a manly voice. I had nowhere else to go, so I had to suck it up. I went upstairs to unload all my things. I was still on a high from graduating, but now I had to figure out what I was going to do next.

My dad got a gun charge scare for using the gun when those thieves came into the house. He was really worried about it. It seemed like Mouse's daughter was going to get off for setting it up. There was no proof she had anything to do with it, but my dad already knew she did it and my cards were saying it.

I got a reading to confirm the whole situation. The reader said Mouse was conflicted between her lover and her daughter. She said Mouse knew more than she was telling, and she was trying to cover up for her daughter.

I wanted to be a smart-ass, so I left the playing cards out on the table with the three queens so Mouse would know I was on to her daughter. I was sitting in the kitchen telling my dad I was a witch. Then Mouse said, "I knew you were a witch," with a snarl. She was usually very quiet, so it was odd she even said anything. I noticed she was staring at my Archangel Michael medallion too.

Later that day, I was watching a movie with my dad, and she came in with an attitude and threw something over my head and into the kids' play pin. Her behavior was very strange, but I knew if she would have hit me with something, I was going to drag her ass across the floor, right in front of my dad.

There were so many times I wanted to punch Mouse right in her fuckin nose, but I didn't because I didn't want my dad to kick me out. I knew if I fought her, I would try to kill her. That's how much I hated her. I heard her one day when I was upstairs saying that she hated me. I didn't give a fuck; the feelings were mutual. She even had her grandchildren acting funny toward me. They both loved me, but now the oldest one started shooing me away. Every time I would see her, she would say, "Go away." I knew Mouse put her up to it.

I got in the shower to wash my hair. I was very particular about my hair. My hair was always really long. I took after my dad in that department. My dad had really fine, curly hair. My hair wasn't as nice as his though. I had a nappy version of it because of my mom. My mom's hair was frizzy as hell and so was mine. I hated that shit. The summertime was horrible. I could never wear my hair out because it would frizz and curl right up. I would waste my money going to hair salons. There were no products that could tame my lion's mane. I tried a relaxer before and it worked when I was younger, but when I got older, it just ruined my hair.

When I got out of the shower, I put some conditioner in my hair and placed a plastic cap over it for several minutes. When I was done, I placed the cap in the garbage.

I went upstairs to my room and got dressed, then I went downstairs to the basement to wash clothes. I noticed an old pair of tennis shoes I thought I had thrown away were sitting neatly in the basement. *'That's weird,'* I thought. It had been a while since I had thrown those shoes away. I knew something was up. Something strange was going on.

I remembered my dad telling me that Mouse fixed my room up for me. We didn't like each other, so why would that bitch get my room together? I started paying attention to her behavior. I purposely put a bag of my garbage in the kitchen garbage. I stayed out of sight until she went into the kitchen. She opened the garbage and found my bag and started going through it. I hurried to the kitchen, and she rushed to put the bag down and put the lid back on. This bitch was going through my garbage. What the fuck? I was so tired of her.

I decided to do a spell on her. It was a new spell I had never tried before. After the spell was done, I went to sleep. I woke up the next morning and noticed it was unusually quiet in the house. After a while, Mouse didn't come down to watch TV and smoke up the house. When my dad got up, I asked him where Mouse was. He told me she went to the hospital because she was having pain in her stomach. I was so ecstatic; I wanted to jump for joy. Yes, the spell worked! I wasn't trying to cause her to have any pain though. The purpose of the spell was to cause chaos. I was just happy she was gone, and I had the living room to myself.

The phone rang and it was Mouse calling for my dad. He came downstairs and said, "Mouse has to get her appendix out." I couldn't believe what I was hearing. She was definitely getting karma from all the shit she did to me. My dad said there had been a lump by her belly button a week before. She was on her way to get surgery and he left to go see her. It was a real high for me. My dad looked sad before he left, and I didn't know what the fuck for. When my dad got back, he said Mouse was staying the night in the hospital.

The next day, Mouse came home with her other daughter, the one with the kids. I went downstairs and then went back up and started laughing so she knew that it was me who put her ass in the hospital. Everybody got quiet and there was a weird silence. She definitely tried to make me feel sorry for her, but I wasn't falling for it. Somebody called me on the house phone. Mouse answered it and called me. She acted like she was in so much pain walking up the steps and tried to put on this sad face. *'Bitch, please,'* I thought.

I got a reading with the YouTube reader again. I told her about Mouse's weird behavior. "She paid someone to do magic on you," she said.

"What?" I said. I was very confused. "Are you sure?"

She told me it was a couple who did it. The guy did most of the magic, and the woman backed him up. I asked how long ago this was done. She started to stutter – six... six... six months ago. It all started to make sense.

Souls, remember when I was having those dreams about Mouse putting her grandkids' shit in my room? That was part of the spell.

The reader told me Mouse had paid them a lot of money so I would fall out with my dad and never be in his life again. "She's getting a woman to help her," she said. "It's a woman that asks your dad for money all the time."

She was talking about her dusty-ass daughter, the one with the kids. She always asked my dad for money. Like, where the fuck was her own dad? My dad mostly helped because she had kids but fuck that. She didn't even like him. My dad was way too generous to the wrong people, and they took advantage of him. You couldn't tell him shit though. These people were out there embarrassing him, and he would get mad if I said something about it.

The reader told me there was something attached to my scalp and my throat chakra. I was terrified. I noticed that the plastic cap I put in the garbage was missing. That hoe took the plastic cap and used it to do magic on me. It was already planned before I came home from college. That's why I kept missing the bus when I tried to look for places when I had that section 8 voucher. She wanted me out of my dad's life, was fucking ridiculous, but she wanted me to come to the house so she could do black magic on me. I couldn't believe that sneaky coward-ass bitch hired someone to do magic on me. She knew she couldn't do it herself. She was a scaredy-ass bitch.

I wasn't quite sure what to do next. I was stuck in a house that was booby-trapped. I noticed there was a broom at the bottom of the steps of the basement and it was placed diagonally. It looked like some kind of trick or something. There was no way I was going down there. I told my dad about it. He got angry with me. "I put the broom down there," he yelled. "I threw it down there." '*Why would he throw a broom down the steps?*' I thought. '*Why would it land the way it did?*' He was full of shit. He eventually moved it.

I went to the other room – the kids' playroom – and there was a toenail in the middle of the floor. Then, I looked around the room and saw toenails in the base of the wall. For some reason, I picked them up and put them in a bag. Then that bitch came running in the room to see if I picked them up. She started giggling. That night, I started having really bad dreams again. I assumed it was because I touched those toenails.

My friend from college invited me to come to her house for a couple of days so I could get away from them. I packed some clothes to take with me. Then I put all my other stuff away and locked up everything so Mouse could not get it. It was a nice little break spending time with my friend, but I knew I had to go back to my dad's. I was dreading it.

When I got back home, my whole room was moved around. The kids' toys were in there. My dad was surprised that I came back. Mouse was pissed. She walked past me real fast, and I could tell she was angry. I cleared all the shit out of the room and put my shit back where it was.

The next day, I saw the plastic ties I used to tie my suitcase up lined up on the basement floor in a row. Obviously, she went in my garbage to get those. I started leaving my garbage in my room. I'm not sure why, but I picked up the ties. I kept touching things with my bare hands. When I went to sleep that night, I dreamed about the man and woman who were doing magic on me. I couldn't see their faces though. The setting was at a bar that was cold and smelly and dirty. They were trying to fight me, but I was whoopin' their asses with a chair. I had several dreams about them after that.

I spoke to another reader I had been going to for years. I had to talk on the phone very quietly so Mouse didn't hear. I put a blanket over my head and sat in the corner of my bed. He told me the magic was supposed to get me to leave the house without saying why I left. So that's why Mouse was angry when I came back. The spell hadn't worked completely. He said she was doing magic on my dad too. She was turning him against me, and I could tell. She put a love spell on him as well. She knew my dad didn't want her. He'd been trying to get away from her for years. She was using him for money because she was unable to take care of herself financially. He had been with her since she was twenty-five, so he took on the father role for her, I guess.

My dad did the same for me. He took care of me financially way longer than he should have. He always helped me if I needed it. He always sent me money or bought me stuff. He was a really good dad, but I knew his behavior was off. I didn't know she was doing spells on him too, but it all made perfect sense. The reader said she was acting like an evil stepmother even though they were not married; she was jealous of me.

That was the second time I had heard that from a psychic. She was jealous that my dad paid more attention to me, and she felt left out. She was competing with me. She felt like if I wasn't around, she and my dad would get married. She was most certainly delusional. The reader told me it was going to backfire on her. He gave me a couple of spells to do to protect myself. One was to buy a doll to protect my dad and the other was to protect me in the house.

When I got off the phone, I went into my dad's room, and when I came out, I could hear Mouse downstairs walking around, but like she was dragging her feet. It was inhuman, like she was a zombie or some kind of monster. I could tell she was eavesdropping on me and my dad's conversations. I went downstairs and looked her dead in the face and noticed one of her eyes was rolling around uncontrollably. '*What the fuck*?' I thought.

The YouTube reader told me to take a spiritual bath with goat's milk. So I gathered all the ingredients and took the bath. I let the milk air dry on me and put my night clothes on. She instructed me to save some of the bath and pour it out at a crossroads. I went to sleep and got up early in the morning. It was cold outside, and it was still dark. I walked far away from the house getting hit with a chilling wind. It was icy out, so I had to make sure I didn't slip. I found a crossroads I felt comfortable with. I dumped the bath over my shoulder and walked away and didn't look back. Later that day I did the other spell work I was instructed to do, but I waited for Mouse to leave for work. I was nervous because I wanted to make sure I did everything right. Then I had to watch my surroundings and my every move.

I got my dad this big-ass card for Valentine's Day. I wanted to sneak it in the house so Mouse wouldn't see it. I put it under my coat and then put it in my room. I tried to give it to him early, but he wouldn't take it because he was being an asshole. He was so embarrassed that he had a sorry-ass girlfriend who never bought him anything. Somehow, he thought this would make her feel uncomfortable. We all knew what a piece of shit she was.

I went back out to grab the rest of the groceries I had bought. I also stopped by Eat'n Park to get some breakfast while I was out, and I set that on the table. Mouse and her daughter were in the living room with the kids. While I was at the car, Mouse's daughter came out and sat in her car. She just sat there for a minute, and I noticed she didn't pull off right away. I saw that she was on the phone, but I finished getting my things and went back inside.

The bag with my food looked like someone opened it and tied it back. I wasn't completely sure though. I thought maybe Mouse did something to my food, so I gave her grandchildren a piece of my sausage just in case. If there was something in my food, it would affect them too. I went upstairs to eat my food in peace. A little bit later my throat started hurting like I had strep throat. I thought that was weird because it came out of nowhere. I knew something was up. *'Did that sorry-ass fucking bitch put something in my food?'* I needed to know immediately.

I contacted the YouTube reader and she confirmed it. "She did it to control you," she said. "She wants you to keep your mouth shut."

She crossed the fucking line with that one. It was going to get physical. I didn't care if my dad kicked me out. I needed to come up with a plan. I needed to find somewhere to stay because that shit was unacceptable. I had to figure out when I was gonna kick her ass and leave. She was not getting away with that shit. My throat seemed to feel better but then got worse again. My throat never does that.

A while later, Mouse was downstairs washing dishes. I told myself I wasn't going to say anything, but I couldn't help it. "Yeah, I know about the two people you paid to do magic on me."

Her eyes got so big. "What two people?" She looked guilty as hell.

I told her, "That shit is gonna come back on your ass, watch." She rushed to leave the kitchen.

I continued to do shit to piss her off, but she acted like she didn't care. I sat in the living room with her. I was being annoying and loud; she just ignored me. I wished I would have punched that bitch right in her fuckin face, but I knew I would get kicked out. I was in one of the bedrooms and I could see her in her bedroom. I saw her staring at my picture while smoking a cigarette. *'This bitch is on my dick,'* I thought. My dad had several pictures of me near his side of his bed.

That night, I heard her tell her granddaughter to go wake me up. The bitch thought I was sleeping but I heard her. The little girl said, "No." That little girl was smart because I was gonna send her ass right back out. The next day, I told my dad what Mouse did and later, she made it seem like she didn't do it. My dad tried to take her side and I was sick of that shit.

Then my sunglasses went missing. Now mind you, I never lose anything. I tried to remember where I left them. After hours of thinking, I realized when I had come in from the store that day Mouse put something in my food, I had put them on the table next to the bag. I didn't like people stealing my things. So, I was going to confront her funky ass. I waited until she came home from her break at work. My dad was at the bar, which was perfect as he couldn't help her. I heard the door slam when she walked in. I had my sneakers on and my hair up in a ponytail. I was nervous but more nervous about getting kicked out of the house and about smashing her head on the ground and getting blood everywhere. I went downstairs and said, "Where are my sunglasses?"

"What sunglasses?" she said.

"You know what I'm talking about, Bitch. You stole my sunglasses." I began to move towards her and get in her face. At that point, I put my finger in her face. "Bitch, I told you not to touch my stuff," I yelled.

Mouse then grabbed her phone and called my dad. She told my dad I was in her face screaming at her. She began to tremble in fear. "I don't even wear sunglasses," she said.

I began to yell, "You stole my sunglasses and I know you did."

She hung up the phone and I grabbed it and threw it on the floor. Then I pushed her. She then ran into the bathroom, and I went after her. She closed the door. I kicked the door, but I should have kicked her. I could hear the shower running. I then went back upstairs and waited in my room for her to come out. Thoughts of kicking her down the steps filled my mind. I heard the bathroom door open and her feet coming up the steps. She was wrapped in a bath towel, and she entered her bedroom. I wanted to hit her right in the damn head, but I didn't. She shut the door behind her. She wouldn't come out of that room for shit. An hour went past; I yelled for her to come out, and I started to kick the wall. I started packing my things and waited for my dad to get home.

My dad finally got home and was intoxicated. I could feel the tension in the air. He went straight to the bedroom. I stood by my bedroom door so I could hear their conversation. "Did she hit you?" he asked.

"No," Mouse said.

"You want to fight her? Go fight her," he said.

"Yeah, let's fight," I yelled. I began to go off at the mouth saying all the fucked-up shit Mouse had done. Nobody came out of the room for the rest of the night. I went to sleep.

The next day, I stayed in my room mostly. It was unusually quiet in the house. Mouse had left and I went into my dad's room. "You got to go. Mouse was going to call the police on you," my dad said.

"For what," I said. "Go ahead and call them, then."

"You got to go," he said.

I was very angry and upset. My dad had never kicked me out of the house before. I went into my room and slammed the door. I started calling people to come pick me up. Unfortunately, my only choice was to go back to my mom's house. I needed a ride there. I called my college friend and asked her if she could come get me. She said she had to see. I began to cry. I told her Mouse was making up lies about me and my dad was kicking me out. She told me she would call me later. I called one of my dad's friends and she said she couldn't come get me that day. I was running out of time and just wanted to get the hell out of that fucking house. It seemed like nobody was going to come. What was I going to do? My college friend then called me and said she was on her way. I was so relieved. It was an unfair and fucked-up situation.

I made sure to leave my dad and Mouse a parting gift before I left. I went downstairs and grabbed some milk and poured it all over the bed I was sleeping on and behind the bed, and on the walls. I grabbed some juice and poured it all over Mouse's grandchildren's toys and all over the room. "Fuck them," I said.

I went downstairs and Mouse walked past me and started laughing. *'Ohhh she was so lucky.'* I said to myself, "Okay, Bitch, I got you." So, I thought about something I could take from her since she took my sunglasses. Hey, fair is fair. I went in the bathroom, and I took her and my dad's dentures. I thought about taking her deceased mother's picture off the wall, but I didn't have time to grab it.

My college friend came, and she helped put all my stuff in the car. I had to leave some of my furniture behind, but I didn't give a fuck. I was just happy to be gone.

On the way out, my dad handed me my sunglasses. "Here," he said. "I found them in the car."

I knew for sure they weren't in the car. I had OCD. I never left anything behind, and I always checked. The bitch stole my sunglasses and then placed them in the car when she knew he was leaving. The bitch set me the fuck up. "Just because Mouse don't wear sunglasses don't mean she didn't take them," I said. He had no idea what was going on. He was brain-washed and Mouse was doing magic to keep him that way. There was nothing I could do at the moment.

We stopped at the mall before we went to my friend's house. I emailed the YouTube reader to tell her what had happened. She said Mouse was an evil witch. The reader said she fixed my throat for me. I did notice my throat stopped hurting. I thanked her for all her help. The next morning, something white came out of my throat. It looked like a long white worm. I had never seen anything like that before in my life. My dad called and left me a message complaining about their dentures missing. He thought it was a sick thing to do, and I thought it was a clever thing to do. Plus, I needed something of hers in case I needed to put a spell on her. "What sick person would take false teeth?" my dad asked.

I stayed with my friend for a couple of days, and then she asked her other friend if they could drop me off at my mom's.

I went to my mom's house, and she was being a bitch as usual for no reason at all. The house was still in the worst possible condition. I hated it there. There was black mold and nasty dirt for centuries piled up. Plus, her nasty attitude was not going to work for me. The plumbing was not working and the fact that I had to walk up the street to go to the bathroom was fucking ridiculous. I had nowhere else to go, though. The house was so old and falling apart. I didn't know why she just didn't move. I started feeling sick immediately. The mold made me sick from breathing it in. It even blurred my vision. The house got worse and worse every time I went there.

I told the YouTube reader and told her where I was. I told her I took their dentures, and she busted out laughing. She told me to get rid of them and anything I had of Mouse's because she was doing work on them, which meant she was doing magic. I told her about the condition of my mom's house. "You can't even use the bathroom there. You need to go to a women's shelter," I said. That house was unlivable. I already felt like I was homeless.

When I got off the phone, I noticed my mom was eavesdropping and heard the whole conversation. "Yeah, your dad kicked you out," she said.

My mom kept getting on my fucking nerves, so I said, "Fuck it. I think I will go to a shelter." She was threatening to kick me out like she always did. Plus, there were pieces of black stuff falling from the cracks in the walls. I kept feeling like something was in my eye. I realized those black piece were falling in my eye. I ended up getting a brown stain in my eye because of it.

I called a shelter, and they wouldn't let me come because it was for domestic violence victims. So I changed my story and said I was being abused by my boyfriend. They allowed me to come after that. My mom knew I had nowhere else to go so she felt like she was entitled to treat me like shit. I felt like she enjoyed it. She wasn't just mean to me. She was like that with everybody.

I started having dreams about Mouse. She was doing black magic and astral projecting into my dreams. Now I had somebody else coming into my dreams harassing me. Mahogany had slowed down with her interaction but now this bitch was picking up where she left off.

I packed all my belongings up and was ready to go. I was nervous about going to a shelter, but I was happy to leave my mom and her house. I had known that shit was going to happen; it happened every time I went to stay with her. I was worried about what I was going to do after I got to the shelter. I didn't tell my mom shit. I made her think everything was cool and then when she went to sleep, I called an uber and left.

When I got to the shelter, I did not know what to expect. I was worried about my room and roommates; luckily I got a room to myself. It wasn't the best, that's for damn sure, but it was better than my mom's house. It was gross, especially the bathroom. It had boogers on the walls and nasty floors. The shower was disgusting. The bathtub was torn up and you could see pink shit and rust. I showered once with flip flops on. I didn't even want my flip flops to touch the damn tub. I had a membership at the YMCA, so I started to shower there.

I was so mad I even had to be in this fuckin position. Like, I was really in a fuckin shelter. It was peaceful there, though. The bed was hard as a rock. I ended up buying a mattress pad to put over it. That was so much better. While I was there, I stopped having visions of aliens. I was still having dreams of Mouse though.

They told me there was a program that helped women find housing. I was so grateful because I had no idea where I was going to go. They also had a program that paid off any amount due that was left over from previous apartments. I owed $400 to the apartment in Texas. They wanted to make sure we didn't have any blockages so I would qualify for a place. That took a lot of stress off of me. I was ready for my own place again. I was so tired of living with folks.

I got along with the women at the shelter for the most part. It was interesting to hear their stories when we had our group sessions. These women talked about abuse and how hard their life was. I couldn't imagine being in an abusive relationship. I felt bad for them. One of the women talked about her boyfriend punching her in the stomach while she was pregnant. He was a professional boxer. I thought, *'Why didn't she throw hot grits on him or something?'* I probably would have tried to put a hex on my boyfriend if he was doing that to me. I saw the sadness in her eyes. I decided to give her some something to use to protect herself from him.

I was at the shelter for only two weeks before they found me an apartment. I was so excited. *'That was fast,'* I thought. By then, most of the women at the shelter were against me. I'm not sure what I did to make them turn on me. I heard one of the women call me a simple bitch. I honestly thought it was hilarious, but I went out in the hallway so she could say it to my face. She walked up to me and said, "Hey." I said, "Hey, girl." Women were too catty and fake for me. I was just cool with this woman and now she didn't like me. I knew it was time for me to go.

# Chapter 12:
# Jody

I moved to a new town right by the water. I didn't really know anything about the area, but I had heard it was a drug town. Regardless, I needed somewhere to live. I was happy to be on my own again and out of that shelter. I was hoping to start my life over. It was a small apartment, but it was in good condition, and I was on the top floor. I had three other neighbors on my floor. It seemed to be a very quiet place. The first night I didn't have a bed, so I slept on the floor. The floors had no carpet, just tiles. I really didn't sleep that well.

The next day, I grabbed my things from the shelter. I was so happy to be leaving. I told those bitches at the shelter goodbye because I was sure I would never see them again, but deep down inside I truly hoped that they escaped their abusive situations. The shelter paid for a cab for me to get back to my apartment. I went to the office and got my key and settled in.

The people were really strange. They would gather around almost every night and fight each other. That shit was insane. I would hear screaming and watch people fight outside the window. I mean crowds of people. It was a big drug town, and I was smack in the middle of it. I watched their little operation going and the fiends just walking around. I had never seen anything like it.

There was a fat prostitute who lived downstairs who was nice to me. She called me pretty every time I saw her. There was an older white woman next door to me. I spoke to her sometimes. Nobody was in the apartment across from me but eventually a black lady moved in there. Across the hall there was a guy my age who was a stalker.

I saw two men standing by the steps that left my apartment to go outside. When I came back in, I saw one of them squatting down and straining. I looked at him and said, "What are you doing?" I could tell he was going to the bathroom on the floor.

I ran out of the building and went to the management office. I told them what was going on. I went back upstairs with the maintenance man and saw diarrhea and piss all over the floor. I was so disgusted and so was the maintenance guy. I couldn't believe that shit. Why didn't he just go use a restroom somewhere? The maintenance man later told me he did it because he was too embarrassed to go in the lady's house and poop. That shit stayed in the hallway the whole weekend. The smell was fucking horrid. One of the neighbors poured something on it to stop the smell. It still stunk. Maintenance did not want to clean it up.

There was a couple who lived in another building, across from me, and they fought all the time. She would get beat up and even her friends tried to help her but the next day everybody would be cool.

The neighbor downstairs, she would fight almost every day and she was always drunk. I felt bad for her. I felt bad for all those people. This was their way of life.

I quickly came to the conclusion that these people were literally invoking demons by doing all these drugs and alcohol. I was surrounded by nothing but demonic energy. They looked like zombies. They would walk all funny and it was scary. That shit was not fuckin normal, and I wanted to stay far away from them; I did for the most part. '*Who the fuck lives in a place like this*?' I thought.

One night I was sound asleep and I heard arguing outside as usual. I walked to the living room window and saw two girls arguing. Some guy's side chick had pulled up to his girlfriend's house trying to fight. The girlfriend had a knife and everything, but I could tell she didn't want no trouble. The guy was out there too. I remember the girlfriend asked, "How did she know where we lived?" The arguing continued and one of the other neighbors stepped in to help and her daughter was there too.

All of a sudden, I saw all of them running and heading for the door. That side chick woman was driving towards them trying to run them over. They were all safe and they called the police, but that shit was crazy.

I had never seen so many fights in my life. It was not a place for kids.

The following week I was able to get the rest of my things out of storage. I had a camping cot I slept on until I was able to get furniture. The shelter paid for me to furnish my entire apartment with used furniture from a non-profit agency. I was so thankful. I knew I couldn't afford any on my own. The agency was fast with delivery. It was a Saturday, and movers were putting my furniture in the apartment. They were trying to get my couches up the steps, but they were too big and wide to fit.

That's when I saw him: Jody. He was looking at me through the hallway door and eyeballing the shit out of me. I really wasn't paying him any attention. I was just trying to get my furniture moved in and enjoy it. Jody opened the door and kindly tried to help the movers move the couch up the steps. Jody's phone rang and he was on his way outside of the building. When he walked past me, I looked at him, but he purposefully didn't look at me. I knew he wanted to be seen.

The movers gave up on the couch; they told me I would have to get another one. As they were leaving, Jody said, "Y'all couldn't get the couches up there?" They said, "No." I knew he didn't care about the couch; he was just trying to get my attention. The movers were able to get my bed inside; I was excited to have a real bed and not have to sleep on that cot anymore. It had dust mites all over it and I was allergic to them. I decided to throw the cot away. "Are you throwing that away?"

Jody asked.

"Yes," I said.

"Is there something wrong with it?" he asked.

"No, I just don't need it anymore. I got a bed now."

"Oh," he said in a nasty tone. I think he thought I was being smart with him, but I truly wasn't. "Wait a minute don't throw it away."

I set the cot right next to the dumpster and left it there. I came back out to throw away some more trash and I saw Jody with the cot. "This looks new," he said.

"Yeah, I hardly use it."

He said, "I'm gonna use this for my kids."

"That's cool," I said.

"Thank you," he said.

My first couple of weeks at the apartment were very challenging for me. I had an issue with the furniture. There were some kind of chemicals fumigating from them, especially the loveseat. My whole place had a disgusting, sickening smell to it. It was horrible. I tried everything. I tried cleaning the furniture and spraying neutralizers, but the smell was too strong.

I made spaghetti one night and the fumes got into my food. After I ate that spaghetti, it was curtains for me. I threw up all over the fuckin place. I couldn't stop; I was so dizzy. I realized those chemicals were on all the furniture and even the bed. The bed was brand new too, but when I would lay on it, it burned my skin. As I continued to throw up everything in my body, I realized I needed to make a trip to the emergency room. I went outside to get some fresh air, but I could barely stand up. I had vomit all over me as I waited for an uber to arrive.

I saw Jody again. It was dark outside, so I was hoping he wouldn't see my dinner on my shirt or smell it. He looked at me, and I secretly hoped that he would ask me if I was okay and help me. I felt so weak and the uber was taking so long to arrive. I stared at him as he walked down the street.

I finally got to the hospital and began to break out in a rash on my face. The doctor gave me the medicine they always gave me to make me stop throwing up, but it made me puke even more. Being sick like that was such a burden; I was already stressed out. I couldn't catch a break. I was still having nightmares about Mouse. *'I wonder if she did something to make me sick,'* I thought. I couldn't stay at my place for a couple of days because of the fumes. I had to get rid of all the furniture and get all new stuff. Thank goodness the agency was okay with it.

A couple of days later, I checked my mailbox and stopped to read my mail on my way up the steps. Jody walked into the building. We made eye contact and I started to run up the steps. "Hi," he said abruptly as he waved to me. He said it in a shy manner as if he wanted me to feel sorry for him or as if he wanted to come off as innocent.

"How are you?" I said cheerfully.

"I'm good. How are you?"

"I'm good," I said.

"That's good," he said.

I could tell he still wanted to continue the conversation, but I hurried up the steps and he stared at me as I left.

A couple of weeks went by, and I could hear Jody's voice in the courtyard. My apartment was right in the middle, and I could hear and see everything. His voice was loud and had a very strong, mature tone to it. At first, his voice annoyed me.

I grew to like his voice, though, and that's what attracted me to him. I would look out my window and see him. He was shorter than I liked, and I could tell he was an attention seeker. I found myself increasingly becoming attracted to him. I told myself he was going to be my boyfriend, but I always said that about any boy I was attracted to. I would see him out with his children and family. I would also see him with a white woman, but they never stood close together. I thought maybe it was his sister or another a family member.

At the time, I thought Jody was with his babies' mom. She looked Hispanic from far away. She looked very young, too young to have so many children. She was a lot younger than him. She never spoke to me or even looked at me. She didn't come off as being very friendly. I mean none of the women up there were friendly. I was from out of town, and they didn't like that. She and Jody didn't really get along and barely spoke to each other.

One night, I got home from work and some of the people in the apartments were sitting outside. I looked over and saw Jody sitting outside with his children. I took the garbage out and I saw Jody coming in my direction. I was on my way up the stairs, and he called out to me. "Hey!"

"Hey," I said.

"Did you see my kids?" He was standing by the hallway door, and I proceeded to walk towards him.

"Yeah, I seen them when I was coming in." I looked out the door and saw them outside playing.

"Do you have a man?" he asked.

"What," I said. I began to put my head down and stare at the floor. I couldn't believe he asked me that. I had never had an attractive guy ask me if I had a boyfriend. I always got hit on by ugly guys, so it was very weird for me. It made me a little uncomfortable because I wasn't sure where the conversation was going. I didn't answer him. I started talking about other stuff.

"What's your name?" he said.

"I'm Brandi."

He said, "My name is Jody."

I thought, '*That's a* girl's *name.*' We continued to talk. I went to the top of the steps, and he stayed downstairs. I asked him what his zodiac sign was and told me he was a Scorpio. I said, "Oh hell no."

He said, "What?"

I said, "I don't fuck with no Scorpios."

He smiled.

I said, "Scorpios are *very* vengeful. Are you vengeful?"

He said, "Yes," still smiling.

I told him I read playing cards and I needed to practice.

"Oh, okay," he said. I'm not sure if he knew what that meant. He said, "Alright, I'm gonna get back outside,"

And then I said, "No, I don't have a boyfriend."

He was like, "You don't?"

I shook my head no. "Well, are you gonna ask for my number or what?" I said.

"Oh, yeah." He ran up the steps in a hurry. He was so eager to get my number. He reminded me of an excited dog, and I was a treat standing on the top of the steps. He startled me a little bit. He was way too close to me, too close to my face, so I put my arm out and backed up.

"Don't get too close to me," I said.

He said, "I won't bite."

I gave him my number and a few minutes later, he texted me. He was definitely coming off a little too forward for me. He said, "When can I see you?"

I said, "I just saw you."

He said, "I know but I want to see you again."

I pretty much told him if he was looking for just sex, he wouldn't find it here. He said it wasn't like that, but the conversation quickly ended after that. I definitely wasn't looking for a sexual thing, and I wanted to let him know upfront.

A couple of days later, I texted him and asked him if he still wanted me to read his cards and teach him about astrology. He said, "Yeah," but I didn't think he was really interested, to be honest. I didn't see or hear from him for a couple of weeks. I did some readings on him to see what was going on with him. I saw there were three women around him. One of the women was very angry at him. I saw that he had a girlfriend, and he was already in a relationship, which I had figured. However, I ended up finding out it wasn't with his baby mom: it was with that white lady I had seen him walking around with.

I was on my way home from the store, and Jody was staring me down hard. He started walking towards me. I wasn't sure if he was looking at me, so I turned around to see if anybody was behind me. He smiled and tried to give me a hug, and I pushed his arm away. I saw that his babies' mom's mother was looking at me. I said, "No, your girlfriend."

His eyes got so big like he didn't expect me to find out. He completely ignored what I said. He grabbed my arm and said, "Come meet my kids."

I said, "No," and snatched my arm away. *'Why is he introducing me to his kids?'* I thought. I didn't feel important enough to meet his kids plus I knew I wouldn't be around him that long. I asked him about the card reading again.

He agreed and told me to bring the cards outside. I didn't feel comfortable doing the reading outside, so I told him to come up to my house. He said he had to get someone to watch his kids. He soon came up to my apartment and we sat in the living room. After pulling a few cards, I noticed the joker card came out, which was the devil card. He said, "What does that card mean?"

"It's the devil," I said.

"That's me," he said with a smile.

I said, "No, that just means you have an addiction or something negative in your life." Now since I had just started reading, I wasn't sure what I was doing. I saw that angry woman in the cards again. I said, "I see a woman lookin at me crazy."

He asked, "Like, how?"

I said, "She lookin at me like, 'Stay away from my man.'"

He started laughing.

I said, "I see things are going okay with you guys."

He said, "No," in a clear tone. "We're about to break up." He told me things weren't working out with them. He said every time he was at the house, she would leave and act like she had to go somewhere. He said she didn't work, but he didn't work either. "I gotta get back to my kids," he said.

I said, "Okay."

He got up and walked towards the door. He looked at the bag of garbage sitting on the floor. "Let me take your garbage out for you," he said. He picked up the two-day-old bag and said, "You're gonna be my next girlfriend."

"Yeah, okay," I said. I knew he didn't know me that well. I knew I was a handful and hard to get along with.

He walked out the door and came right back in and yelled, "I want you." Then he left back out.

I was on my way to work one morning. I was riding the bus as usual and in deep thought. I heard someone calling my name. It was Olivia. I had gone to high school with her, but we never really talked to each other. I worked with her before too, briefly at a daycare. She was dressed really nice. We were the same age, but she was much more mature than I was. That was something I admired about her. She carried herself in a very sophisticated way. She was a kind person, but she also gave off the energy that she was not to be fucked with. "How are you?" she said.

"I'm doing good," I said. I told her I had just moved. I told her the name of the apartments I lived in.

She said, "That's where I live too."

I thought, '*Wow, what a coincidence.*' We decided to exchange numbers before she exited the bus.

We didn't communicate much after that, but I saw her a couple of weeks later standing at the bus stop by the apartments. I told her that I read playing cards. She said, "Me too. I've been reading for years."

"I just started reading not too long ago," I said. I was excited to find another person that was spiritual like me and that read cards. We both shared our spiritual experiences.

After that day, we started to hang out more. I went over to her apartment; I had no idea she lived on the floor beneath me. "How didn't I run into you?" I asked her.

"Girl, I don't ever be home. I be at work all day," she said. Her place was similar to mine. I was instantly drawn to her aunt that passed away. She had a picture of her hanging on the wall.

Olivia gave me a reading, but she used tarot cards instead of playing cards. She said, "It's been a while since I did a reading."

I asked about me and Jody. She pulled three cards. The first card was the queen of cups. "There is a beautiful woman standing there, but she is not open emotionally. There is nobody around her," she said. That was true; I was alone most of the time, and I didn't let people in. I forgot what the second card was, but the last card was the ten of swords. That's what I was afraid of. The ten of swords represented a betrayal. I was afraid if I got involved with Jody, he would play me, but that was a worry I had with all men. She basically said he would betray me, but for some reason, I ignored that part, or I didn't take it seriously because I completely forgot about it. Olivia read with such clarity and accuracy. I thanked her for the reading and headed back to my place.

I continued to read on Jody and what I saw surprised me. I saw that his girlfriend was doing black magic on him. I started to panic. '*Oh no*,' I thought. I told myself I wasn't going to tell him, but I couldn't help it. I felt like I had a duty to warn him. I saw him the next day, and I just kind of blurted it out. I avoided making eye contact with him. "I wasn't going to tell you," I said.

He said, "What?" looking all concerned.

"I think your girlfriend is doing black magic on you."

He said he didn't believe in that, but his girlfriend's friend was just talking about people putting period blood in spaghetti.

My eyes widened as if that was a confirmation that I was correct. "Really?" I said.

"Yeah," he said. "I need your help." He placed his hands on both of my shoulders.

"I can't help you. I can recommend someone."

"I want you to help me," he said. I could tell he didn't fully believe me. "I'm gonna call you," he said. "Okay?"

I just wanted to help him. I didn't see him for a while after that. I wondered where he was. He never called me either. I texted him to see if he was okay, and I sent him a link to help him find a job. He had previously told me he was looking for a job and he needed help with that. He told me he had a criminal record and that was blocking him. Olivia sent me a link that helped felons become employed.

One night, I heard Jody's voice outside. I had just put my pajamas on for the night. I looked outside my window and saw him standing with a group of friends. I decided to give him a piece of black tourmaline and a white sage incense. I went outside to greet him. "Jody," I said. He tried to act like he didn't hear me, like he was trying to avoid me.

He finally came over. "My phone was messed up. Sorry I didn't hit you back."

I wasn't sure what he was talking about at first. Showing my confusion, I said, "What?" I assumed he was talking about when he didn't call me back, but I didn't care about that. "Here, I got you something." I explained to him what everything was. I told him it was for protection.

"Aww, thank you. Give me a hug," he said.

For some reason, I felt comfortable hugging him. I didn't hug very many people, and I really didn't like people touching me, but this felt okay.

A few hours later I heard Jody arguing on the phone with his girlfriend. "You fat white bitch," he yelled. "I'm done. No, I'm serious this time."

I ran and looked out my window. I wasn't sure why they were arguing. I saw Jody slyly look up at me occasionally like he wanted me to know they were breaking up. I couldn't believe he was talking to her like that.

I got a reading from a psychic from Canada. I asked her about Jody. I told her about his girlfriend doing magic on him. The psychic confirmed that she was. She told me to be careful about Jody because he was not who he appeared to be.

Me and Olivia decided we wanted to go out to lunch at Eat'n Park. We hopped on the bus. I showed her a picture of Jody and his girlfriend. Olivia was really good at reading pictures.

Souls, if you don't know what that means, it means she was able to see and predict things by reading a person's energy through a photo.

Olivia stared at the photo. "Umph," she said.

"What?" I asked.

"I see death. He has to get away from her," she said.

I couldn't believe what I was hearing. "Oh no, we have to help him," I said. I was so worried. Olivia could predict death and everybody she predicted would die, actually ended up dying.

We got to Eat'n Park and ordered our food. I couldn't even focus. All I could think about was Jody being in danger. I had to help him. I couldn't even enjoy my food. "You have to tell him, Olivia. He won't listen to me."

She agreed to do it. It was a serious matter.

When we got home, I saw Jody outside drinking. Olivia and I agreed to talk to him inside her apartment. I called his name while I stood by the door. He made his way over and started to jog. He said, "I hurry up for you." He looked at me and then turned his head and said, "You're so beautiful." I had worn lipstick that day. I rarely wore make-up; I honestly didn't need it. I really didn't know how to apply it and I was just lazy mostly. My mom never taught me how to put make-up on. Jody caught me off guard; he had never called me beautiful before. I was confused as to why he was even saying that.

I asked him if he knew Olivia. He said, "The girl they call the Oracle." I told him we had something important to tell him. He said that he would be up in a minute. Olivia and I waited for him, but he never came up. One of his kids was having a birthday party. It was getting late, so Olivia and I decided to go outside and tell him. We saw him standing with his baby mom and his baby mom's mother. We both looked at his baby mom and she seemed to be very irritated. Jody looked up at both of us and said, "Perfect timing." He was clearly intoxicated, and he grabbed two beers and hid them inside a bush.

We walked over to the side of the building. Olivia was very hesitant to tell him. She looked so scared. "I'm Olivia, and I'm a psychic medium, and I have to tell you something." She hesitated again.

"Just tell me," he shouted.

"Your girlfriend. You gotta get away from her," she said.

He was like, "I know. She's crazy. I'm gonna end up in jail."

She said, "No, death."

Jody got quiet for a second.

"Is there somewhere else you can go?" she asked.

"You mean for a lil a while," he said.

"No, for good."

He assured us he had somewhere else to go.

She basically told him if he didn't leave her, he was going to die. Olivia said, "Now listen to Brandi."

I said, "Your girlfriend is a witch. She's in a cult."

He looked at me and said, "That's not my girlfriend."

"She is a witch," I said, but I could tell he really didn't believe me.

He went on to tell us how she always argued with him and gave him problems. He made a reference about the moon, saying she tried to bring him down and block him from happiness.

Later, Olivia told me that meant he was spiritual. I could tell Jody was smart and had great potential, but for some reason he was choosing to live a very reckless life. As we were having this conversation, Jody's speech was slurring, and he could barely stand up straight. I felt bad for him but at the same time I found that very unattractive. I wasn't into alcoholics because of their unexpected behavior.

He thanked us for sharing the information. He gave Olivia a hug and I stood there waiting patiently for mine. I thought, '*I know he better give me a hug too.*' He then leaned in and gave me a hug. He said, "You have to stop being afraid of me."

I wasn't afraid of him physically, but there was something about his energy that frightened me. I wasn't sure what it was at the time, but he was a Scorpio and they had very intense energy. Before he departed from us, he looked directly at Olivia and said, "This will bring us closer together." I didn't like that he said that to her at all. I felt like he was flirting with her in my face. I told Olivia how I felt about it. "I guess I kinda like him a little bit," I said. I got a little jealous. She assured me she wasn't interested in him.

I was still concerned about Jody and wasn't sure if he took us seriously. I texted him later that night and said I hoped he would be okay and good luck. I told him if he had any questions about anything to let me know. I felt the least I could do was warn him, and hopefully, he would make the right decisions.

It was 5:00 in the morning. I woke up and couldn't get back to sleep. I thought Olivia and Jody were going to hook up. I was so frustrated that I started to cry. I felt like I never got anybody I wanted and I was tired of it. I had previously watched a horoscope on Taurus and Scorpio and it said those two signs were going to get together. Tears streamed down my chubby-cheeked face. '*Why is this happening, God? Why does this always happen to me?*' I thought. Then I went into a rage and threw my sheets on the floor. I got up and fell to the ground. I screamed and hollered and was so angry with God. I got up off the floor and ripped my Jesus poster right off the wall and a corner of it tore off. I threw the poster down with force and then sat back on the bed.

Suddenly, I got a text message. It was from Jody. The text read, "Good morning. Can I come over?" I wiped the tears from my eyes and replied back. I asked him if everything was okay. I thought he was scared and needed someone to talk to. "You can say no if you want," he added.

"Okay," I said. I figured because it was 5:00 am, it was okay for him to come over. I mean it was morning even though it was still dark outside. Plus, I thought booty call hours were late at night around 1:00 or 2:00 am, and I was definitely not having sex with him. I was just trying to help him with his situation. I heard a light knock at the door. He came in quietly and sat down on the couch. "So, what's your plan?"

He slowly responded in a nonchalant manner, "I plan to find a job."

"No, are you planning to move? Let's make a plan."

He seemed very uninterested in planning anything and looked like he didn't take anything we told him seriously.

"Do you even remember my name?" I asked.

"No," he said, then he blurted out, "Brandi," and then he rolled his eyes.

I laughed. I really didn't know him or see him that often, so I wasn't sure. I felt really comfortable around him, comfortable enough to let him in my house and stay the night if he needed to. I felt safe. We continued to talk.

He got a call and said he had to leave for a minute. "Can I come back?" he asked hopefully. He said it as if he wasn't sure if I would let him.

I said, "Yeah," like it wasn't that big of a deal.

He came back shortly after that. He sat down and took his shoes off.

I thought, '*Why is he taking his shoes off?*' I told him I wasn't having sex with him.

He started using pussy tactics and saying shit like, "I'm falling in love with you," and the shit went right over my head.

I was like, "What are you talking about?"

He was a fast talker. I was getting tired, so I told him I was going to bed and grabbed a blanket for him to use on the couch. "As long as it smells like you," he said with a smile. I was on my way to my room when he said, "Give me a hug first." I didn't mind hugging him, and I figured he might just try to kiss me or something.

I said, "Okay, one hug." I leaned into hug him, and he wouldn't let me go. Before I knew it, he started kissing me and he stood up and pressed me up against the wall. As he was swirling his tongue around in my mouth, I had my eyes wide open staring at the wall. Jody grinded on me softly. I was thinking, '*God, you're letting this guy kiss me.*' I was surprised and caught off guard. What the hell?

I started to feel a little uncomfortable, so I turned my head. He stopped kissing me for a moment, then positioned his mouth to find my lips and continued to kiss me with my head still turned. He stopped again, realizing I wasn't kissing him back. Then he lifted me up with my legs spread open and pinned me against the wall. My body tensed up. "No!" I yelled. He gently released me. '*What does he think he's doing?*' I thought.

"Are you okay," he said.

"I feel uncomfortable."

He quickly backed up from me with his hands up as if he was being arrested by the police. Then he sat back down on the couch. "I'm sorry."

I said, "No, that's okay." I did feel uncomfortable, but I didn't want him to feel bad about it. I told him I wasn't kissing him back and that should have been a clue for him.

"You didn't stop me either," he said.

I didn't want to get into a debate about that; it really shook me up. I got a lot more comfortable after that. I wondered why he didn't leave. He decided he wanted to lay his head on my lap, and I said no at first; then I let him. "Is that how it starts?" I said with a giggle.

He quickly turned his head, "Are you a virgin?"

"Yeah," I responded with a smile.

He was searching through his phone. It looked like he was looking for another girl to hook up with. I didn't pay attention at the time. He smiled and quickly put his phone away. He grabbed both of my hands and put them on his face. I told him previously I was a witch. "Are you doing magic on me?"

"No," I said. "I'm a retired witch."

He assured me that there were good witches too and that it was okay for me to be one. I really didn't consider myself to be a good one. I was probably a neutral witch. I did good and bad spells. That was all behind me now. Doing magic was not helping me at all. So I put my hat down.

Then he began to lick my stomach. "You feel that?"

"No," I said.

"You have no soul," he said.

Maybe fear made my body have no feeling. I'm not sure, but I felt nothing. Then he undid my bra and started to lick on my nipples. He licked his way down until he got to my underwear.

"No!" I yelled.

He started to move his way back up. He then tried to pull my panties down.

"No!" I screamed. I told him I didn't shave down there. I was using that as an excuse, and I really didn't want him to see my head full of hair down there. I had never had a reason to shave my vagina hair. It was so long and thick that I could braid it and put ponytails in it if I wanted to.

Then he tried to take off my sock. I said, "No my socks are dirty." I tried to make up any excuse I could think of so he wouldn't take my clothes off.

Then his finger entered my vagina. He forcefully moved his finger in and out. I screamed so loud, but it felt so good. I was thrusting my body back and forth. When he was done, I just laid there for a second to collect my thoughts.

When I turned my head, just like that, there he was standing naked right in front of me. I didn't even notice he had left the couch and took his clothes off. "Touch him," he said.

I stared at his erect penis and slowly reached my hand out because I was unsure what I was doing. He demonstrated how I needed to stroke his dick. I went to stroke it, but I used my left hand and was unable to get a good grip. I was right-handed. He then climbed on top of me and pulled my panties halfway down. "No! Don't take them all the way off." I was really nervous. Plus, I had my granny panties on, and I just didn't want him taking them off.

He tried to penetrate me but was unable to because the panties were blocking. He looked a little frustrated and slapped both of his hands down on his legs. He removed the cushions from the couch and threw them on the floor.

I said, "I want to take my underwear off on my own." I went to my bedroom and came back out with just a shirt on. I was bottomless and he was waiting on the couch still stroking his penis. I laid on the couch.

Then wham! He stuck his dick right inside me. I let out a sigh like I always saw women do in the movies when they lose their virginity. He started to stroke me with a steady pace. The force was hurting me. I placed my hand on his stomach and pushed him to get him to stop. "Jody, it hurts really bad," I said. I pushed on his stomach even harder and tried to push him off of me, hoping he would stop.

He then stopped and looked right into my eyes and said, "Relax."

When he said that, I completely let go. I became more relaxed. He continued to pump his penis in my vagina. I screamed so fuckin loud. My goodness it was amazing. There was no more pain. It actually started to feel good. I watched him hover over me and then I closed my eyes. I screamed louder, "Fuck my pussy."

He turned his head and looked at me while still giving me pleasure and whispered, "Oh baby."

I could tell I was giving him pleasure as well. I yelled, "Oh baby." I yelled and squirmed the whole time.

He stopped and pulled his dick out and started to rub on the tip of his penis and he came in his hand. I turned my head and just laid there. *'What the hell just happened? Did I just have sex?'* Thoughts raced through my head. I couldn't believe what I'd just done.

"Look at me," he said. I kind of felt ashamed like I had done something wrong. "Please," he said in a pleading tone.

I slowly turned my head and looked into eyes. I was uncomfortable making eye contact, but I looked in his eyes and they were watery. He still had his sperm in the palm of his hand, and he leaned over and kissed me.

He got up to dispose of it. Both of our bodies were dripping with sweat. He asked me if I had a condom. "No," I said, "I can't use those."

"Why not?" he asked.

"I'm allergic to them," I said. Years before, I wanted to see what a condom felt like, so I put one on my finger and put it in my vagina. It was very painful, so I took it out. A couple of minutes after, my vagina swelled up and I started getting a lot of discharge. It felt like my vagina was falling out. "I feel like a slut," I said out loud.

"Don't say that," he said. He sat on my couch naked. He said, "Give me a kiss."

I said, "I don't know how."

So, he demonstrated for me, "Just do this." We kissed each other and he stared into my eyes. Then he said to kiss him. He was referring to his penis. I had no idea what to do. I just stared at it out of curiosity. I grabbed his penis and began to examine it to see if I saw any bumps or any signs of STDs. His dick was perfect, the size and thickness. There were no bumps, nothing weird about it. It was pretty. Then I gave it a sniff. He stared at me and began to laugh because I was being so weird about it.

I started to say something, and he cut me off with a nod of his head gesturing for me to go ahead and put it in my mouth. So, I gently licked the tip of his penis. Then I began to suck on it and stroke it up and down. After a couple of minutes, he started to instruct me on how he wanted me to please him. He told me to play with his balls and to be very gentle. So, I took my left hand and began to massage his balls but had a hard time multitasking, so I just focused on taking him in and out of my mouth. I asked him if I could spit on it, and he nodded his head yes. I always wanted to do that! I couldn't believe I was actually sucking somebody's dick. I thought I would never do something like that. I had always made excuses for why I didn't want to do it. I thought it was gross, and I thought I would get lockjaw or something.

I began licking the tip of his penis and he started to squirm and looked a little as if he were in pain. I looked at him to see if I should stop, but I continued. He gently pushed me on my forehead and pushed my head away and said, "Come on."

We quickly moved to the bedroom. We began to have sex again, and that time it felt even better. His dick slid right in. There was no pain, only pleasure. I yelled, "Fuck me. Yes, Baby." I always thought the women in the porn videos were faking those screams and hollers. I thought they were exaggerating. Now I knew they were real because mine were definitely real! I couldn't keep quiet. I looked down and watched him fuck me. I watched his dick go in and out, I saw the precum starting to build up. He tried to get up, but I held him closer to me because I wanted him to keep going. He did a circular motion with his dick, and it hit all around the walls of my vagina. "OMG," I yelled.

Then he rushed to get up and began to rub his penis; he came into his hand again. He held the cum in his hand for a minute and smiled at me and kissed me on the lips. He told me he had strong sperm because he had a lot of children. He then went to the bathroom to get rid of the remains of his semen. He came out and I laid on the bed. I got up and we both started laughing. He then leaned over and kissed me on the forehead.

We decided to go for round three. I sucked his dick again. He went even harder this time pounding my pussy. I screamed so loud. It hurt a little, but it felt good at the same time. He pulled me close and repeatedly slammed into me. While he was slamming into me, he began to make this evil demonic face. I was confused by it, and it scared me a bit. It was like he was trying to punish my vagina. Then I began to get dry down there and it began to hurt. I called his name and shook my head no. I couldn't take the pain anymore.

He stopped and got up and looked really disappointed. "I need a shower," he said.

"Okay," I said.

He headed to the shower and took his clothes off. I watched in the doorway. "What?" he said.

"Can I shower with you?"

"Yeah, come on."

I hopped in the shower with him, and I noticed the water was turning coal black. *'Wtf.'* I thought it was poop at first. It was actually dirt. It seemed like he hadn't bathed in months. I began to kiss him, but he didn't kiss me back. He pulled away. I decided to wash him up myself. I didn't have any clean wash rags, so I used a bar of soap. I rubbed it all over his body. I had no idea what I was doing. I had never showered with a guy, but I had always wanted to. I washed all over his body and made sure he was clean. It was almost like I was washing a child; like showing him: this is how you do it.

Then I washed myself. We both dried off with our towels. We then got dressed. He stood in front of the mirror, and I stood in the hallway watching him. He put his sunglasses on and then he said it. "You just made a deal with the devil."

"Why would you say something like that? Who says shit like that?"

He just stared at me. We walked towards the door, and I told him he better not play me.

"What do you mean by that?" he asked.

"Like, I better talk to you, and you say, 'Hi.' Cause if you don't it's gonna be two Scorpios fighting each other."

He agreed to not ignore me and act funny since we had sex. On his way out he said, "You're Jody's now." Like I was one of his hoes or something. He was claiming ownership. He started smiling and he seemed to be excited about it.

After he left, I couldn't wait to tell Olivia. I called her immediately. I told her it was important and ran down to her apartment. "Girl guess what? I had sex three times and took a shower with Jody." She had to gather herself. "It didn't hurt as bad as I thought. It hurt though, at the beginning. I bled a little bit. I had little drops of blood in my underwear."

"What, wait a minute, let me grab my cigarettes," she said.

I told her everything. She couldn't believe it. We both couldn't believe it. Finally, I had sex, after all those mothafuckin years. Olivia seemed to be a little jealous. "Everybody havin' sex except me, even a virgin," she said.

While we were conversing, Jody kept texting me. "Do you have oodles and noodles?" the message read. I guess he was making his kids some breakfast. I told him I didn't have any. I was hoping he wasn't going to start asking me for shit.

I was a real woman after that. I never thought in a million years that it would happen. Later that day, me and Olivia went to do some laundry and he texted me for like the twentieth time. "What are you doing?" he said.

"At the laundry mat with Olivia."

He told me he wasn't doing very good, and I asked him, "What's wrong?" He wouldn't tell me. I wanted to hurry home to see what was going on. As soon as I made it home, I texted him. An hour later, he knocked on my door. Jody hugged me as soon as he came in. He whispered in my ear that his baby mom had left him with the kids. '*What*?' I thought. Apparently, she had moved to another state and left him with all of their children. I was shocked and really didn't know what to do. "Go look at your cards," he shouted at me.

I scurried back to my room as he shut the door and left. I pulled my deck out and started shuffling. On one hand, I really wanted to help him, but I also wanted to enjoy the fact that I lost my virginity. So much was happening so fast! I laid the cards out on the table. I wanted him to see the cards, so I texted him to hurry up and come look at the cards with me.

He came in the door drunk and fired up. "I have to work," he shouted. I assumed he was speaking about selling drugs. He was all sweaty. The question I asked the cards was, "Where is his baby mom?" I tried to tell him his girlfriend put a spell on him, and it came up again. As I was trying to explain, he shouted, "What does this mean?" while pointing to the joker card, which represented the devil.

I said, "It's your girlfriend."

He said, "No, follow your first instinct."

I started to back up slowly away from him. He was scaring me; he was intoxicated, and he was yelling. I was confused about what was even going on. He soon calmed down and gave me a hug. Then he started shouting again and he told me he was coming back later and was spending the night. "And set your alarm so I can wake up in the morning so I can get my kids up for school."

I just stood there as he walked away. Did this nigga just tell me what to do? Who did he think he was talking to? "Come lock the door," he shouted. It startled me and I ran to lock the door. Later that night, I waited for him to come back, but he never showed up.

The next day, I was coming back from the store. I heard Jody calling my name. He came over and I looked at him with an attitude. "What's wrong?" he said.

I told him I didn't understand what was going on. I was very disappointed he hadn't shown up the last night. He immediately started to whine, "My kids needed me." He said, "You're mad."

I covered my mouth and laughed a little bit. It wasn't that serious, not the way he was acting. He told me he broke his phone and got a new one and needed my number. He told me he would be up in a little bit; he had something to do. I waited for him patiently on my bed in my bathrobe. I wanted to have sex again. In fact, I expected to have sex every day now. He knocked on the door with a cigarette in his hand. "I'm laying down on my bed," I said. I proceeded to lie down, and he lay beside me. "Why didn't you come back."

"My kids needed me," he responded. I knew his phone had been broken so he'd had no way to contact me. We stared at each other for a while. He gently picked the lint off my robe. He was showing a caring gesture, I guess. His baby mom's mother called him to go find his son's bike. "I gotta go get my son's bike," he said.

I blurted out, "I want to have sex again."

He said, "Okay," and dropped his pants and boxers and his dick stood straight out. "I want to give you want you want." He stood in front of me with his dick and said, "He needs your mouth."

I began sucking on his penis. He moaned and gently tapped my forehead to let me know to stop. He pulled me close to him and laid on top of me. He slid inside me with no hesitation. He stared into my eyes. After two minutes, it was over. He came so fast and a lot. He came in his hand again and showed it to me so I could see what it looked like. He said it was a good thing he came fast. He went to the bathroom and got dressed.

I asked him, "Why don't you kiss me, like a real kiss with your tongue?"

He began to whine like a child. "I knew you were going to ask me that. I have to get to know you first," he said.

I didn't argue with him about it. "I was just curious," I said.

He said he would be back later and headed out the door.

I was already in pain but later that day I realized I was in so much pain that I could barely walk. My body was extremely sore. I couldn't even eat anything, not even soup. It lasted for three days. I laid in bed with aching pain. I wanted to cry, but what was the point? I wanted to have sex and now I felt like I was being punished in some kind of way.

While I lay on my bed, I saw Jody outside in front of the building across from me. I peeked out through my blinds and stared at him. He was talking to Ms. Ruth, his baby mom's mother. He made eye contact with me and started smiling. I pulled away from the window. I saw Ms. Ruth look up and roll her eyes. I wondered if she knew about us.

When I felt better, I went to Olivia's place to talk more about the sexual experiences I had with Jody. I took a journal with me and thought about how I could help him.

Out of nowhere, I told Olivia my angels wanted me to go back to my apartment. I left not knowing what the hell I was talking about. As soon as I got to my room, I heard people screaming and yelling outside. My nosey ass looked out the window and I saw Jody getting ready to fight another guy. There was a big crowd of people standing around. They were yelling at each other, but Jody was coming off as the aggressor. I heard a guy telling him to stop. "You got kids, Jody, go in the house," the guy said. It was apparent Jody was intoxicated. The guy mentioned he was showing off in front of the young girls who were standing outside in the crowd. Jody took off his shirt and the two guys got in each other's faces.

I was so worried and scared. I ran back down to Olivia's place. "We have to help him! Jody's in trouble," I said. Olivia was very hesitant to come out. I could tell she didn't want to get involved. We went downstairs to see what was happening and as soon as we stepped out the door, the fight began.

Both guys ran towards each other. The other guy ended up getting Jody on the ground and then another guy came and kicked him right in his head.

"We have to do something!" I pulled Olivia's arm; she stood there solid. "Cover me!" I knew I was going to get my ass kicked if I even attempted to help him.

Olivia looked at me and said, "No, stay here."

I ran quickly to the church right beside the apartments and stood in front. I prayed that God would let one of my angels protect him.

Olivia came to see where I was. I went back to where they were fighting. Nobody was helping him. I ran to my house and called the police, but the police never showed up. Jody and the other guy finally calmed down and they started hugging each other. I think they may have been related. That was a very stressful night. Olivia gave me a hug and went back to her place.

The following day I really thought about what happened to Jody. I didn't want that type of drama around me. I felt like he started that fight. I decided to tell him that I really hoped he was okay, but I thought it was best if I removed myself and we parted ways. He never responded back. I saw some of his family members outside. I asked his cousin if he was okay. "Yeah, he's at the hospital," his cousin said. "He broke his pinky." I was very concerned. "Much worse has happened to him, so don't worry," he said. After a few hours, Jody was outside discussing the fight with his friends. I just wanted to make sure he was okay. I texted him to stop by when he had time. He still didn't respond.

A couple of days went by, and I hadn't heard from him. I waited for Olivia to get home from work. "I have a message for you from Jody," she said. I wasn't too thrilled to hear it. She told me he said he had a lot going on in his life and now was not a good time for us to be together. I wasn't falling for that bullshit. I felt like he was just trying to get rid of me. I rolled my eyes at Olivia. I felt rejected even though I was the one who rejected him first.

When I got home, I was fuckin furious. He just thought he was going to get rid of me. I called one of my other friends to talk shit about him. I sat in my bedroom and went on and on about how he used me. I said I was going to tell his girlfriend to get him back. When I went to bed that night, I heard Jody outside singing. He was giving me a message saying we should be friends, and he had a lot going on in his life. He must have heard me before when I was on the phone. He must have thought I could hear him because my window was open. I quickly got up and shut the window. I wasn't trying to hear that shit.

The next morning, I got up and went to the store. I needed some fresh air and some time to think. On my way back, I saw Jody about to cross the street. He looked really cute that day. "Hey," I said, "If you didn't want to talk to me, you could have told me yourself."

"I saw her first, so I just told her," he said.

"I think there is some kind of miscommunication," I said.

"I'll be up after I go make like forty dollars."

"Really," I said. I was surprised.

He then moved towards me to hug me. I backed away. He seemed to be a little frustrated. He grabbed me and put his arms around me.

"No, somebody will see," I said.

"So, I don't care."

I went home and changed my clothes and flat-ironed my hair. I wanted to make sure I looked cute. I was hoping to have a conversation about what happened between us. When he got to my apartment, he went straight to the window and looked out. *'Hoping nobody seen him come in here,'* I thought. He sat on the couch. I told him if we were going to see each other, he would have to spend more time with me.

He agreed that he would. I don't think he was paying much attention to anything I was saying. He stood up and opened his arms and I ran to him and hugged him. We kissed each other and I could feel his tongue moving around fast in my mouth. I could tell there was no emotion involved. His mouth tasted nasty. It was a gross, foul taste. I could also feel that his dick was already hard, and I thought that was weird.

We both ran to the bedroom. He picked me up. I was trying to stop my glasses from falling off. He threw me on the bed. He went to take my panties off. "No! Let me do it. I'm spotting is that ok?" I asked.

"That's okay, you're not pregnant," he said.

I went to slide my panties to the floor, and he turned his head to give me privacy. He took his boxers off. He placed his dick in front of my face. I began to suck on it. It had the same sour taste that his mouth had. It smelled sour too. Minutes later, he pulled me by my legs and got on top of me. He laid there for a second and then he tried to put his penis in me, but it hurt because I had gotten a pap exam. I clenched my body up. He attempted several times with determination and then it got in there. It was very painful. I laid there and stared at the ceiling hoping it would be over soon. I looked into his eyes and noticed the sleep in them. *'He didn't even wash his face today,'* I thought. We stared at each other, and he continued. Two minutes later he was done and out of breath.

"You ok," I asked.

"Are you ok," he said. He said when I clenched my vagina walls it made him come fast. He showed me the cum in his hand again. It looked different this time. It was clear and watery. It wasn't a lot either. Like he had been having a lot of sex with other people. He got up and said he was taking his kids fishing.

"I'll be back later." He ran out the door.

Like, damn, he didn't even invite me. I knew he wasn't coming back, but I was still hopeful.

Later that evening, I called Olivia and told her Jody and I had sex again.

"Wait, y'all had sex this morning?" she asked.

"Yes," I said.

Since Jody never came back, I wasn't giving him any more pussy. I texted him to tell him I was done for real this time. This was bullshit.

He texted me some dumb shit saying, "Whatever you want."

# Chapter 13:
# Plethora of Pussy

I watched Jody outside my window. He was all up in other girls' faces regularly. I saw him talking to any girl that walked past. He seemed to like younger girls, or they were just easy to him. "Blue shirt," he yelled to a girl who walked by.

One time, I saw him staring hard at a young girl. She barely looked eighteen. She seemed shy, but she stared back at him. I was so disgusted and surprised that was something he was interested in. I mean, Jody was older than me. The young girl walked into the building, and he followed her like a dog in heat. I thought, '*This guy is so gross.*' I felt bad that he was taking advantage of young girls, including me.

Later that night, Jody and his friends were sitting outside. He asked another girl how old she was. She said she was eighteen, and he asked her if she had a boyfriend. She didn't seem that interested. She was smart, or maybe she already knew about this nigga and his behavior.

Jody was drinking, as usual, and I saw him get all up in yet another woman's face. She ignored him like she was used to it or something. He followed her into her building. Then twenty minutes later I saw him come back out; he was leaning all up against this guy. The guy seemed to be irritated and pushed Jody off of him. I was so embarrassed for him, but I felt bad at the same time. He seemed like he didn't care about himself. I still wasn't talking to him; I just observed his behavior for a while.

It was 11:00 am the next morning and I saw Jody outside throwing up. I assumed it was from drinking, but he continued to drink. I told Olivia about it. She responded with, "Maybe he got somebody pregnant." I thought her saying that was interesting. It seemed he slept with anybody.

I got a reading with one of my regular readers. He told me Jody was scared to leave his girlfriend, and that he got a younger girl pregnant.

'*What*?' I thought. I couldn't believe it. I was furious. How in the world did I get involved with a guy like this? The girl he got pregnant lived in another town. That was too much; Olivia had been right.

I saw Jody arguing with Ms. Ruth. She was a really nice lady until she started drinking. She seemed to be a good grandmother to her grandkids. At night, she would drink and get into fights with everybody. Even her own kids sometimes. It looked like she made Jody leave her house. "Bye, asshole," she said. Jody and his girlfriend were standing outside. They kissed each other and she left. Then I saw Jody peeing on the side of a building. He was trying to get someone to help him with Ruth. He asked some girl for help. The girl yelled, "I'm not getting involved in that domestic violence shit." So, I assumed Jody and Ruth had gotten into several physical altercations. Jody was wild as fuck.

I decided to get a reading with a new reader. Her YouTube videos were very accurate, so I wanted to give her a try. I asked her about me and Jody. She basically told me there was nothing more than sex between us. She said he and his girlfriend had a toxic relationship and that she was going to find out about the other girl who was pregnant. "When she finds out, she's gonna light that motherfucka up," she said. She also told me he would eventually go back to his baby's mom. She said they were life partners. I definitely didn't want to stand in the way of that. I had no choice but to remove myself. He had a lot of shit going on and I felt like I was caught in the middle. He just seemed like he went around destroying people's lives.

Me and Olivia were having a conversation about me moving on from Jody and never having sex with him again. I was so sure of myself. I was going to say, "No," if he ever tried again.

I went upstairs to my place and grabbed a snack. It was hot as fuck outside, so I had all the lights out and all the windows open. It really sucked that I didn't have central air. I couldn't afford an air conditioner. I had a box fan, but that didn't help much. I looked outside because it was packed. There were people everywhere. I happened to see Jody outside and he saw me in the window. I'm not sure how he saw me. Our eyes connected instantly. He started blowing kisses at me. *'What is he doing*?' I thought. He pointed towards the door telling me to meet him. I hurried to my door and looked out. Then I heard Jody running up the stairs. We met each other in the hallway. I went and gave him a hug. "How did you see me in the window?"

He never answered, he just pushed me up against the wall. He picked me up and I wrapped my legs around him. He started to kiss me and flicked his tongue in my mouth. Again, I could tell it wasn't a real kiss. There was no emotion behind it. He was intoxicated, as usual, and his mouth smelled and tasted like alcohol.

He was grinding on me, and I yelled, "No, someone will see."

He quickly dropped me with an attitude and started to walk away.

I didn't want him to be mad at me, so I said he could come inside my apartment. When he came in, I told him to excuse my house because it was a bit messy.

He said, "What," like he was irritated.

We both walked into my dark bedroom. I moved some things out of the way, and he just stood there. "What are you doing?" he said. It was clear he was getting upset because I wasn't fucking him fast enough. I told him to turn his head while I was taking my clothes off. I just didn't feel comfortable with him watching me. He took his clothes off quickly while I lay on the bed.

He gently rubbed his penis on my vagina. He was taking too long to put it in me, so I grabbed his dick and tried to put it in myself. I couldn't get it in. "Move your hand," his tone was nasty. I moved my hand to the side quickly. He tried to enter me, but it hurt so badly that I kept clenching my vagina walls together. "Open your legs," he yelled. I felt so uncomfortable because he was being mean to me and yelling at me. I thought he meant he wanted me to change positions and open my legs in a different way. "No," he yelled.

At that point, I didn't want to have sex, but I was too afraid to tell him no. He was super wasted, and I was scared he was going to get even angrier and try to hurt me. He finally pushed his penis in, and it was so painful – more painful than when I lost my virginity. I grabbed the sheets tightly and balled my fists up, still trying to keep my legs open. I didn't want him to yell at me again.

"There you go," he said.

I laid there hoping for it to be over soon. He moaned twice and then it was over. "Thank God," I mouthed to myself. *'That was not enjoyable at all.'* I couldn't wait for him to leave.

He came in his hand and went to the bathroom to rinse it down the sink. I followed him. I saw him looking at himself in the mirror. He told me he was coming back later, but I didn't believe him. "You have to come back, I want to try different positions," I said.

He turned his head and looked at me. "What?" he said. I didn't like his tone. I didn't like him like this; it scared me. He hurried out of the apartment. "You got some good pussy, it's rare," he said.

I didn't respond. I was just happy he was leaving. I hurried to close the door. I wanted him to go because of how he was treating me, and I didn't understand why he was doing that to me. On the other hand, I wanted him to stay so we could talk about what was going on with us. I wanted to ask him why he kept running in and out of my house having sex with me. I started to look at myself differently. I started to feel insecure. I wasn't sure how to handle the situation. I just knew it was not good for me.

I headed down to Olivia's house to tell her I had sex again.

"You just had sex again after we just agreed you weren't gonna have sex with him again?" she asked.

"When did I say that?" I had completely forgotten. I leaned in towards Olivia and blew my breath in her face. "Smell my breath. It smells like dick," I said.

"No, get away from me," she said while laughing. We both laughed.

I decided to make peace with the situation between me and Jody. After talking with Olivia, I texted him. The message read, "I hope you are okay and be safe."

A few seconds later, I got a call from a private number. I usually didn't answer private calls, but I thought it was Jody. I answered the phone, and I heard a woman say, "What are you doing texting my nigga?" She sounded like she was a black woman. She also sounded like a linebacker that played on a football team.

I thought, '*Is this his girlfriend or a football player?*' I told her we were just friends. "Oh, y'all just friends. Well, where do this friend live?" she said.

I said, "In the area," with a rude voice. Then she called me a bitch, and I got very angry. "Don't call me a bitch," I yelled.

"I'm calling you a bitch, Bitch." She told me, "Don't call my man, don't text him, don't talk to him." I could hear Jody in the background sounding like a little bitch asking, "Who is it?" He knew damn well who it was.

I said, "No problem," and hung up the phone. I couldn't argue with her. I was in the wrong. I was sleeping with her man. I felt horrible. I'm not that kind of girl. I don't sleep with other women's boyfriends. I was becoming someone I didn't like.

I knew after that conversation it was over with me and Jody. I mean,

I didn't expect him to leave his girlfriend for me. I didn't know how to be a girlfriend and plus I wouldn't put up with his bullshit. I wondered if she would come to my house and try to fight me. I would have fought her fat ass too. I kept a small baseball bat behind my door just in case any intruders tried to run up in here.

I was lying in bed one night and had a vision of a green monster in my bathroom staring in the mirror. The monster turned around and stared at me with a mean look on her face. She had red hair. I had no idea who that was, but it scared the shit out of me. I thought about it for a while. *'Who has red hair? Wait a minute...'* I went on Facebook and looked at Jody's girlfriend's page. She had red hair. She was that green monster. I hadn't been sure what color her hair was. I told Olivia about the vision, and she said it meant she knew about me.

Two days later, I saw Jody and his girlfriend sitting outside. Later on, I heard them arguing. They were fighting over their baby. He was holding the baby, and the girlfriend was pulling the baby out of his hands and she yelled, "Give me my baby."

He let go of the baby and then he dropped everything else in his hand. The girlfriend put the baby in the stroller and Jody yelled, "You junkie."

"You have four kids, take care of them," she said. Then she pushed the stroller away from her not even caring that her baby was in there.

It was a complete mess; he was a complete mess.

I went to visit Olivia. She said, "I have to tell you something. Ya boy's a crackhead."

"What? Like a real one?" I asked. I was so dumbfounded. I had no fuckin idea. I mean the guy looked like he was in better health than me. His teeth looked nice, his skin was clear, and he had a healthy weight. He looked normal. I couldn't fuckin believe it. Olivia couldn't believe it either. I never knew a young black guy who smoked crack. I thought maybe it was a 'sometimes' thing. I couldn't believe I had sex with a crackhead. Why would God let me have sex with a crackhead? How did I end up having sex with a guy who was at the bottom of the barrel? It was insane.

Olivia had also heard he kept cheating on his first baby mom so she decided to cheat and ended up getting pregnant by another guy. Then Jody ended up getting his second baby mom pregnant. So, he left his first baby mom to be with her. It was like some *Days of Our Lives* shit.

I saw Jody a few times after that from my window. Then I didn't see him at all anymore. I looked outside for him, and I even thought I heard his voice. Weeks went by and nothing. I wondered what he was doing. I figured he was at his house with his girlfriend.

I wanted to text him and tell him about himself. I asked Olivia for advice. I didn't want to go off on him. I wasn't good at talking to people.

I tried to be as polite as possible. I told him I didn't like how he treated me and how he just ghosted me. I told him he needed to be responsible for his actions. I didn't expect him to respond so I just went about my day.

I got a reply from him hours later. He apologized to me for what he did. I felt a lot better after that and I thought it was over. I felt like I could move on. Later that night, he texted me that he would be back soon. I asked him when. He just said, "Soon." I had no idea where he was.

Olivia had been saying she felt he moved away. I wasn't sure though. I had a dream that Jody was moving into this big house, and I was just standing there watching him carrying boxes up the steps. He was so happy. On the other hand, I was sad. He was ignoring me, and I had tears in my eyes because he had moved on. He was getting married to someone, but the woman was invisible.

That morning, I told him about the dream I had.

He said, "No, that's wrong. I'm with my family." Jody had moved to another state and was staying with a family member. Olivia was right again. The reader was right as well. Jody's girlfriend must have found out about that baby because otherwise why would he have just up and moved to another state? He took his kids with him too.

I was really hurt. I couldn't believe he moved and didn't tell me; like I was a nobody. Well, maybe to him I was. He just took my virginity and skipped town.

Souls, remember I said I was a retired witch? Well, I started doing spell work again. I couldn't handle Jody being gone. I decided to do a spell that would make him come back to me and want to have sex with me again. I was still inexperienced, and I didn't truly know what I was doing. I saved a cigarette bud and a bottle of water he drank. I carved his name in a candle. Then, I took some of my vaginal fluids and rubbed it on the candle. I wrote what I wanted him to do on a piece of paper. Then I lit the candle. I read what I wanted him to do out loud. I began to masturbate. When I was done, I put out the flame of the candle. That was a big mistake.

I went into my room and got into the bed. I started having pain in my feet. It was like a tingling sensation. It felt like some kind of nerve pain and then I began to sweat.

I repeated the spell for three more nights. The pain became more intense each time I did it, spreading over my whole body. I stopped doing the spell after that.

A couple of days later, I texted Jody and asked him if it was okay for me to be friends with him on Facebook. It was then I realized I didn't even know the guy – not even his last name.

He asked me if I still liked him.

I hesitated to answer. He had done so much shit that I had lost interest. I didn't really want to answer that question.

He asked me again.

I told him because of all that had happened, not really.

He also asked me if I was doing magic on him.

I told him no. I honestly forgot I did the spell.

He said he had a dream that I tied him up and tried to have sex with him. He thought it was funny.

I continued trying to stay in contact with him for some reason. It was like I didn't like him anymore, but I still cared about him. I was worried about him and wanted to make sure he was okay.

But after that, I didn't hear from Jody again. I texted him and asked him if we were done and he never responded. I sat in my living room and cried. I knew I had to move on. I thought the spell worked, but since I turned Jody down, I messed it up.

After that, other people tried to have sex with me too. Some old-ass man who owned a store tried to talk to me. I was definitely not into him. Then one of my friends asked me if I wanted to have a threesome with her and her boyfriend. That was completely out of the question. I thought she was playing at first. A threesome was too advanced for me. Plus, I never wanted to have sex with one of my friends or their boyfriends. It was weird to me. I didn't want to have sex with anyone but Jody.

I started to get really depressed. I cried almost every day. I could barely eat. I couldn't think right. I felt like I hated Jody. I wanted him to die. The fact that he couldn't even tell me he didn't want to talk to me anymore pissed me off. He just ghosted me again for the second time. I asked God why this was happening to me and why he was allowing it. I felt I hadn't done anything in my life to deserve the situation.

I was alone in my apartment and then all of a sudden, I couldn't breathe. I was having a panic attack. I went to Olivia's, and I just busted out crying.

She stared at me and watched me fall on top of the pile of clothes she had on the floor. She kept calling my name, but I ignored her because I could barely speak. I was hurting so badly. Hurt like I had never been hurt before and that guy didn't give a fuck. "Brandi what's wrong?" she said.

I wasn't exactly sure. After my brief episode, I sat up with tears still falling from my eyes. I couldn't even look at Olivia because I was so embarrassed, but I couldn't stop crying. "I can't breathe," I said.

Olivia looked at me like she didn't know what to do. "Brandi, look at me."

I said, "No."

She tried to help me calm down. She did a therapy technique on me. She told me to picture myself somewhere safe and made me look at something and identify how it made me feel.

I calmed down a little bit after that. I told Olivia I needed to go take a walk. I went outside and walked around for a few minutes. It was getting dark, so I went back in. I honestly didn't know what to do.

I was losing a lot of weight. I couldn't keep any food down. I was in so much pain and started to get sick. The weight just melted right off of me. I had never been that thin in my adult life. I wasn't sure if I was going to die or not. At that point, I was the one out there looking like a crackhead. I got down to 128 pounds where it had been 155 before. I felt sorry for myself.

My symptoms started to worsen. I was having terrible nerve pain and eating made it worse. It seemed like it was happening because I did that love spell on Jody. I was working at a daycare, and I could barely focus. I was in the nursery with the infants, and we had to take our shoes off. I could feel pain all through my feet. I needed to go to the doctor to see what was going on.

After a bunch of tests, they still couldn't figure out what was wrong with me. My hair was falling out like crazy. My doctor told me it wasn't a good idea for me to work at that time. I ended up getting let go from my job. I had no money; I was depressed; my life was going downhill.

I was lying in bed all day and crying. I thought it was the end for me.

I hated waking up in the morning. Thoughts of Jody ran through my mind over and over. I couldn't even watch movies anymore, which had been my favorite thing. Getting out of bed and showering was a hard task for me. Most days I would just lay there and forget I hadn't eaten all day. I tried to eat even though I wasn't hungry, but my stomach rejected everything I put in my mouth. The nerve pain was still present. I didn't know how I was going to pay my rent, so I called churches for help. They weren't able to help me. The summer went by so fast, I didn't even know what day it was.

I was so angry with God. "How could you let this happen to me?" I cried. "He gotta go," I said. "It's either him or me, God." I gave God an ultimatum on who he was going to keep on this earth. "Kill him," I screamed. I told God I wasn't talking to him anymore and to leave me alone. "Fuck you," I yelled. I didn't have any more energy or faith left in my body. I felt like I was dying or already dead. It was not fair to me. I got up and grabbed my Bible, crucifix, and poster of Jesus and headed to the dumpster. I threw everything away. I was done with God; I was done with having faith. I was fucking done. I wanted everybody to die. I wanted Jody to die. I wrote on a piece of paper, '*I want Jody to die,*' over and over again. Then I taped it to my wall. I would get up every morning and read it. '*Jody got to go,*' I thought. I didn't give a fuck about anything at that point. Either he was going to die, or it was gonna be me.

All of my friends and family got tired of me talking about Jody, especially Olivia. I felt bad that I kept bringing him up to her, but I couldn't help it. She tried her best to help me, but she had work and her own life to deal with. Our conversations got shorter and shorter. She did readings for me and tried to make me look at the situation differently. "I honestly don't give a fuck about Jody," she said. "I was trying to help him because of you."

"I know, Sis," I said.

"I don't think he's a bad guy. He takes care of his children, so he can't be that bad."

"I don't care," I said. "I still hate him."

"Brandi, I don't think he meant to hurt you on purpose. He is on drugs, so his behavior is going to be unstable."

I didn't want to hear that shit. I knew the whole situation was taxing on her and it was draining her energy.

I decided I needed to go to therapy. That was my last resort. I needed help. My depression wasn't letting up. I made an appointment, and they gave me a male therapist. He was a young guy but because he was a man, I felt like he didn't understand my point of view. "Are you okay?" he said.

"No," I said and just sat there and cried. I could tell he felt bad for me. I told him I really cared about Jody. "I never cared about another man except for my dad," I told him.

After several sessions, I could tell the therapist was getting tired of me talking about Jody too. He let out a sigh at one point during a session. That was my cue to change my therapist. I preferred a woman anyway. Plus, I didn't feel like therapy was helping me. I needed to accept that Jody was gone; that was so hard to do.

# Chapter 14:
# Serpents in the Shade

I started working at another daycare that was within walking distance from my house. I needed something close by so I wouldn't have to travel far. I was still very depressed, but I needed to make money. It was a small center and it paid $4.00 per hour less than my previous job. A woman owned it, and there were two other women employees: Ivy and Margret.

I connected with Ivy right away. She was a year younger than me, and she was pregnant. She immediately told me the issues she was having with her baby's dad. She said he had left her for a younger woman. I could tell she was still hurting from the situation. She told me they were friends first while he was in jail, then they started dating. They planned to have a baby together, but I guess he changed his mind, and then he left her. She wanted to get an abortion and he threatened to kill her. After hearing her story, I felt comfortable enough to tell her my story.

"Do you know Jody?" I asked.

"Yeah, I know him. I used to see him walking past here with his kids," she said. She then went on to tell me she had moved to the area when she was sixteen. He had lived downstairs from her with his mom. "Girl, they were like family."

I told her everything that had happened between us. She was so supportive. I felt like God made us meet so we could help each other with our bad situations. She said she heard he moved out of state to go to rehab. I didn't believe it. I believed what the psychic told me.

I showed her pictures of the house he was living in which I had found on Google. "Wow," she said. The family member he was living with had several jobs.

Ivy said, "Wow, she's doing all those things." She looked surprised. She said she knew the family member as well. She told me she was not friends with Jody on Facebook, so she did not know everything that was going on.

I asked her to send him a friend request so I could look on his page and she agreed. On his page, I saw old videos of him. One that stood out was that he had a broken finger and a black eye. I thought, *'Gee, this guy was nothing but drama.'* He was saying something about people talking about him behind his back and how he was going to come to their house.

Ivy looked at me with care in her eyes. "Are you done? Did you see what you wanted to see?" She said there was a rumor going around that he started a lot of drama with people.

On my way home from work, I saw Ms. Ruth walking down the street. I just wanted to know if Jody was okay. "How's he doing?" I asked.

"He's okay. He has the kids with him. He got a job and a car and he's doing great," she said.

I was happy for him that he was getting his life together.

"I'll tell him you asked about him."

"No," I shouted, "You don't have to."

I had to be at work at 6:30 in the morning. It was cold, but it was a quiet and peaceful walk. I left the daycare around 9:30 am and got back in time to get the daycare kids from school. That was a good schedule for me. I tried so hard to concentrate at work, but I was so distracted. I just couldn't stop thinking about Jody.

"I can't believe you waited that long to lose your virginity," Ivy said.

It's not like I waited that long on purpose. I had been wanting to have sex, but my connections with men were short-lived. I could never find someone I had a true connection with. I'm not sure how Jody slithered his way in. I'm pretty sure if he really had gotten to know me, he would have left since I wouldn't have sex with him right away. I wanted to lose my virginity to a guy who actually liked me and cared about me. Honestly, I had wanted a relationship first.

I was thirty-one years old at that point and had never had a boyfriend. I thought that was strange. Then to lose my virginity to a stranger was even weirder. Why the fuck did I have a coming-of-age story in my thirties? I hated Jody so much, and I was still in a lot of pain.

Ivy really helped me through the situation, and I tried my best to help her.

She showed me a post Jody had made on Facebook about his baby mom not helping him with the kids. It reminded me of how my mom was. My mom put all the responsibility on my dad. I knew Jody was with family, and they were helping him with them. On the other hand, I was so angry that he got to move and stay in a nice house. The house that he was living in was huge. Whoever he was living with was wealthy. I didn't understand how he got all those blessings after everything he did to me. He was living the life, and I was still living in the projects barely making it.

"It's not fair," I whined to Ivy when we were talking about it.

"You don't really know what is going on behind the scenes," she said.

She was right, but still, I felt it was unfair. I guess he was the one who needed the most help. I guess that's why God allowed him to have that experience. I still felt like God betrayed me. Jody had pictures on Facebook of him going out, going to the casino, and having fun.

"The psychic said he and his girlfriend were going to break up," I told Ivy. "She said he was going to get back with his baby mom and that they're life partners. As far as I know, him and his baby mom don't get along."

"I don't think he fuck with her like that," Ivy said.

I told Ivy I was going to talk to Ms. Ruth and ask her more about Jody. I was on a quest to find out who he really was. Who was the guy who took my virginity and then moved to another state? I had so many questions and wanted answers. I wanted closure too.

I was in my apartment getting dinner ready and saw Ms. Ruth outside sitting across from my building as usual. I was so nervous and afraid to talk to her. I saw her walk back and forth, and I wondered if she would blow me off or be rude if I brought Jody up. I called to her from my window. "Ms. Ruth," I said, "can I talk to you for a minute?"

She replied with, "Yes," and came right up.

We sat down in the living room, and she looked at me with curiosity. I started off by saying I wasn't sure if it was okay to talk to her. I mean, it was a weird situation, and I was talking to Jody's baby's mom's mother. Then I just blurted out, "Jody took my virginity."

"Honey, I know," she said. I had no idea she knew. She went on to tell me that the night Jody took my virginity he came to her house and woke her up crying. She said it as if she really didn't want to tell me that piece of information. I didn't know he felt bad for taking my virginity. "Now, are you pregnant?" she asked.

"No," I said.

She told me he was on drugs and it was bad. She said he was on crack, he was poppin pills, and he was drinking a lot. "It's good that he left," she said.

I still couldn't believe he was really a crackhead. I believed it more when it came out of her mouth. I had been hoping it was just a rumor, but it was the truth. I didn't say anything to her, but the thoughts in my head were racing. I never really knew a lot of drug addicts and I was never around any, or none that I knew of. It was all a shock to me.

"His mom died, and his aunt just died too," she said.

It seemed like Jody's life had started going downhill after he took my virginity. I felt bad for him. She gave me a hug and said if I needed anything to just let her know.

I thanked her and she left. I called Olivia to tell her about the conversation. I felt a little relieved after that. I was glad I had talked to Ms. Ruth. I got some closure.

The next day at work, I told Ivy what happened. I told her Jody was on drugs and he wasn't in rehab.

"What kind of drugs, coke?" Ivy said.

"No, crack," I said.

Ms. Ruth started acting funny after that. She looked at me with guilt and then she completely stopped speaking to me.

I knew something was off, but I didn't know what. I bought a deck of Oracle cards and Olivia was teaching me how to read them. I asked the cards why Ms. Ruth was ignoring me, and I saw she was covering something up. I couldn't figure out what that was.

I wanted to get rid of any feelings I had for Jody. One of my readers told me to do a spell. I needed some carnation flowers and some lemon juice. I did the spell that he instructed me to do: perfectly, actually. After I completed the spell, it felt like there was a spirit standing by my bedroom door. That night, I dreamed about witch shoes – like the ones the original witches wore in Salem. *'This is a real witch spell,'* I thought.

I noticed when I was leaving for work in the morning, there was a young guy asleep out in my hallway. There was always some shit going on over there. He would sit right in front of the hallway door. I ignored him at first, but I was concerned. "Do you need a blanket or a pillow?" I asked.

"No," he said. He told me his girlfriend kicked him out of the house and he had nowhere to go. I wasn't sure why he chose my building and floor to sleep on. He asked me if his sleeping there made me uncomfortable, and I said, "No."

I went back into my apartment and grabbed my couch pillow and gave it to him. He was reluctant to take it, but he did. I started to see him more often just hanging out in the hallway. When I would leave during the day, he would be standing by my door. I looked at him and his eyes were dilated. He looked like a fucking zombie. It was then he began scaring me. I thought maybe he was trying to break into my house. I was worried so I said, "The next time I see you, I'm going to call the police." I came home and he was sitting on my steps. I yelled, "I don't feel comfortable with you here," and then he ran off and I called the police. I didn't see him again after that.

My boss had surgery done and when she came back to work, she was acting weird. She started complaining about dumb shit. She made a comment about us needing to use a new dish rag every day.

"I don't use a new dish rag every day," I said.

"Who does that?" she said. Then she went on to talk shit about Ivy. I tried to stick up for Ivy because she wasn't there to defend herself. Plus, Ivy always stood up for me.

We got into an argument after she called me incompetent. I got up quickly and yelled, "Who you think you talking to like that?"

She told me to leave and that she was firing me. I didn't give a fuck. I was tired of working at that daycare and tired of her. I grabbed my coat. "I've been running this business for a long time," she said.

I told her, "Good luck because you're doing a horrible job." I called Ivy and told her what happened. I was pissed off at my boss, so I reported her ass to the state. Plus, she had many violations in her center.

My reader told me Jody was going to return, but it would be to apologize. Since Jody and Ivy were friends, I made comments on her post hoping he would see them.

He did.

Jody contacted me and said he missed me. He gave me his number.

I couldn't believe it; the psychic was right. I texted Ivy and asked her if she thought I should call him. She said, "Yeah."

I called Jody back.

"Hi," he said.

"How can I help you?" I asked.

"I just wanted to see how you were doing."

I told him how I was doing, and I was completely honest. I told him about the weight loss and losing my job.

"I didn't even know you liked me all like that," he said.

I didn't like him at first. I hadn't known he would affect me like that either.

"You know, I wasn't all there," he said. I assumed he meant about his drug use.

We got into a conversation about his baby mom.

He told me how lousy of a mother she was. He said she never cleaned up the house. He said he would come home from work, and he would have to do all the cooking and feed the kids. She just sat there, he said. There was a big age difference between them. He basically had a child with a child. Also, I pointed out the zodiac sign his baby mom was; they were known to be lazy.

"Wait a minute," he said. "How did you know her zodiac sign?" He had caught on to the fact that I had done research on her. I started to laugh. That mothafucka was smart. He asked if I had a boyfriend and said that he was done with his girlfriend.

"What?" I asked. Why on earth did he think I would be interested in him again? I didn't have the energy to go through any more bullshit with him. I told him I was okay with us being friends. I asked him if he had a baby on the way.

He paused for a second. "Naw," he said.

I wasn't convinced with his answer, and I knew he was lying.

We started talking again. He called me and texted me every day. He seemed to be making a real effort.

One morning, he told me he wanted to see me. I told him he lived too far away. I decided to go see him anyway. I wanted to have sex with him at least one more time. I knew it was very risky: I was gonna go visit a guy who hurt me and who had the potential to hurt me again.

"Do you think that's a good idea?" Olivia said.

I knew it was probably not the best idea, but I really wanted to see him. I also told Ivy I was going.

We talked on the phone while he was on his way to go pick up his kids. "I pick my kids up every day after school," he said. I told him I was going to buy my ticket to come see him. He said, "Okay, and when you get here, I won't touch you."

"What," I said. "I want to have sex again."

He said, "You sound all distraught." Then he said, "I do too." He said he remembered how warm my vagina was and that he had a boner. "It won't go down. I gotta call you back."

I went to the store to buy things for my trip. I bought some cute little shirts and some cute boots. I knew he would be surprised at how much weight I had lost.

Thanksgiving Day, I didn't hear from Jody all day. I was upset. I called Ivy and told her that he didn't even call me. "Girl, you don't need him," she said. It was fucked up he didn't even call me on a holiday, knowing I was planning to go up there. Ivy was right: I didn't need him and his bullshit. He didn't care about me. I was done for real this time.

Then Ivy blocked me on Facebook, and I wasn't sure why. *'That's weird,'* I thought. I looked at my cards and I got the ten of swords: a betrayal. It didn't make sense to me; I thought we got along well.

February 2nd, 2017, I called the doctor to get my test results. The doctor wasn't in yet, so I waited for her to call me back. I was really nervous and worried. She finally called me and told me I was diagnosed with HPV. I couldn't believe that shit. I got silent and I started to black out. Tears started to stream down my face.

I was in shock, but really, I had known something was wrong. I had a lot of unusual discharge, it felt like I was peeing on myself all the time, and the discharge was sour-smelling and flaky. I kept seeing crust in my underwear. My coochie wasn't the same anymore either. I could hear the doctor saying, "Hello," several times as I gave her the silent treatment. It seemed like she had an attitude, so I hung up the phone. *'My life is over. I'm going to die. I'm going to get cervical cancer.'* So many thoughts raced around in my head.

I sent Jody a message telling him that he gave me HPV and that I was telling the truth, and I would show him the papers. I also told him I hoped he died, and I meant that shit. He had totally ruined my life. The cards had been right. I cried the whole day thinking my life had gone down the drain over some sorry-ass nigga. He never responded.

I talked to Olivia and all she could say was she was sorry. I talked to my mother about it and, surprisingly, she was really supportive. She said, "You will be okay, just pray about it." I knew exactly how I got HPV. The day when I sucked Jody's dick and it tasted sour, that was the day. It all made sense.

I pulled out my cards and asked about the STD. It said Jody had sex with someone else before he came to my house. The woman he had been with was a white woman and she was in her forties. She was a nasty-looking bitch. She looked like she was sick. She'd had something and she gave to him, and he put it right in my mouth and my cooch. I was so fucking disgusted. He hadn't even showered before coming to my house. I remember him saying he was about to make some money. I thought, *'He was prostituting. Omg!'*

I made fake Facebook pages with his picture displaying that he had HPV.

About a week later, I was on Ivy's Facebook page. She had just had her baby. I had decided to block Jody's page for the last time. I saw that somebody had left a message under Ivy's post, and I couldn't see who. *'Wtf?'* I thought.

I went back and unblocked Jody and saw he had wrote, *'Congrats, you're a wonderful woman.'*

*'Hold the fuck up,'* I thought. *'What the fuck is going on here?'* That's exactly what he had said to his mom.

She replied with, *'Aww, thanks, hun.'*

I thought maybe he was trying to flirt with her, so I sent her a fake Facebook page I created to let her know he had an STD.

She liked the post he sent, and she blocked my fake page.

I had seen in my cards there was communication between Jody and Ivy. I saw a friendship and a relationship card. I decided to ask a reader what exactly was going on, because it wasn't clear to me.

The reader said that Ivy stabbed me in the back, and she was seeing Jody. "She did you dirty," she said. The reader told me Ivy and Jody were really close friends but would soon be in a relationship. She called her a fake friend. Then she said Jody was going to drop her and go to someone else and she was going to be devastated. "That's her karma, girl," she said.

I couldn't fuckin believe it! *'What the fuck is going on,'* I thought. I swear my spirit came out of my body and was looking at it. How hadn't I known about this? Why hadn't my angels or spirit guides warned me? I was completely flabbergasted. I had no clue. Damn, that shit was cold-blooded. I sat on my bed for a while in shock and then tried my best to go to sleep that night.

I finally did, but I woke up to an unusual feeling inside my vagina. It felt like something was falling out. I got up and panicked. I looked down and something was coming out, but I didn't know what it was. I could barely stand up. I thought my cervix was falling out, so I called my mother. She told me to go the hospital. I wasn't even sure if I could make it there. I was too embarrassed to call the ambulance; an Uber was my only option. I then called my friend because I was supposed to go to court with her. She was trying to divorce her husband and needed my support. She also told me to go to the hospital.

I scheduled an Uber and could barely walk outside. I was so stressed out and was scared I was dying. I got in the car and the police called my phone. I told them I was dying, and I was on my way to the hospital. The operator asked to speak to the Uber driver. He kept telling me I was going to be ok. He was driving as fast as he could. I told him what happened between me and Jody, and I could tell he felt bad for me. "Hang in there," he said.

"The angels will save me," I said.

I got to the hospital, and they checked me into a room. Three doctors surrounded me. One of them told me to stay still. Whatever was in my vagina fell out while was on the emergency room bed. They looked and stared at it and had no idea what it was. Then they told me it was a piece of something they put on the cervix when you get a Colposcopy. It must have gotten stuck to my uterus, they said. After that, I was okay and ready to go home.

I was so fucking livid when I got home. I posted a picture of that bitch and Jody on Facebook and said what they did to me. Then I deleted it. I looked at my cards later that day and saw that they were pissed. I didn't give a fuck. I couldn't believe the fat bitch did that to me.

After that, I started noticing whenever I left my house, somebody was following me. I purposely went outside and as I was coming in, a guy out of nowhere started following me. I started getting followed every day by different people. I noticed people would follow me to the bus stop and sometimes even get on the bus with me.

Meanwhile, Jody and Ivy were keeping quiet about the whole situation. I would read her Facebook posts and she would make little comments about me without mentioning my name.

I friend requested Ivy on Facebook. She accepted my friend request. She pretended like she was happy to hear from me, talking about how she got a new Facebook. She said she didn't work at the old job anymore at the daycare. I wanted to cut the bullshit, so I told her what she did was grimy. She said, "What. I don't know what you're talking about."

I said, "I know about that other shit you did too." I was talking about her telling the owner of the other daycare I reported her.

"I didn't do any of that," she said.

"You pretended to be my friend so you could get information about Jody so you could date him."

She said, "I don't want that nigga." Then she started trying to talk tough saying we could meet up because I was disrespecting her. She then called me a low life.

A low life? If anybody was a low life, it was her for sure. I didn't even qualify to be a low life. This piece of trash bitch called me a low life. Excuse me?

I made a joke of it and said, "You're a wonderful woman," which is what Jody had said to her.

She threatened me by saying we were going to meet up, and I didn't like being threatened.

I got serious; I said, "If you gonna pull up, then pull up." I told her to stop all that talking.

She said, "I'mma see you."

I wasn't scared or worried at all. I was waiting for her to come to my house. I was going to fight her and not because of Jody; but because she had the fuckin nerve to think she could do that shit me. The conversation ended and then all of a sudden, I got a notification that I was tagged in a Facebook post. She framed me. The post said that I was crazy, and I was accusing her of seeing Jody and it wasn't true. Then she put, "Where you at now, lil bitch."

I hurried to block her, and then I went on my fake page and saw that she had it set up where I couldn't respond. I was fuckin pissed that bitch set me up. I called one of my nephews and told him what was going on. He was like, "Fuck that shit." He tried to comment as well.

I read all the comments, and her ugly-ass bestie, who looked like a skunk squirrel combination, said, "Who are you talking about?" Then Ivy posted a picture of me. Her bestie said, "Jody live all the way in another state, the bitch is dumb. People will say anything." Then she made a comment to Jody because he had commented as well and said, "We all love you, but that's all his ex-girlfriend." Her friend tried to say I was ugly. I looked nothing like that nasty crack-head bitch, and I wasn't anywhere near ugly, but she sure was. She had some motherfuckin nerve.

Ivy's other friends started to comment. One said, "I know she ain't that stupid," talking about Ivy. She basically said Ivy would be stupid if she fucked with him.

Then Jody replied cussin' the girl out. He said, "Shut the fuck up before I beat your man up."

She quickly changed her tune. Then she apologized. This nigga was a straight clown, and everybody knew it. All their friends and family knew they were dating but were keeping it on the low. Later, Jody's cousin commented on the post and said, "This bitch is dumb," referring to me. They all tried to cover it up.

I knew I was going to get that bitch back; I just didn't know how or when. I did not like people getting over on me. She tried to embarrass me on Facebook; there was no way I was letting that shit go.

People continued to follow me, but I started ignoring them. At first, I thought somebody was going to rob me or cause me physical harm. They weren't doing anything, so I just went about my life. They expected me to live in fear and become depressed but that was not happening. I came into my power, and I started to get a lot of self-confidence. Since I lost all that weight, I looked good. I looked really sexy, better than Jody and Ivy. She was overweight and ran through. She looked like a fat-ass pig. I started to call her Peppa Pig from that cartoon on Nickelodeon.

I was still upset and I was telling everybody about what that bitch did. I told my nephew's girlfriend. She said, "Oh hell no, that's fucked up." So, she decided to send her a message. I didn't tell her to do it, but she did it on her own. I did a tarot reading for her, so she did me a favor in exchange. She sent Ivy a message on Facebook that said she was a rat-ass bitch. She also told her she need her ass whooped. My nephew's girlfriend told me she didn't respond, and she blocked her. Yeah, I bet she did.

My nephew sent her a message too calling her a rat. I looked at my cards and saw the bitch was scared.

The next day, I was coming home from work, and I got off the bus and headed toward the store. As I was walking, I saw Ivy and her no-neck-ass sister parked in front of the store. I suddenly stopped in my tracks. I immediately went and hid behind a car hoping they wouldn't see me. I was thinking they were gonna try to jump me. Shit, I didn't know those skanks, and that area was known for jumping bitches. That was the first time ever in my life I hid from someone. I had never run or hidden from a fight, even though I didn't get into many fights. I did when I was younger. I wasn't no punk, but I felt like that was best at the time for my safety.

I watched those bitches get in their cars with their kids. Then I angrily walked into the store. I was like, '*Okay, so I got to strategize.*'

I still had Ivy's number and gave it to my nephew. He decided he would call her. She answered the phone with her fat ass.

"Yeah, since you wanna be out here hoeing, y'all going to get the fair one just you and her this weekend and we gonna put it on live."

I was definitely down to have a fair fight. He hung up the phone and then she texted back saying she didn't take threats.

My nephew said, "Let's go to her house."

The next day, my nephew and his girlfriend came to stay the weekend. I also invited a guy I was talking to. All of us went to my house. I was a little nervous, but I was glad they all came to support me. My nephew's girlfriend was known as a good fighter. She was known for beating several bitches up at the same time. Just in case I got jumped, I knew she would have my back. I didn't know her that well, but I knew about her. They had dated for a few years.

We were all in the house and nothing was happening. So, I decided to go outside with my nephew and walk around just so those mothafuckas knew not to fuck with me. Some of the people who lived in the projects started coming out, but they just walked past us.

My nephew and his girlfriend decided to go outside and look for weed. I didn't want them to go. I started looking at my tarot cards and worrying myself. I didn't want anything to happen to my nephew.

I started reading my cards again and the tower came out. The tower meant an explosion or something unexpected happening. My nephew started to worry. His girlfriend stayed cool and calm the whole time. "It's whatever," she said. She was ride or die for sure. I went into my room and my nephew said, "I'm not feelin this, man." Then he grabbed his book bag and pulled out a gun with a bunch of bullets. I don't think I had ever seen a gun that close before. I thought, *'You said you didn't bring it.'* He lied to me. I was glad he did, though, because I would have been worried. He started to load the gun. I was excited. I thought the gun was cool.

I couldn't sleep that night. I was worried about my nephew; I didn't want him to get in trouble. The next morning, they were up laughing and having a good time. They decided to walk up to the store. I didn't think it was a good idea, but they left anyway. "We're not scared," they said. When they came back, they said nobody bothered them. We went back and forth to the store several times. When me and my nephew's girlfriend went, somebody made a weird noise like they were signaling that we were leaving.

On the way back, we walked past my neighbor who sold weed and his friend. My nephew's girlfriend was holding her shoulder. I asked her what happened. She said he pushed her shoulder real hard. So, we told my nephew, and he said, "Why didn't he do it when I was out there?" My neighbor had done a punk-ass move. Why hadn't he done that to my nephew, I wondered? Better yet, why hadn't he pushed me? I was the target.

My nephew went to get more weed and said the people were so friendly. He said, "You need to get out and talk to people. That's why they don't like you." He didn't understand those people were watching him and purposefully being nice. He said a guy in dreads followed him. They laughed about it. It wasn't funny though. They didn't have to deal with it on daily basis like I did.

Me and my nephew went to the store; a guy was following us, but my nephew didn't notice it. I suddenly stopped and the guy abruptly stopped too. He didn't expect me to stop. He looked stupid and like he almost tripped. I was starting to pay more attention to their patterns and behaviors.

It was time for my nephew and his ex-girlfriend to go but absolutely nothing happened. My nephew wanted to stay, but I had to go to work. Plus, I didn't trust him. He would probably have those fools over to my house not knowing they were setting him up. He didn't think anybody was following me. They left and things were still the same. I was still being followed as usual but not harmed.

I was on my way back from the store when I noticed Ivy's car parked in front of the police station. I saw her kids trying to duck down in the backseat. She had an ugly-ass car. It was an odd color, and it looked like a hearse to me. I then saw her walking to her car. She just looked at me and got in and drove off. I hurried to take pictures of the vehicle. I walked back up the street and went looking for her to see if I could catch her coming around the corner. Stupid bitch. I wish I had known I was going to run into her so I could fight her funky ass.

I figured I could charge her ass for harassment because that's what she was doing. I had to get her in trouble in some kind of way. I went home and called the police. The police came and I showed them the pictures. They weren't good pictures, though. They didn't show her in the car well enough, but the police officer believed me.

Ivy got her court papers in the mail and tried to make a joke about it on Facebook. She made it seem like she didn't care. The day of court, I made sure I looked really cute. I was just ready to get it over with. She walked in and had the ugliest jumpsuit on I've ever seen with an ugly-ass design on it. It looked like she got it from a thrift store. She looked a hot-ass fuckin mess. She was talking on the phone huffing and puffing and shit like this whole thing was stupid.

We got called into the court room. I told the judge what happened. It was my first time in court, so I didn't know what to expect. All I knew was I was telling the truth.

While I was telling the judge my side of the story, Ivy shouted, "Oh, oh, can I say something?" and was waving her hand around like a fat-ass whale. She was acting completely different than when I was around her. She said, "I'm not dating him. I was pregnant at the time."

"And what does that have to do with anything?" I said. I explained how she and her big forehead-ass sister tried to scare me at the store.

"I don't even shop there," she said.

She told the judge Jody was a cokehead, like she wouldn't be interested in someone who did that.

That really threw me off.

"Wow," I said. '*This bitch is dirty,*' I thought. Of course, she denied everything.

She then told her side of the story saying she stopped talking to me because I got fired from the job. I showed the judge a picture of the car and she said, "I want to see." The officer showed her the picture and she laughed. "That's not my car," she said.

This bitch was a straight up piece of shit for real. Nobody else had an ugly-ass car like that around there. The judge seemed to be very familiar with Jody and her; I mean, it was a small town. He asked me if I was still involved with Jody, and I said, "No."

He said, "Then it doesn't matter."

This bitch Ivy said, "Yeah, that's right."

I ended up losing the case, and then I started smiling because I knew it wasn't the end. '*Next round, bitch*,' I thought.

Ivy said out loud, "See look at her, see she's smiling. She wants me to get in trouble and go to jail."

I continued to smile. I really wanted more than that to happen. I was pissed off; I felt like she wasn't getting her karma for what she did to me.

I called my cousin and told her what happened. I walked around outside just so people wouldn't hear my conversation. As I was walking back towards the court building, I heard somebody say, "I don't even shop there." It was none other than Ivy's big ass. The judge had told us to stay away from each other, or next time we would be charged with harassment. So I kept walking and said, "That's why he cheated on you. That's karma." I knew that had to hurt. That's what the fuck she gets, too. Weak-ass bitch.

A couple of days passed, and I was on my way to the post office. The maintenance man stopped me to talk. I felt like he was in on stalking me too. The whole neighborhood was. When I stepped inside the post office, I saw Ivy walking out. '*That bitch is lame as fuck*,' I thought. I was so unbothered by her, and I knew she wasn't gonna do shit. I didn't see her after that day.

I looked on both Jody's and Ivy's pages and they regularly said smart-ass comments. I knew they were talking about me. They tried to rub it in my face that they were together, and nobody knew about it. But people did know because I was telling everybody I saw. I think they just didn't care, honestly. I knew he was giving her money; well, money from whomever he was staying with. He didn't have any money. He was broke and didn't work. He helped her get that ugly-ass car she got.

She wrote on Facebook, "I got two cars, gotta sell the other one. Don't need two cars." She was trying to brag about him getting her a car. That bitch was making $8.00 an hour at a daycare at thirty years old. So that was an upgrade for her. He was on Facebook flashing money thinking he was a big boss nigga. I knew he was trying to piss me off. I felt like he didn't deserve a better life after what he did to me. '*Why is this nigga still alive?*' I thought.

On Mother's Day, she made a post about how she got herself diamond earrings. In reality, I knew Jody got them for her. She definitely upgraded when she got with him. Her wardrobe changed. She started wearing better clothes. She started going more places. She got that car. That bitch thought she was all that when she got with him. She thought dating a crackhead was cool. She was fuckin delusional. Those people were completely sick. She thought she was some Facebook model, but really, she was just a small-town slut. She was not the same girl I met who was crying about her baby dad leaving her.

I got a reading on both of them hoes. I still had trouble reading my own cards; I could only read for other people. The reader told me Jody and Ivy thought they were soulmates, and he was buying her gifts and giving her money, but he realized he needed to be more responsible with his money... well, his family member's money.

I got another reading from a different woman, and she referred to Jody and Ivy as the Joker and Harley Quinn. She told me Jody was going to leave her for another woman. She said he was going to drop her and go back to his baby mom. The baby mom was trying to get revenge on him for what he did to her. She was smart enough to know he was seeing Ivy after Ivy had posted about me and tried to embarrass me on Facebook. She was Facebook friends with Ivy, so she knew something was up. The reader said she would pretend to get back with him just so he would break up with Ivy.

I started looking at my cards and saw something similar to what she said. Shortly after that, Ivy started posting things like, 'I don't want a relationship, I'm just worried about me and my kids.' Her posts started getting sad and negative. I knew Jody had left her ass. I bet he ghosted her and stopped returning her calls. That was her karma but that wasn't enough karma for me. I wanted her to have more. So you know, I went on Facebook talking shit, posting things like, 'Hahaha, he left your ass for another woman.' I was so happy too. Jody then tried to go back to her shortly after that because his baby mom played him. I saw the tower card and saw them getting into an argument. Ivy ended up finding out why he ghosted her, and she was pissed, but she deserved every bit of that shit.

They were both stalking my page and seeing what I was saying about them. Jody was getting really angry, so he started posting videos of the house he lived in and all the cars he had. He was trying to clown me for living in the projects when he had been there his whole life. I could tell he was mad because he looked like a hot-ass mess. He didn't look healthy at all. He kept bringing up one of his girl cousins. She was around his age, and she was really rough looking, especially her face. I wasn't sure why he kept saying her name, but I didn't give a fuck. That nigga was mad and hurt, and I was loving that shit.

Jody and Ivy went on break with their relationship, but she was losing interest in him because he cheated on her. I could tell it wasn't the same. After that happened, she calmed her ass down. *'Yeah, bitch, humble yourself,'* I thought. She had thought she was the shit, and he wouldn't cheat on her. This was Jody we were talking about. He fucked the whole neighborhood, but from what I heard, she did too. They were both town sluts.

A guy that knew her told me she was a hoe on the low. I said, "Really."

He said, "She's definitely about that dick."

It made sense. She had told me she used to be a player, and he was one too. She started making her page private after that and would rarely post publicly. When she did, she still looked a mess. She was constantly showing pictures of going to the gym but not losing any weight. She tried to portray she had the perfect life. That bitch was a phony, and I didn't understand why I hadn't seen it when I first met her.

I finally came out as a witch. I was so happy because I felt free. I didn't have to hide anymore. Most people were accepting of it, but there were a few who didn't understand or believe in witches. I wasn't sure how people would take it, but it turned out to be good. I had retired being a witch until Jody did that fucked up shit to me. Then the witch returned. The witch was my dark side, my shadow side. He had brought that out of me. I didn't give a fuck about anything anymore.

I gathered up all the information about Ivy and Jody and I thought it was the perfect opportunity to get them back.

I still hated Jody and Ivy. I began to go on a very dark path. I was constantly talking about killing people and dead people all the time. I could tell people were trying to avoid me, but I just didn't care. The situation was unfair, and I wanted justice. I became dark and sneaky just like them. I started matching their energy and moving like they did. I also found Ivy's police records, and I wasn't sure if I would get in trouble if I posted them, but I thought, '*Fuck it.*' She put me on blast; it was her turn. I posted her criminal record. She had some charges for shoplifting. That's a broke bitch trait. I was surprised to see it. She had also posted a picture showing her titties which was fucking disgusting. I posted that too. That bitch was trifling as fuck. Her friends and family started liking my posts – like they were trying to scare me. I did not give one fuck.

I was washing clothes at the laundromat so I wouldn't get bothered at the one in my apartment building. A man looked inside the window like he was waiting for me. I didn't have time for that shit. When I was leaving, a man across the street spoke to me. He said, "Hi." I didn't say anything back. He was weird as fuck. He looked weird and sounded weird, just like all the weirdos around there.

I went home, and I saw three girls across from me. They were all carrying grocery bags. One of the girls was Jody's cousin. I recognized the color of her hair. I had looked at her Facebook page a few times and had seen she dyed it. I went into my building, and I noticed all three of the girls started walking over toward me. I just kept walking to my house and started laughing thinking, *'This is a wild goose chase.'* When I got upstairs inside my home, I shut the door. A few minutes afterward, I looked out of the peephole and saw that Jody's cousin had come up to my floor. Then I saw her leaving with the other girls and I heard her call somebody a bitch.

I looked at my cards to see who they were looking for. It said me. *'Me?'* I thought. *'She was probably just trying to scare me,'* I thought.

Afterward, she started coming over to the projects almost every day. I really didn't pay her attention, but then I noticed she would show up right after I went into my apartment. I thought if she was gonna do something, she would have come to my door. She did that for the whole summer. It was weird because I would see her out there, then I would come down, and she would disappear. Finally, I saw her while I was going into my house one day and she didn't even look at me. Then I went back out. I saw that the goal of those motherfuckers was to inflict fear. They wanted me to be in a state of fear all the time, but I wasn't. I had finally decided to start a tarot business and I was too excited and busy with it to be scared.

I bought a regular deck of tarot cards and taught myself how to read them. I practiced a lot and read for people for free. Then people started offering to pay me. That's how I knew it was time to start my business. I registered with the state and got an LLC. I was so proud of myself. I knew Jody and Ivy were going to be mad. They weren't doing shit with their lives. They motivated me to start the business.

I did a photoshoot at a cemetery so I could put pictures on my website[ref] The pictures turned out amazing. I felt like God made that photoshoot happen. I was being my true self. I was a witch, and I was embracing it.

I got this girl to do a love spell for me. I was tired of not finding someone I could connect with. Within a couple of days, a lot of guys were friend-requesting me on Facebook. It was mostly guys I wasn't attracted to, but it was still really fun.

Since I was in the process of starting my tarot business, I was looking for someone to do my business logo. A friend of mine had just gotten hers done and recommended me to the man that did hers. His name was Zeke; he had long dreads and was very talented. I asked him to do my logo for me, and I really liked it. It was a moon with broken glass over it.

I thought he was cute, and I was interested, so I started talking to him. Our first phone conversation was great. We had a lot in common. We both had the same last name. He had Crohn's disease like my mom. I had never met anyone else who had that. The last person we were involved with both had the same fuckin name. We both had our own business.

He thought that we were soulmates, and I was happy I had met him and that the girl had done the spell for me.

It didn't bother him that I was a witch even though he said he was a Christian. He seemed to be really interested in me.

A week passed and he wanted a relationship. I thought it was too soon. He wasn't even sure if he liked me yet and, with my history, we decided to go out on a date to see where it would go.

He picked me up from work, but he had an attitude because of something with his job. He said he needed to stop at his house first. As we were walking inside the house, one of his friends was coming out. I noticed his friend had this shiny glow over his face, so I said, "Hi," to him. Me and Zeke went into the house, and I met his brother and his cousin. Then we went to Friday's to eat.

The date was okay. It was the first date I had ever gone on. Like my first real date. How was I thirty-three years old and just going out on a date?

After our date, we sat in the car. He showed me some of the shirts he made and a picture of his friend. He said, "There go your boy."

I said, "No." I asked him who his friend was. I said he look like a player.

He said, "He is a player, but he has a girlfriend though."

I had only asked because of his face being shiny.

When we left, I knew I didn't want to go on another date with him. I wasn't really interested, at least not then. I wanted to stay friends and get to know him better.

He told me after our first conversation that he couldn't sleep that night because he couldn't stop thinking about me. I laughed. We faced-timed, and he said I was so naturally beautiful. He wanted a relationship and said he didn't want me as just a friend. I was only open for a friendship at that time, though. He had to grow on me. He agreed, so I told him I was going to help him organize his business, because he needed it. We planned for him to come pick me up the next day.

As I was getting dressed, he canceled on me saying an unexpected project had come up. I was fuckin pissed. That was a deal breaker for me. Anytime someone canceled on me I was done with their ass. I didn't play that shit. I told him goodbye, and I was very disappointed in him. "Damn, Brandi over that," he said.

Zeke really pissed me off, so I decided I was going to get him back by talking to his friend, Juelz. We were already Facebook friends, so I asked him if he wanted a reading. Then we exchanged numbers. He didn't seem to mind that I had gone out on a date with his friend. I honestly would have never talked to a guy's friend, but I had only known Zeke for two weeks and he shouldn't have pissed me off. I didn't expect anything out of Juelz and wasn't paying that much attention to him. It was purely revenge.

Our connection started out slowly and was on and off, especially since he was in a relationship. I really didn't feel comfortable with talking to a guy with a girlfriend because I knew it wouldn't go anywhere. We talked about meeting up and I was kind of nervous. I mean, I was getting comfortable enough to see him in person and possibly have sex. It had been a while, but I was looking forward to it.

Then, we were talking every day from morning until night. I wondered when he spent time with his family because he spent most of his time on the phone with me. We talked on the phone a few times, but mostly it was through text. I felt like he wasn't taking me seriously and I wasn't taking him seriously, so I didn't care.

I asked him if he had a girlfriend, and he said, "A little bit."

I told him I didn't feel comfortable with him having a girlfriend, and then he called me and somehow talked me into being comfortable with him. He was in his car, and he had very long dreads just like Zeke. They were neatly done. He was dressed very nicely. He went on to tell me how popular he was in high school and how he won prom king.

He was over at his friend's house, and we did a video call. We were more comfortable with each other. I could hear his friend in the background asking me if I had some friends. Juelz answered for me. He said, "Naw, she don't really fuck wit nobody like that." We had a nice conversation, and I felt like we started to click.

He was on his way home and he texted me and said, "I like you."

I said, "I like you too."

He said, "I'm serious I really like you."

I could tell he was serious, and I really didn't know how to react because I was honestly surprised. I figured I would have sex with him at least twice and then just go my own way. I told him to call me back and he said, "I can't." I knew it was because his girlfriend was around.

I mean, we talked, but I guess when he saw me on video, he liked me even more.

We made plans for him to come over to my house so we could have sex. I was really excited and worried about his dick being big. He had sent me pictures of it. He had a nice one. I was also worried about there being some sort of spiritual interference. I hadn't had sex in a year.

He texted me the day before he was supposed to come over and told me his friend got shot in the face. '*Wait, what?*' It had been the friend whose house he was in when we video chatted. I couldn't believe it. He told me a lot of his friends get killed. There was death all around him.

The first thing I thought was, '*This is the interference I was worried about.*' I was like, '*Damn, y'all killing people so I don't have sex? It's not that real.*' I didn't know his friend, but I wanted to be supportive. Getting shot is a horrible way to die. I believed he got robbed. Juelz said, "That's crazy. I was just at his house, and I was talking to him."

I could tell he was devastated, so I tried my best to be there for him and not think about my own selfish needs.

He asked me if he should go to his friend's mom's house or come see me. Of course, I told him to go over there. I was very disappointed, but more disappointed at spirit. I talked to him when he was in front of the guy's mother's house. "Thank you for being supportive," he said.

"No problem," I said. I felt a little badly for only thinking about myself because I really wanted to have sex.

"That's crazy someone would shoot a person in the face. I won't be in here long. Maybe tomorrow you can stop by my job and come see me," Juelz said.

"Really?" I said with excitement.

"If you happen to be around, and you're not busy." He made sure I wouldn't get too excited.

I was surprised he wanted me to come to his job. The next day, I made sure I looked cute. He worked at a college. I caught a bus down there. The college was well-known, and I saw all these young college girls and started to feel insecure. I wondered if he was talking to the girls.

I waited for him to meet me. I saw him standing tall with smooth brown skin. I walked towards him and gave him a hug. He looked different in person, definitely more attractive. We sat down on a bench. He was on his lunch. We talked for bit. I could tell something was a little off, but I wasn't sure what it was. He seemed kind of distant from me. He still held the conversation, but his body language was off to me.

I left and he seemed to have changed his whole energy. He didn't want to meet up anymore. I wondered if he hadn't found me attractive. I'm not for everybody, but we already had video chats, so he had seen my entire face. I thought maybe it had been my clothes, and I was confused.

I got a reading done and it said that he had just broken up with his girlfriend and he had been feeling down about it. That's why he had been acting funny.

That wasn't enough for me. I still felt like he hadn't found me attractive. How the fuck did a person want to have sex then all of a sudden change their mind? I honestly didn't take into consideration that his friend had just gotten murdered. I just got so angry.

He kept acting funny and was not texting as much. I went off on him. I told him exactly how I felt. I told him if he didn't find me attractive or didn't want to have sex with me, that was all he had to say. I also insulted him by saying he thought he was all that cause he had been prom king. I said, "You're forty, nobody cares."

Oh, he was mad. I had known exactly how to piss him off. He said he was spending time with his children, and they came first. I knew he was lying, and I didn't like that he was trying to put people in front on me. Even though kids were more important, he didn't have to say that; I already knew.

We stopped talking to each other and after two weeks, I missed him. I wanted to apologize and make up. I had already unfriended him, so I sent a request. I also did a spell so that he would come back. When I did the spell, my candle holder broke into pieces, and glass flew everywhere. That was definitely not a good sign.

I waited for him to respond to the friend-request and thought about how I missed him, but honestly, I just had obsessive behavior towards him. I had known our connection wouldn't go anywhere. All my readings had said it, and even my cards said it.

He finally accepted my friend request. I was surprised. *'The spell worked,'* I thought. I apologized to him in his inbox. He forgave me and asked if I wanted to start over where we left off. I agreed, and we got back to normal.

Then I bought up the topic of us getting together again, but only if he wanted to.

He said he did, but I felt like he was playing a fucking game with me. He told me would take off of work so we could meet up on the same day. Our work schedules didn't allow time for us to meet. I asked him what day and time, and it took him so long to respond. I was at work, and I couldn't take it anymore.

He said he was in trouble at work and that's why he hadn't responded. I knew he was lying, so I snapped. I felt it too. Something inside my brain just did. I tried to keep calm, but if I hadn't gone the fuck off at that moment, who knew what would have happened. That guy was leading me on and playing mind games with me and I wasn't mentally stable enough for that shit. I was a fuckin emotional mess. I was still fucked up from Jody and then that mothafucker was playing the fuck out of me.

I went off on him so badly, I sort of blacked out while going on a rant about him on Facebook. I called him a loser and started posting photos of him. He ended up blocking me. I even went as far as to say I hoped he died. I knew after that I would never talk to him again and I didn't give a fuck. I knew what I said was fucked up.

He responded later and said, "I didn't do anything to you."

Oh yes he had, and he was trying to play dumb. I also sent him the death card in tarot. That was the last fuckin straw for me. I also decided to contact his friend Zeke and tell him he was talking to me behind his back. First, I sent him the dick pic Juelz had sent me.

Zeke asked, "Who is this and why would you send me something like that?"

I revealed who I was and told him what was going on.

He instantly took his friend's side and said, "I told you he was a player. He has a girlfriend. What did you think was going to happen?"

I felt like I had helped Juelz and given him support and he had played me.

Zeke said, "I knew there was something between you guys. You're not the only one who is psychic. I told him, 'I think she like you.' I told him it was okay to talk to you, and I wouldn't be mad."

I wasn't sure if he was telling the truth or not. I knew that Zeke thought I had stopped talking to him to talk to Juelz, but that definitely wasn't the case. Zeke had also just pissed me off.

I threatened to tell Juelz' girlfriend.

"Please don't tell her. I don't want them to break up," Zeke said.

"He should have never fucked with a witch," I said.

I came to the conclusion that something was wrong, and it wasn't me. Guys would want to have sex with me and all of a sudden change their mind. I was fed the fuck up. I wanted answers. I asked my reader what was going on. "You have a love hex on you." That made sense.

My reader recommended I see a Baba Lowa. He was from the US but had moved to Africa. I booked a reading with him. After all those years, I finally got my answer. He told me I had a relationship in a past life and the person never moved on and was blocking me from relationships and sex. I had never in my life heard of shit like that before. It was always an excuse for why I couldn't have a relationship. Why had this never come up before? I had been getting readings for years. He said I also had two hexes on me that were blocking me.

So that was the culprit.

He gave me instructions on what to do. It was a very long list. Some of it involved candle spells, of course, and I was able to do those.

There was a guy on Facebook I had gone to high school with named Enoch. I remembered having a class with him, but I hadn't seen him after that because he moved to a different school.

He was spiritual and into everything I was. I thought he was pretty cool. After sending each other messages for a while we became closer. I wanted to talk to him more and we eventually exchanged numbers. He was so smart. We talked about everything but mostly spiritual stuff. He was very supportive and positive.

He had a girlfriend who he had kids with, but she wasn't spiritual at all and that bothered him. He felt like he had outgrown her and was ready to move on. I wasn't okay with a man leaving a woman for me. I wanted him to leave on his own and then start something with me. Our connection happened naturally and at the perfect place. I had never had a connection like that with a guy who was on my level spiritually.

We talked every day, all day. He worked at a gym and was an assistant manager. He was also starting his own business fixing up houses and selling them. He knew a lot about everything. He was an Aquarius so he was an intellectual. We talked about having children. I told him I didn't want any but that a psychic had told me I would have some.

"You think it will be with me?" he asked. He wanted more kids.

"No," I said, "it will be with my husband."

"Oh, I thought maybe it would be with me."

He seemed to be disappointed, but he already had kids.

I wanted him to stay the night at my house; I just wasn't sure what was going to happen. I invited him over one night, but I specifically told him I wasn't having sex with him. It had been years since I had seen him, so I wasn't comfortable yet.

We talked some, but he seemed to withdraw after I set that boundary.

He came over and was shocked when I saw how tall he was. He looked the same from high school but a little different. We sat in my living room and talked. He wanted to sit next to me on the couch. I told him no because I didn't want it to get sexual. Then he tried to touch me, and I wasn't comfortable with that. I felt like I didn't have control in the situation. Sex was out of the question because I wanted to be in control.

"I know I'm into you more than you're into me," he said.

I said, "That's not true." I was into him, but I just didn't want to have sex that night. I wanted to get to know him more and get more comfortable. I was ready for him to go before it went too far. I walked him out and he tried to pick me up. "No!" I yelled. "The neighbors will see us." I could tell he was getting frustrated with me. Maybe he felt like I led him on, but I had told him no sex.

That night, I had an unpleasant dream about him, and it scared me. I dreamed we were dating, and he was cheating on me and making me feel horrible. Then he tried to make me have sex with him. I didn't like that at all. I thought he was doing magic on me to make me have sex with him. I was so angry and felt violated. I sent him so many texts when I got up. He said he hadn't done anything. He stopped talking to me, but I didn't care.

On August 18th, 2018, my business was up and running.

I reconnected with one of my cousins from Texas. I had talked to her briefly when I had lived there. She wanted a reading, and it was a very powerful one. She had a brother who died from cancer, and I contacted him through the cards for her. Her brother wanted her to start a non-profit foundation in his name. She was having a really hard time over his death. We both cried, and overall, it was a very good and accurate reading. We became closer after that and started talking every day. We had a lot in common. I found out she was a witch too and she also practiced magic. Shit, she knew more than me. She told me how to do the candles properly.

I began to get a lot more clients. People from different states were contacting me for readings. It really made me happy reading for people. I felt like this was something I was meant to do. I helped so many, and I was surprised at all the things I could see in those cards. I was becoming more well-known and more comfortable talking with people.

I made sure I looked nice every time I left my apartment to show those stalkers, and that sorry-ass neighborhood, I didn't give a fuck — because I didn't. My energy started to change. I started to feel happier. I was waking up happy every morning.

# Chapter 15:
# The Stalking Gang

There was a guy following me and he got on the bus every morning like I did. He looked strange and like a crackhead. Bums and crackheads seemed to follow me. He talked to me a few times, but I ignored his ass. He would sit behind me on the bus and would look at my phone. I think he just wanted to scare me and make me think he was tryna be in my business. He told me one day I looked just like his daughter. I could tell somebody was making him get up early to follow me because he would fall asleep on the bus. I assumed they were paying him in crack.

One day, I was on the bus, on my way home, and he was getting off the bus. He grabbed my shoulder and said, "Hey there."

"Don't touch me," I yelled.

He quickly got off the bus and then walked towards the store.

I was pissed. Who did that fiend think he was touching me and shit? He crossed the fuckin line. I called my dad immediately. I told him what was going on.

"What is he touching you for?" my dad asked.

Then I saw the guy come out of the store. I took some pictures of him, and he turned towards me as if he didn't care. I walked right to the police station and reported him. They needed time to figure out who he was. I was trying to figure out a way to get the asshole in trouble.

A week went past and then I started seeing him again at the bus stop but with other people. I could tell by their energy they were trying to intimidate me, but I wasn't afraid, not afraid at all. The police had told me the next time I saw him to call the police. I figured this was my chance. I got on the bus and decided to sit in the front this time. The guy sat in the back with his friend. I secretly called the police. Then the bus pulled over on the side of the road. Nobody knew what was going on, not even the bus driver. We sat there for a while waiting for the police to show up and the other passengers began to get restless. "I gotta go to work," one woman yelled.

After about twenty minutes, a sheriff showed up. The bus driver yelled, "Did anyone call the police?"

I ran over to him and said, "I did." I could hear the groans and moans of the passengers. I stepped off the bus and told the officer what was going on. I told him a guy was following and harassing me and asking me for my phone number.

"Who is he?" the officer asked.

I got back on the bus and pointed him out. He had his head turned like he was trying to hide.

"You," the officer said.

"What, I didn't do anything," the guy said.

Then I heard someone say, "I didn't see him do anything." The passengers were siding with that clown.

"Just get off the bus," the officer said.

I sat down and waited for them to get done talking. I knew the man would deny everything.

The guy got back on the bus and popped his collar as if he got away with something. The officer then called me back out to talk. He basically told me the guy denied everything. I heard the fiend yell, "Get off the bus!"

I looked at him and said, "No."

Then the officer got an attitude and told me to get off. He told me there would be a court date set up. I did not feel comfortable getting back on that bus, especially since the passengers were against me, and I wanted it to look like I was really scared. Another officer came and took me to work.

I decided to go back to the women's shelter because I knew they would help me find another place to live. That was the only way I could think of to get out of that dump. I couldn't afford to move by myself, and I was so tired of that town and their bullshit. I was tired of the stalking and the following. I was tired of the fighting and arguing. I was tired of catching two buses to work.

I packed some of my clothes and headed down to the shelter. It looked very different because they had remodeled it. It looked just like a hotel. I quickly made myself at home. I had a roommate who seemed to be very quiet at first. The beds were so uncomfortable it made me ready to go back to that town, but I knew I had to stay to get housing. Since I was staying there, section 8 put me on the top of the list to get a voucher.

I wanted to read cards for the women at the shelter because I wanted to help them. I read for a spooky woman with some big-ass eyes. She said she felt her kids were in danger. I saw that they were okay. The woman looked at me, and she looked like she could barely keep her eyes open. I saw her later in the kitchen. She kept nodding off while she was talking to me. She asked me if she could have some of my milk.

"Sure," I said. I had almond milk and she said she wanted to try it. As I was pouring her some in a cup, I looked up. Her head was tilted down and her eyes were closed, and she had drool coming out of her mouth. She looked like a zombie. "You okay, Sis?" I asked.

She then opened her eyes and said, "Yeah." She said her doctor had put her on a new medicine and it made her sleepy. I went into the office to tell the workers about something, and she followed me. She said something and some of her drool got on me. I was so disgusted.

Me and my roommate were really cool. We got along very well. She was much younger than me and she was running from her boyfriend who abused her and her baby. She had been there for a while – the longest of all the women. We ended up getting another roommate. She was there because she was addicted to pills, and she had lost everything. She carried herself with so much class, though, that no one would have known about her addiction.

A few days after she moved in, the new roommate told me she was getting kicked out. "What?" I asked.

She said they found an empty pill bottle in her drawer, but that she didn't have any pills in it. We were not allowed to have any medication in our room. She started to cry, "I don't have anywhere to go."

I felt so bad for her, and I wondered who snitched on her.

When the old roommate left the room, the new roommate said, "I think it was her."

"Really," I said.

"I heard she gets all her roommates kicked out," she said.

"She never tried anything with me," I said.

There was a rumor going around that my old roommate was an informer for the shelter. She would rat people out so she could stay longer.

The new roommate packed her things up and called other shelters. I wanted nothing to do with the old roommate. I was done with that bitch. I started to ignore her and didn't say another word to her. She tried for days to talk to me, and I stayed silent. I was worried she would try to get me kicked out, so I had to watch my back.

I went into the room one day and there she was sitting on her bed crying. I knew she was just trying to get attention from me, and I didn't give a fuck. I walked right past her and let her cry. It was curtains for that hoe. She moved out a week later.

Another woman came to the shelter. She was a tall bitch with masculine energy. She was very friendly and talked to everyone. We were having a conversation and then she mentioned she was from the town I had just come from.

I looked at her and paused. "Did you say you were from that town?" I asked.

"Yeah, I was born and raised there."

"Do you know Jody and Ivy?" I asked.

"Yeah, I know both of them," she said.

"That's why I'm here. I'm here because of Jody."

She didn't say anything about Jody, but she said she didn't like Ivy and she didn't trust her. "What's your name?" she asked.

"Brandi," I said.

"Oh, you're Brandi," she said. "Yeah, he's going around telling people you're stalking him."

"I'm stalking him? He's stalking me, and he's getting other people to stalk me too."

"Yeah," she said. "He tried to pay my daughter to beat you up, and I said no."

I told her the whole story of what happened between us. She went to sit down in the TV area, and I followed her. "He took advantage of me," I said. I went into the graphic details. I told her the last time we had sex he was yelling at me, and he kept having sex with me while it was hurting. While I was talking, I could remember him yelling at me because I hadn't opened my legs wide enough. It was still a scar in my mind.

She told me she knew his second baby mom and she was going to her house because she owed her some money.

I said, "And tell her that Jody and Ivy are together and they're hiding it."

She asked if I could give her a reading later. She agreed.

Later when I gave it, it seemed to go well. She wanted me to contact her dead brother.

I read for another girl, and after that, I headed back to my room. I started to think about the masculine woman, so I decided to read cards because something wasn't right. I saw that tall bitch was being deceptive in some kind of way and she was connected to Jody. '*That bitch,*' I thought. So, they had planned that shit. Otherwise, how would I have just happened to run into a bitch that knew him? I caught on to her scheme and I tried to play it cool.

I got up the next morning and made sure I saw her before she left. She looked at me and then turned her head. She tried to avoid me. She wasn't sure if I knew she was setting me up. I told her Jody was going to jail for bothering me.

Two more women came to the shelter after that, and they were both her friends. They all stayed together and one of them roomed with me. I thought it was weird the roommate came with no belongings. She asked me if I had some money so she could get some clothes. She had to be out her damn mind.

The women continued to harass me, and it became even more clear that these women were here for Jody. My roommate became afraid. "They might do something," she said. The tall masculine bitch kept trying to talk to me, but I ignored her. I had to watch her closely. At group, I told the women there my story and what happened with me and Jody. I told them that's why the tall masculine bitch was here. The women assured me that I got raped. "You said no," one woman said. The tall masculine bitch was furious. I rolled my eyes.

Souls, I never said that this man raped me, but I was trying to figure out why it felt like, and why everyone was saying he did. I didn't lie about what happened and was open to sharing. After, getting countless readings and doing research, I realized I was attacked by a demon. Since Jody did drugs, he invoked demons, and he was used for the demon to attack me. At first, I wasn't sure if Jody was a demon, or a demon possessed him. After talking to a guy friend of mine, he told me "That sounds like a spiritual attack, that was a demon."

It all started making sense. I wasn't raped by Jody but attacked by a demon.

I needed to get those bitches out of the shelter because I didn't want them to fuck up my moving. I managed to get two of the women kicked out, but the tall masculine bitch was a challenge. It became a game and the she started getting the women I was hanging with kicked out. She was trying her best to turn people against me but then I got my section 8 voucher.

I called my mom and told her it was time for me to leave and that I was coming to stay with her. She was okay with it. I didn't really want to move in with my mom and her boyfriend, but I was ready to get out of the shelter. I wasn't leaving because I was scared; I was leaving because the shit they were doing was getting old. Plus, my job was too far away, and that town had nothing to offer me. I was relieved to be going back to the city and closer to family and friends. I paid movers to move my belongings.

While I was getting things ready, a younger girl asked me if I needed help with anything. They had just moved in next door, and she hadn't ever spoken to me before.

I told her, "No."

She was very strange looking – like someone you would find out in the woods somewhere. I could tell she was off, and she was ugly as hell. One of her friends had come to her house, and I heard her whisper, "That's the girl who…" and I didn't hear the rest. That let me know Jody and Ivy were making up rumors about me and telling lies. All those people in that place knew about me – people I didn't even know.

The movers came and I was a little nervous because I didn't want anybody to steal anything off the truck. The men came up to get the boxes. I told them I wanted them to lock up the truck each time they put a load on it. We decided that would be too much work, so me and one guy grabbed boxes and the other guy watched the truck. I locked the door every time we left the apartment though.

People were still following me as I was trying to move. I was a little annoyed, but more worried about my stuff. I asked the guy that was helping move if he noticed people were following us, and he said, "Yeah."

There was a girl in particular following us who was really good friends with Jody. Every time we went outside, she would walk past us. "Did you notice that girl following us?"

"Who, that girl in white?" the moving guy asked. "Yes, I did. It's definitely weird out here. I'm trying to get out of here," he said.

When we were finished, I was so relieved. The movers headed to my mom's house, and I caught an Uber. I got everything moved in and squared away, but I had to go back and drop my keys off.

The next day, I went back up to the shelter. I was happy and cheerful, and I was ready for all the bullshit to come to an end. I dropped my keys off and the phone rang in the office. The manager answered and the person hung up. Then the phone rang again. I knew they were trying to fuck with me, but I didn't care. Somebody kept walking past the window. I didn't pay the rent I owed the apartment either. Fuck them and all the shit I had to go through down that mothafucka. Shit, they owed me some money.

On my way out, I said bye to the people who were stalking me just to be a smart-ass. The stalking gang had the weird girl and her boyfriend follow me to the bus stop. They had a little boy with them too. I saw they were training children to do the crazy stalking shit. I said bye to them as well. The guy was very surprised because I never spoke to him.

I was back at my mother's again. I wondered how many times I was going to live with my parents. I was too old for that shit. I was tired of moving and I really didn't like being around my mom. She was really draining. I remembered what the psychic said: I wouldn't be there long, so I decided to try my best not to argue with her or let her bring me down.

Souls, my mother isn't very bright. Thank God I got my brains from my dad. He is really intelligent. There isn't anything he doesn't know or can't do. My mom, on the other hand, needs some more schooling and a brush-up on the basics.

I immediately started looking for a job, but I was pretending to go to my old job. I cut my hours at work down to two days. I just couldn't stand working in a daycare anymore. I was actually going to my old college and sitting in the library for hours.

There was a guy who lived across the street from us. He lived with his guy friend and his kids stayed with him part time. I would see his kids playing out in the yard. He would sit on his porch sometimes. I couldn't really see his face up close, but I began to take interest in him. I'm not sure what it was about him. When he would be outside, I would go outside too. He really wasn't paying attention to me.

I asked my mom about him, though her response was negative about everything. She said, "Yeah, he got all them kids over there and they're bad. They be playing outside all loud and shit. He's probably on welfare. He don't seem like he go to work. He be having loud parties over there with all these women running in and out." She already had a dim view of him, but she viewed everybody that way, so I didn't pay her any attention. "Listen to me, don't talk to no guys over here." She started to raise her voice.

I said, "Calm down, I was just asking about him." I was not about to let her tell my grown ass what to do. She didn't like him, and she made that clear.

I decided I wanted to talk to him. I saw him on the porch one day, so I went outside and sat on the porch too. I said hi to him.

"Hi," he said back. We continued the conversation. He asked me, "Are those your parents?"

"That's my mom and her boyfriend," I said. We added each other on

Facebook. We began chatting there and then exchanged numbers.

He was out of work and was laid off because of an injury. I went over to his house and sat by the steps. I didn't want those stalker assholes in my business, so I went over without my phone. He was cleaning his yard. He looked kind of scary up close. He had these thick-ass coke bottle glasses on. I mean I wore glasses too, but they weren't that thick. "Why you got those glasses on?" I asked.

He said, "Because I wear glasses."

I had never seen him with glasses on, so I was just asking a question. He wasn't cute at all; he was strange looking. I wasn't sure what the attraction was to him, but it was strong. We talked for a bit, and I told him if anybody asked him about me to ignore them. I told him I read cards so I could see if he was doing something behind my back. Some weird guy walked past us with a long black trench coat on. I just stared at him because it was hot as hell outside.

The guy stopped and looked at me and said hello with an attitude. My neighbor spoke to him. The guy was suspicious. Then I realized it was one of those stalkers. *'How the fuck did they know I was out here without my phone? Maybe somebody is watching the house and they saw me walk out the door,'* I thought.

"I can't believe you are over here talking to me," my neighbor said.

"Why?" I asked.

"Because I didn't think you would come over here talk to me and we were gonna chop it up like that." He was quite smitten by me.

I figured I would give him a chance and just see where it would go. Plus, I hadn't had dick in eons. I was hoping he would be around long enough for me to suck his dick or something at least once.

He called me the next day and we had a deep conversation about feeling connected to each other. He said, "I know something is there."

I mean, I was interested in him, but I had to get used to his face. I went over to his house again, but just in the backyard. I spoke to his children. "You can come over anytime," he said. "I cook too. You want something to eat?" He was big on cooking food on the grill. I told him maybe some other time.

He had mentioned that he thought there was a ghost in his house. I insisted on giving him a reading, so I went home and grabbed the cards. When I got back to his house, I pulled my deck out and his eyes got so big. He looked scared of them. He was hesitant to get the reading. I saw there was a woman there, but she was not trying to harm him. I saw that she had died from tuberculosis and was young. He asked me if she liked his guy friend who stayed upstairs, and she said no. He said he could tell. I could tell he was impressed by the reading I gave him. "I should pay you for this," he said. I told him it was fine and that he didn't have to pay.

A few days later my mom was getting on my nerves as usual. I asked the neighbor if I could come over to get away from her ass. I had just got home from work, and I hopped in the shower and headed to his backyard.

"I said hi to your mom, and she ignored me. I don't think she likes me," he said.

"She doesn't," I said. "She said you be having all these parties with all these women over here."

"What?" he said. "I have get-togethers for holidays and stuff and those girls are my cousins. I pretty much keep to myself."

He seemed like a pretty good guy. He always had his kids over and I saw him spending time with them.

"Your mom is wrong about me," he said. He looked upset, and I knew he felt judged.

I had been thinking exactly what he had said about my mom and her view of him. "Yeah, she is like that with everyone."

As we were talking, I got a message on Facebook from Jody's fat-ass baby mom ex-girlfriend asking me how I knew Jody. I thought, '*What the fuck. Why is she just now contacting me?*' I told my neighbor I was going to tell him what had happened when I was at my last place. All of a sudden, his neighbor slammed the back door. I went over to the door to see who was there. Then I sat back down, and it happened again.

"You wanna go inside?" he said.

I normally didn't go into stranger's houses, especially a guy's house, but I felt like it was okay. We went inside and sat in the living room. I started telling him what happened with me and Jody. He started asking me questions, but they were kind of strange. I told him about the stalkers. He took his shoes off and his feet looked like hooves. Looking at his face and feet was strange. I wondered if there was something wrong with him. When we were talking about the stalkers I said, "At first, I thought they were going to kidnap me."

He said, "No, we wouldn't do nothing like that." I didn't catch on at first, but it seemed like he had some device on him like someone was telling him what to say.

'*Who the fuck is we?*' Again, it went over my head.

He said he looked at women like flowers. "They are delicate."

I was thinking, '*What the fuck is he talking about?*' He started asking me about my tarot cards and how I read them. "I don't know, I just can," I said. I went home to get my deck of cards to give him another reading.

He seemed to be nervous, even more nervous than before. In the reading, I saw him talking to another girl, but it wasn't me. "I don't see me in your future," I said.

"I wonder why," he said.

I read a few more things, like what was going on with his job and what his future looked like. He then started asking me about magic and what kind of magic I did. I told him about all of the spells I did and how I did them. He seemed to be really interested.

We started talking about sex. I told him I was open to it, but it would have to be on my time. We did have a sexual attraction towards each other, and I felt comfortable enough to talk about it. We talked about having a relationship with each other as well. I could definitely see myself having a relationship with him. I knew I had just met him, but I felt like he could help me get away from my mom until I found a place of my own. I thought I could just stay at his house sometimes. I would also get in-house dick. It seemed like a good idea to me.

I told him he had to be gentle with me. "The last guy I was with was too rough and he took advantage. I really don't like talking about it," I said.

"Then don't," he shouted. For some reason he didn't want to hear that part of the story; he seemed slightly uncomfortable.

"No," I yelled, "I have to tell you. I have to tell you what happened to me." I finished telling him and he was silent. I figured he didn't know what to say. It was very hurtful talking about it; I had to relive it all over again each time.

"That's fucked up," he said.

I told him, "I will come back tomorrow."

That night, I woke up in the middle of the night and I felt something was wrong. It was the same feeling I would get when somebody was setting me up. I looked at my cards and checked my neighbor out again. I saw he was being sneaky, but again it wasn't clear.

I got a reading to confirm everything. My reader told me he did set me up. I thought, '*Like damn, how did they get to him that fast? This is fuckin ridiculous.*' The stalkers were trying to mess up my love life. They were trying to make sure nobody would talk to me. '*Well, there goes my chance of having sex,*' I thought.

I asked the reader why he would agree to do it.

She said it was because it made him look important. They hadn't paid him or anything.

I was fuckin pissed he did that shit, but then what had happened made sense. The neighbor next to him purposely slammed the door to make me paranoid so I would want to go in his house. It had been likely somebody was telling him what to say, because he been acting strange and asking me a lot of questions on how to do spell work. I had told him a lot of shit too. I knew those people heard how I do everything. Then his ass being scared when I brought my cards over. He was afraid I was going to find out he was setting me up. I honestly didn't see it at the time. That mother fucker. I warned that fucker not to set me up.

I was like, "Okay, I'm gonna get his ass back." So I texted him and said, "I know what you did," and, "that was fucked up."

He said, "Wow, why would you think I would do something like that?" and, "I just met you."

I wasn't falling for his bullshit. I told him he missed out on some good pussy. He basically denied everything and didn't even try to stop me from walking away. Which was another sign he did it. That guy was really into me at first.

My reader told me Jody and Ivy were behind that shit. I just wasn't sure how it reached over there so fast. They just didn't want me to have a relationship because theirs was fucked up. Hatin-ass bitches.

That's why Jody's baby mom ex-girlfriend had sent me that message. They had wanted me to tell my side of the story so they could see what I was telling people.

I cussed her ass the fuck out calling her a crackhead bitch and saying she had a big-ass forehead. I told her, "Don't ever fucking contact me again."

She said, "Imma see you."

I wondered if Ivy had broken into Jody's baby mom's account since the message was so similar to something she had said before. I wouldn't have been surprised since she had tried to break into my email at one point. Anyway, that's why that message was sent to me: so I would tell the neighbor about my situation.

After that, I would see my neighbor sitting on his porch and I would stare out my window looking at him, just to fuck with him. Then I would go outside and pretend like I was doing spells on him. I could tell he was scared and was getting nervous. That's what the fuck he got for fuckin with me. He would try to sit on the porch with other people to try to intimidate me, but I would sit right on the porch without hesitation. I wasn't scared. He had a couple of sisters too, but I didn't give a fuck. This was war. When I got angry, I had no fear. My revenge was ruthless. My motto was: whatever happens, happens.

His sisters came over to his house and acted like they were going to do something. One of his sisters dropped him off at his house and I called him ugly out loud so he could hear me. She then turned her car around and drove past and looked at me. Another time his mom and sister came by his house and they both just stared at me with the stank eye while I sat on my porch. They didn't say anything to me, so I didn't say anything to them. Who knew what lies he told them about me.

One of his sisters followed me and my mom to the store. Again, no words were said to me. I started doing my own stalking. I would act like I was coming toward him, but I wasn't. I made it seem like I was going to his house, and then I would quickly go a different way. I did the same shit they had been doing to me. I looked at my cards and he was scared as hell. He was scared I was going to do magic on him, and he was right. He stopped coming outside for a while after that.

I did a spell to get a new job. I applied at this mental health place right by the house. They emailed me back and it went to spam, so I didn't see it until two weeks later. '*Stupid-ass Mercury Retrograde*,' I thought, and, '*Finally, something in my field.*' I got called in for an interview. The place looked like a jail on the outside, like some kind of asylum. They paid only one dollar less than what I had asked for in the spell. My interview went really well, and a couple of days later, the boss offered me the job. I was so excited; I finally got a real job! It was my first full-time job, and they paid the most I had ever been paid.

I guess I was too excited, and my mom couldn't handle it. She said,

"Don't get too excited." Who says shit like that? *'What you mean, 'don't get too excited'?'* I thought. I told her I would not let her negative ass spoil my happiness. I couldn't wait to start so I could save up money and get the fuck away from her and out of her house. When I moved down there, I had the intention of finding a job and a house. I got the job; it was time to look for a place.

I was a psych tech, so my job was to supervise fourteen mental health clients. They stayed at the facility until they found a place to live or a person to live with. The program was only for a couple of months but could be extended. I pretty much made dinner for them and then cleaned up the kitchen and gave out medication. Passing out medication wasn't my favorite thing to do. It took too long, and I had to go and look for them if they didn't come down to take it. Counting the medication was a pain in the ass, but I did it. I thought, *'Hey, this job provides medical insurance.'* I had never had that before at a job. I had medical, dental, and vision. I wrote notes too at the end of my shift. The staff was cool, and the management seemed cool too. I was working ten-hour shifts and had three days off a week.

The place was a little depressing. The clients had therapy all day. They were allowed out for smoke breaks, and they could leave for two hours a day and four hours on weekends. I would get them things they needed, such as if they wanted something out of the kitchen or extra toiletries. I also did intakes sometimes. When a new person came in, I would collect all their things and put them in a machine to destroy any bugs. Then I would take down all their information, show them around the facility, and show them their room. I hated doing that; it took a while.

My mom wanted to charge me more rent because she was being money hungry, but I refused. I didn't feel like I should pay anything at all except my food, but since I was paying rent, I was entitled to my privacy. She didn't think so. She would listen to my conversations and go through my stuff. Her mental health was showing badly. I knew something was wrong with her, but I couldn't quite put my finger on it. I couldn't fuckin stand her nor did I want to be near her.

A new group of people started following me. I thought when I moved from the last area, that would be over, but boy was I wrong. I noticed people were following me when I would get off the bus. Sometimes when I sat on the porch, some guy across the street came out. He looked suspicious to me. When I went out with my mom, they followed us both, and I was surprised since I was with someone. They knew my mom was an idiot. They knew she thought I was paranoid. When I said something, of course she didn't believe me. Honestly, everybody believed me except her and my aunt. I ignored those stalkers for the most part. I was happy and enjoying my life.

Ivy was still talking shit on Facebook taking pictures at this comedy club that was near my house. It was like she was saying, 'I know where you live at now,' as if I gave a fuck. *'Bitch, I don't care if you know where I live. I would tell you myself,'* I thought. I knew she wasn't going to do shit anyway. Her scare tactics didn't work and neither did the group of people following me. They even had a little boy next door in on it.

That neighbor and one of his guy friends were sitting on the porch; he thought he was intimidating me. One of my nephews came over that morning, so I insisted we sit on the porch too. We just sat there, and I brought up the guy's back, because he hurt it at work. Nothing had happened; his back just went out while he was standing up. I made a joke about him falling and fuckin his back up. He looked right at me. I was hoping that mothafucka would fall again. I posted on Facebook saying I had done a spell so my neighbor would find a girlfriend, and I called him a pussy.

My nephew and I laughed and giggled, then I pulled my tarot cards out on the porch and those guys went in the house. I was teaching my nephew how to read. We went in the house after that, and I took a nap.

I woke up to get ready for work. I was about to get in the shower when we heard a knock at the door. It was the police. They said something about a car accident. Neither me, my nephew, nor my mom had left the house, so we hadn't taken the car anywhere. The officer said there had been a car accident and somebody with my mom's car hit someone and drove off. They said a young girl was driving it. "Not me. I was asleep," I said.

My mom said, "Did one of y'all take my car?" Meanwhile, she'd had the keys the whole fuckin time. We would never have taken the car without asking.

Me and my nephew looked at each other and said, "It was that loser across the street. He had something to do with this."

They showed us a piece of the other car that was left at the scene. I had to get ready for work. The officer said, "If you're lying, you can get in trouble."

I walked outside to see the damage. There was a big maroon scrape against the car. It looked like a real accident had happened. There was a big stone underneath the car. We were trying to figure out if they had stolen the car and hit the other one, or if they put a dent in it while we were inside. I wasn't surprised the stalkers had done some shit like that. They were always up to some shit.

The officer then walked over and said, "They said the driver had a ponytail in her hair."

Now, I had just done my hair for work. I had put it in a ponytail, but earlier in the day it was in a bun. Those mothafuckas were trying to get me for a hit and run. I wasn't too worried because I knew I didn't do anything wrong.

My mom on the other hand called me at work talking shit. None of it was my fault. I told her before that those people were going to start fuckin with her too. She hadn't believed me. They fucked her car up and they had someone following her at work. I understood she was mad about her car because she had almost been done paying it off, but it wasn't my fault.

When I got home, I had to listen to a bunch of dumb bullshit about her and her boyfriend having to move. My mom was always talking shit on someone, but she was scared as fuck for no reason. Move for what? I knew they weren't going to harm anybody physically. But I couldn't tell her anything.

I got a reading done by one of my readers and tape recorded it for my mom so she would shut the fuck up. The reader said it was an insurance scam. I was glad to hear that because it made it look like I wasn't the motive. Even though I was.

The reader said it wasn't my neighbor, which I had figured. He was too much of a punk to do some shit like that.

"Did you ever hear of gang stalkers before?" she asked.

"No," I said.

"You should definitely look that up." She also said Ivy and Jody were involved in it in some kind of way.

I let my mom listen to the recording. "I knew it was an insurance scam," she said. She started being a little more pleasant after that. I was worried she would kick me out. I knew how shady she was. She had done it before several times. I always wondered why she was born, and what her purpose was because she wasn't a good person at all. I always thought she was a demon.

I took the key she had hidden on the porch so those gang stalkers couldn't sneak in. She was so dumb that she didn't know how far they would go. She came storming upstairs. "Where is my key?" She yelled.

"What key?" I asked.

"Give me my key," she demanded.

I gave it back to her. I told her I took it so she wouldn't kick me out the house.

"I'm not gonna kick you out."

I went downstairs and my mom said with fake tears, "Brandi, you need help. We need to send you to a mental health facility. Your aunt agrees." Apparently, she had called my aunt who had agreed something was wrong with me.

I almost wanted to laugh because of the performance she was putting on. "What," I said. *'This is insane.'*

I went upstairs and called my aunt and asked her what was said. She denied saying anything, but I knew she had said something. "I don't want to get in the middle of this," she said. The only person who needed to go to a mental facility was my mom. She was telling me one of my sisters was saying I needed to be 302, or involuntarily committed. If she tried that shit, I was gonna 302 *her* ass. I'm sure my mom was making up stories about me and making things seem way worse than they were.

I was perfectly fine and aware of what was going on. My mom was trying to get me back for her car situation. She wasn't even concerned about whether or not I got in trouble from the accident; she was more concerned about the car. She tried to get my dad's number from me so she could talk to him, and I told her ass no. My dad didn't want to talk to her anyway. He couldn't stand her either. I could see why nobody liked her and why she didn't have any friends. She didn't even like herself, and she envied me. She tried to turn everyone against me.

She tried to be a smart-ass and show me an article about schizophrenia. Then she started laughing. It was hurtful that she laughed about it but look who I was talking to: an idiot. I told her *she* had schizophrenia. I had no symptoms of schizophrenia, and she knew that. I didn't hear anybody talking to me and telling me what to do. *'Some people aren't cut out to be a mother,'* I thought. She had no business having children. She was telling all the family I had a mental illness when she had one and was not diagnosed.

Meanwhile, I was working for a mental health facility. I had never been on any medication, and I had been evaluated several times and was not diagnosed with anything. There wasn't anything wrong with me. I was just me. I felt like I had a personality disorder, borderline, but I could control it most times. If anything, I had gotten it from her, but I had more common sense than she did. *She was* the one that needed help.

I did a spell on her ass when she went to work. I was so fuckin tired of her. I had no feelings for her whatsoever and never really did. The spell didn't seem to work. After that, my powers went away.

I tried to put a hex on Ivy and that neighbor guy, but I didn't do it correctly. I had never done a hex before. I had bought some magical ingredients. I wanted my neighbor to pay for what he did. One night, I snuck outside and put the magical ingredients in his yard. It was during Mercury Retrograde. I believed I shouldn't do spells during that time, but I did it anyway.

I went back in the house and started getting dizzy and hot, so I laid down. I started seeing skeletons everywhere. A few hours later I started feeling worse. I wasn't sure if I was going to die or what. I became nauseous and began dry heaving. I could barely stand up. I needed to go to the emergency room. I tried my best to stick it out, but as soon as my mom got home, I went to the hospital. I was fine after they gave me some medicine. Then it rained which probably flushed all the ingredients away. I decided I would never mix those ingredients together again. I later read that you're not supposed to touch those ingredients with your bare hands and that it was poisonous. It was strange nobody told me that, not even the witch mentor I had. She knew I was going to use them and didn't warn me or anything.

I also found out Jody and Ivy were doing magic on me as well. A reader told me they were doing a spell to get me to leave them alone. *They* were bothering me. They were the ones who were getting those gang stalkers to follow me. They should have thought about that shit before they fucked with me. I felt kind of weird, which was how I knew something was off.

One morning, I woke up crying. I was crying about the Jody situation, and I wanted to move on, but I wanted answers. I had saved his new number, which he had put on Facebook. He gave it to some guy, and I had seen it. I texted him first. I asked why he did that to me and didn't say who I was.

He replied, "I don't understand. I didn't do anything to you."

"Why would you treat me like that?" I asked.

Then I finally said who I was, and he said, "Stop playing around." He didn't believe me at first.

I said, "No it's really me." I started bringing up things only he and I knew about. Then I sent him a picture. I told him I would contact him on Facebook so he would know it was really me. I called him but when he answered, I didn't say anything, so he just hung up.

I kept calling. He called me on video messenger while I was at work. I could see him. I hadn't seen him in person for a long time. I didn't turn my camera on; I didn't want him to see me, plus I was on the job.

"Hey, baby girl, how are you? Let me see your face." He always talked to me like I was a little girl. "Let me see your face."

"No, I'm at work." Then I heard a loud noise.

"What was that?" he asked.

"Ummm nothin," I said. I hurried to hang up the phone.

He called back and then he texted me. "I want to talk to you," he said.

Once I was home from work, I kept thinking about how much I wanted to get the hell out of my mom's house and away from her. It was obvious she was against me. I mean, those gang stalkers did fuck her car up, but she was getting it fixed. I could feel that she and her boyfriend wanted me out. I decided I would never again put myself in a situation where I was kicked out of a house.

My mom was acting like she was scared to go outside. I was fine. If the gang stalkers wanted to harm us, they would have already. She didn't want me to leave out the front of the house. She really made me hate her. I always did. She was a nasty person. Her boyfriend complained about people following him in cars. Even he had caught on.

So when I said, "Somebody is following me," I was crazy, but when she said, "Somebody is following me or my boyfriend," it was okay?

See, Souls, don't fuck with people like that. I don't care who it is. She hated herself and tried to spread it to others.

My mom got her car fixed. It looked brand new like nothing ever happened. The insurance company didn't believe we had nothing to do with the accident and gave her a hard time. The supposed victim tried to sue me and my mom, but it didn't work out. I didn't get in trouble and neither did she. She changed her insurance company. I was not sure if the other party got any money. My mom was hiding things from me. I wasn't sure why; she was just being an asshole.

Meanwhile, I was the one with cards and could see shit. '*At least I didn't get in trouble,*' I thought. They wanted me to sign some shit, and I didn't.

I started looking for places. I applied to the same apartment that had decided not to take section 8. I was getting paid pretty well, so I could afford one of those places. I went in, and the residential manager remembered me. When she saw me, her eyes got big. '*Yeah, bitch, I'm back,*' I thought. The place was brand new and beautiful. It was perfect for me. It had hardwood floors, a beautiful kitchen, and a huge bathroom. The building was an old bakery that had been converted for apartments. There was an elevator and an exercise room. It was located near all the stores, so I wouldn't need a car. There were buses all over the place. I had a call shortly after that saying I got approved. I was so relieved. I could finally have my own place again and it was nice. My rent was $800. That was pricy for me, but I could afford it. Within three months, I had gotten a new job and then an apartment.

I called and told my mom and she sounded excited for me, but she was still acting funny. It was like she was thinking, '*All this good stuff happening to you and I'm getting all the bad stuff.'* She was acting like she wanted me to leave so badly, like I gave a fuck. I didn't because I was leaving; she could kiss my ass.

I started packing my shit right away. I needed someone inexpensive to help me move. I had just moved a couple months before. I was tired of moving, but I was hoping I would be at that place for a while.

I looked around to find movers. My mom actually gave me some stuff to take with me: a bed, a couch chair, and a dresser. It was the first time I was moving into an apartment with furniture, and new furniture at that. My mom didn't want to help me move and that was fine.

I put an ad out on Facebook. A guy contacted me. He had a twin, and he said they could help. I read cards on him and saw something suspicious. It wasn't clear, but I wasn't sure. I told him never mind because I did not trust him.

I told my mom that they backed out, and she got mad and started getting an attitude. She said she and her boyfriend didn't want me there anymore. I didn't want to be there either. I shouldn't have gone to her house in the first place because she was a sorry-ass mother, and her energy was horrible. I never did anything to her boyfriend. My mom would talk shit about me to other people to make them see me in a bad light when it was actually her. So I was like, *'Fuck it.'*

I needed to move, so I called that guy again and told him I needed help even with the suspicious reading. He agreed to do it. I was a little nervous because I wasn't sure what was going to happen with those guys. They called me and told me they were on their way and that they just moved someone in the same town I had just come from. That was a red flag right there. They were a part of that gang stalking bullshit.

When we got to the house, they arrived at the same time. I watched their every move. I didn't want them to take any of my stuff. They were actually really cool guys. My aunt loved them. They were very prompt and did a very good job. I had no problems with them, but they were still with those stalkers. Remember, the goal of the stalkers was to scare the target. I paid the guys, and they went on their way. I moved in, and I was finally home.

I was so glad to be away from that dark cloud of a mother. It was nice and peaceful. I woke up in my furnished apartment and looked out my window. I decided to have a housewarming party because my place was so nice and because I had never had one before. I invited all my friends and family and the people who supported me.

I was manifesting the things I wanted and fast. I bought a cute outfit and had one of my friends do my make-up. It was a big event on Facebook. Everybody wanted to come, but I only wanted people who supported me there. My mom tried to make up for her lack of parenting skills by buying me stuff, but it still didn't count to me. 'You can't pay your way out of it,' I thought. She acted like she didn't want to come to the housewarming party, but I knew she wanted to come. I was glad she didn't since her attitude sucked, and I didn't want her to affect the positive energy in my house. She bought some food for the party which I greatly appreciated, but I was glad she was leaving.

Almost everybody I invited showed up. I had so much food. My aunt made some and some was store-bought. I set up entertainment too for my guests. I had an astrology book. I had an angel tarot deck people could ask yes and no questions. I had crystals available so they could see which ones resonated with them and take them home. I played relaxing music. I had a great time, and everybody seemed to enjoy themselves. I got new gifts for the house; it was lovely.

I started noticing some of the people in the apartment were following me. I also soon realized I was being followed in stores again. I had known they were going to find out where I was going because of the tracking of the phone and all. Target and grocery stores were the main stores they followed me in. I recorded them and took pictures, but they seemed not to care. Even in Aldi. There was no point in me calling the police.

Then I started following them back. They would stop following me when I did. I started hitting them with my shopping cart. They would also know when I looked out my window because someone else living in my building would walk outside. I honestly didn't give a fuck. I ignored them for the most part. They were so annoying, but they weren't slowing me down in any way. People were still following me to work: slamming doors, making loud noises, lying on me. There were people that waited for me to get off the bus too. I ignored them for as long as I could. They were trying to intimidate me. This one man stood beside me, and I could feel how dark his energy was; he smelled like sulfur. I started realizing he was not a human but a demon. They definitely did too much and went out of their way to bother me.

On the flip side, I became really cool with the people I worked with. I actually became close with two of the women there. One of them I started calling my work mom. She definitely treated me like her daughter. She gave me the love and attention my mother never did. I went over to her house a few times and she came to my house a few times. We went to the movies together; she gave me lots of advice.

There was a client at work who was cool at first, but he started acting crazy and not listening. He was one of those gang stalkers. I thought, *'How do I know he won't purposely do shit he isn't supposed to?'* Every time I would leave the building, he would show up. One time he was walking up the street to be a smart-ass, so I told my supervisor. The client said he didn't want to be there anymore, and he wanted to commit suicide.

Oh, those gang stalking mother fuckers were pissed. I loved pissing them off. I could tell when they were mad; the energy changed. He would pretend he was on the phone when he wasn't. The same patterns I had seen before. He gave me problems, but at the same time, he was cool. I actually liked the guy. They started to send more gang stalkers as clients. That shit was unbelievable.

I did some research on gang stalkers after that. I read they are a group of organized crime. They prey on people to fuck them up emotionally and make them go crazy. There are a lot of victims out there. They do street theater. They follow you everywhere you go. You're on twenty-four-hour surveillance. They tap your phones, set up video cameras and voice in your home and your job. They try to get you in trouble and smear your name and get people to dislike you. They get your neighbors and coworkers to not like you too.

That shit was stupid to me.

# Chapter 16:
# Book of Psalms

I friend-requested a guy on Facebook named Psalms who was from the town I had just moved from. I was trying to add everyone who was from there so they could know about what happened to me with the Jody situation. He accepted the request. The next day, he waved at me in my inbox. I was going to ignore him, but I asked him how he was doing so I wouldn't come off as rude. We ended up having a conversation about him living in that town and he told me about what was going on with him. He told me he had just come home from prison. He was married and his wife had put a restraining order against him. He violated the order and got charged for burglary and trespassing. He was in prison for a year and a half. I asked him if he knew Jody. He replied, "Yeah, that's my cousin."

I told him I couldn't move forward with this conversation because I hated Jody and was always talking shit about him.

He replied, "What does that have to do with me? He's a grown man." He didn't seem to care, so I continued to talk to him even though he had just gotten out of prison and was related to Jody.

We talked every day after that. We had an instant connection. We were very different, but I enjoyed talking to him.

He told me he got the nickname Psalms because he was always reciting Bible verses and he came from a big family. He had been in and out of jail most of his life. He used to box but after he was hit in the head with a bottle, he was unable to do it anymore. He was very manly and smart and had great potential. He seemed to be a good father to all of his children.

After two weeks, I really wanted to see him; I wanted to have sex with him too. I felt comfortable enough. I also told him about the STD. He didn't seem to have a problem with it. I invited him to have dinner at my house.

I wanted to have sex with him, but I didn't want him to use me for sex. I wanted it to be okay for me. I suggested that we start dating. He laughed.

"What?" I asked.

He replied, "I know what you're doing."

I was confused, I wasn't trying to do anything. I told him I was only having sex with someone who was serious about me. He was hesitant. I asked him if he wanted to date or just have sex, because if he just wanted sex, I wouldn't have sex with him.

"Okay," he said.

I said, "What?" I was surprised. He actually said yes. I couldn't help but smile. I was finally dating someone! The first guy I ever dated at thirty-four years old. I was over the moon. I wanted to make sure he was really okay with dating me. I gave him the option to get out of it. "Are you sure?" I asked.

"No, I'm sure," he said, "I think it's a good idea."

"Do you need some time to think about it?" I asked.

"No," he said.

I asked him if he wanted to date exclusively. "Do you plan on dating other people?" I asked.

"No, because you're going to get mad."

"I'm not going to get mad," I said. I probably would be mad if he said yes but I wanted him to make his own choices.

"No, I don't want to date other people."

Well, it was settled.

We got along really well. As I mentioned before, we were very different, but we had similar interests as well. We had the same taste in music, and we just blended well. We were both Leos so our personality traits were similar. He mentioned he didn't think two Leos would get along. He liked that I was confident, fun, and easy-going just like him. On the flip side, he wasn't into tarot cards or magic. He believed in magic, but that just wasn't his thing. I respected that. I could tell he really liked me, and I think he could tell I really liked him.

I told him I didn't drink, and I didn't like alcoholics. The problem was that Psalms was an alcoholic. Just like Jody, just like my dad. I made it clear I didn't want him drinking around me.

"I got it," he said. "You sound like my ex-wife." Apparently, his ex-wife didn't like him drinking either. He told me he just wanted to drink and relax since coming home from prison.

As we started hanging out, he tried to sneak and drink. "Can you tell I was drinking?" he asked me. Sometimes I could tell but some days I couldn't. When he drank, he would act a bit differently. He would smile a lot more. There were a few times my stomach would hurt when I was talking to him, and I could tell.

One night, I was sick to my stomach. I felt bad for him because I knew he had a problem. He decided he wanted to show me his penis on video chat. I was excited to see what his dick looked like. He pulled it out and it was the smallest dick I had ever seen. It literally looked like a shrimp. I didn't know what to say. He wanted to see my coochie, but there was no way I was showing my private parts online.

A few days before he was supposed to come over, I started having second thoughts about having sex with him. I mean it was the first time I was going to see him in person. I wanted to make him wait until at least the second time I saw him. '*What if I don't like him in person,*' I thought. I wanted to make sure I liked him first.

"Are you gonna give me some pussy?" he asked.

I laughed. "I think we should hold off until our second date."

"No," he said. He then began to laugh.

"You been thinking about this all day," he said.

"No, you're giving me some pussy."

It was funny at first but then I got serious. I told him he had to wait.

Finally, it was the day he was coming over. It was a cold chilly day. I was excited but nervous at the same time. I hoped he took me seriously about not having sex. I decided that if I liked him and found him attractive in person, I would at least give him some head, just to hold him off until the next time he came over. He texted me and told me he was watching the football game. I asked him what time he was coming.

"I'm not sure," he said. He didn't seem very interested in coming over anymore. At least that's what I picked up from his energy. I was worried he wasn't going to show up because of the no-sex thing. I started to get angry.

"Well let me know when you're on your way," I said.

A few hours went by, and he told me he was waiting to use someone's car to get to my house. His license was suspended, and I lived right next to a police station. I could tell he was a little nervous. It was getting late, and my patience was wearing thin. He should have had his shit figured out. "If you don't want to come, just say that," I shouted.

"I'm waiting for the car," he said with an attitude. "You just want me to come on your time."

'*I bought all this food for nothing*,' I thought. I felt so stupid. I really thought he was going to come.

"You're rushing me," he yelled.

"You're a big disappointment," I said. I was disappointed with him and myself. I hung up the phone with him, and I was so angry, I needed to take a nap to calm down. I decided if he didn't come, I was done with him. I woke to a text that said he was so upset that I made him start drinking again. He asked me if I still wanted him to come over.

I texted back, 'If you want to,' and he said he was on his way.

I was still upset about the argument we'd had earlier. He waited outside so I could let him in. I prayed that I would find him attractive and that he would find me attractive. I opened the door, and I was pleasantly surprised. He was much more attractive than I thought. He was a small guy and had beautiful glowing skin. "You look like him," I said as I stared at his face. He looked like Jody, but a better version of him.

"Come here," he said.

I walked away from him.

We looked at each other while on the elevator. "You look like him," I said again. I still had a frown on my face. He just smiled at me.

We started to cook dinner. I had bought steak, asparagus, and sweet potatoes. I watched him as he prepared the food. He could tell I was nervous. "You gonna give me a kiss?" he asked. I slowly walked over to him and kissed him. I really liked it, so I wanted to kiss again. His lips were soft. I really liked them.

He prepared the food. We talked for a while. He knew I was suffering over what Jody did to me. "Don't take it out on me," he said. I stared out the window. "Don't worry," he said. "You're safe with me."

I told him about the stalking situation. I wondered if they were watching us from the window. I wanted them to see us. I wanted them to see that they didn't run my life, and that I made my own decisions. They weren't stopping shit.

We took pictures together. I was excited to be dating. When the food was done, we sat and ate side by side. When we were done, he washed the dishes. I sat on the couch and waited for him. I could tell he was a little nervous because he wasn't sure what was going to happen. I wanted to kiss and cuddle, so we laid down on the couch together. He started to kiss me with a lot of tongue. He kissed me slowly and gently. It wasn't rough enough for me. I wanted to keep kissing and he said,

"You're gonna kiss me to death."

I asked him if he would be able to contain himself if I took my pants off.

He nodded his head yes.

So, I took my pants off. "You wanna see it?" I asked.

He nodded his head yes again.

I began to take my underwear off as he stared at my vagina. He began to move to the end of the couch. I placed my hands over my privates.

He moved my hand and began to lick my vagina with slow soft strokes. I couldn't handle the sensations and I knew I wouldn't be able to control myself. I tapped him on the shoulder and told him to stop. I couldn't take anymore. It had been only a few minutes. I laughed so hard and fell right off the couch and onto the floor. I was so happy I finally received oral sex! It was a big deal for me.

Psalms looked at me confused and frustrated at the same time. He had told me his favorite thing to do was eat pussy. I guess I cut him off too early.

I laughed and threw my underwear at him. "My turn," I said. I was happy to be sucking dick again. I pulled his pants down and pulled his penis out. I began to slide my mouth up and down. I gripped it tightly and spit all over it. His dick was so small that I couldn't deep throat it. I didn't have much to play with, it fit in the palm of my hand.

I kissed him in between and licked all over his mouth. I don't think he liked that, and I think I sucked his dick too fast and too rough. He seemed to be in a little bit of pain. Finally, he came. I still had some of his cum in my mouth and I started kissing him again.

He backed his head up and started to frown. "You're not supposed to kiss me with cum in your mouth," he said. He got up and smiled. "I didn't think that was gonna happen," he said.

I sat there cheesing with cum all over my mouth. I grabbed the blanket we had covering us, and I noticed there was cum all over it. He told me he had to head back home.

He kissed me on my forehead while we waited by the elevator. We got downstairs, and as he was leaving out the door, he kissed me again. "I need tongue," I said. He kissed me again except with tongue that time. He got in the car, and I waved to him goodbye.

He called me the next day and asked me if I had figured out how to suck dick yet. I laughed. "Hey, I did the best I could do." I told him he needed to teach to me.

After that Psalms started acting funny. I told him I was gonna call him when I got off work so we could video chat. I called and he didn't answer. I had seen he was video chatting with someone else. I texted him and said, "I guess you're busy. Have a good night."

He called back after that, and I didn't answer. He then called several times back-to-back. I finally answered the phone. "Yeah," I said sarcastically.

He was surprised at my sassy tone. "I was talking to my cousin," he said.

"Yeah okay," I replied.

"No, for real. My cousin called me, and we were talking about the Bible," he said. His story didn't sound right to me.

I started getting more suspicious as the days went on. There would be times he didn't answer his phone at all. We usually talked every day, but there would be one day a week when he wouldn't answer the whole day. I pulled my cards out to get to the bottom of that shit. I saw another woman. I questioned Psalms and asked where he was when he didn't answer the phone.

He told me he went out of town with his cousin.

"For what?" I asked.

"I be taking care of business," he said.

I didn't know what the fuck he was talking about. I don't know if he was talking about selling drugs or what. Whatever it was, it was a secret, and he couldn't tell me.

I told him I had seen a woman in my cards. "You're a liar," I yelled. "I should have never talked to you in the first place."

"What are those cards telling you?" he asked in distress. He assured me there was no other woman he was seeing.

I called him the next day and he had a mark under his eye. Apparently, he was fighting at the bar. "I like to fight," he said.

His probation officer was visiting him and asked him about the mark under his eye. He made up some lie. So basically, he was going around fuckin with people while intoxicated and fighting them for pure enjoyment. He wasn't that big of a guy. *'Somebody is gonna kick this guy's ass,'* I thought.

Things started going downhill real fast with us after that. It was starting to become a very toxic situation. We began arguing every day. I would question him about his job because he never seemed to go. "I called off," he said. It just seemed like he wanted to lay around the house and do nothing. I expected more from him. I figured since he got out of prison, he was ready to do something with his life. He felt like I was putting him down, but I wasn't trying to. I was going to work and had goals in life. He didn't, and that bothered me. He just wanted to drink. I felt like he was draining my energy, and I was draining his.

He started hinting that I had competition.

"What do you mean competition?" I asked.

"There are other girls who want to talk to me. They are pretty like you and have a nice body like you."

"No they're not," I said.

"Why not?" he asked.

I didn't like to be compared to other people and I figured whoever he was talking about was probably trash. *'How dare this nigga compare these hoes to me?'* "Well, if you want to talk to someone else, then leave me alone," I said.

"I'm not saying I am. I'm just saying you got completion," he said.

I didn't like where the conversation was going.

He went on to tell me he didn't like how I talked to him and how I always accused him of stuff. He had teenage children, and I could hear them in the background. One of his sons got on the phone and started talking crazy to me. "Don't disrespect my pops yo," he said.

I didn't say anything because I didn't know why he had even gotten on the phone. He started talking more shit, and I wasn't sure how to respond. Like, do I cuss the little nigga out, or do I hold back because he was his child? He started saying shit like, "We come first, then you."

"What?" I asked.

"You heard me. We come first."

I never said anything about who came first, but I didn't like hearing that I didn't come first. I sighed on the phone. Then he started saying he would beat up any nigga I would get to fight him. He had totally lost me at that point. I could tell Psalms had raised them to be some hood niggas. I could hear him in the background laughing. I think he put his son up to it because he was mad I was talking smart to him. Either way, Psalms didn't say shit and allowed his son to carry on with the shenanigans.

Psalms got back on the phone and was being an asshole. "I'm psychic too," he said. "You're not the only person who can see stuff." He asked me if I liked girls. I was assuming it was because I lost my virginity so late in life.

"No," I said. I was really irritated at that point because he was bringing up dumb shit.

"No, I think you like girls," he said. "I like that though." He said he wanted to date two women.

I told him I wasn't into that shit and if he was, I was not for him.

He kept calling me gay to piss me off. I thought if anyone was gay it was him. He was in jail for a while; I'm sure he was letting someone suck his dick. Especially with his high sex drive. He told me he was just playing with me, and I better get my shit together if I wanted to keep him.

I was at work, and he called me while he was at the bar. He told me he was talking to another girl. My mouth dropped. I had already known that, but him telling me himself hurt even more. I wanted to cry, but I also had known we weren't working out. He yelled at me like I was one of his children. I just listened to him. He said, "Your attitude is ugly. You telling me I need to get my shit together. No you need to get your shit together. I don't like being told what to do," he yelled. "I would have been focusing on you if you didn't act that way. I had to get that off my chest." He cussed me out for a while.

I told him it was not going to work out with whoever he was with. He told me not to contact him anymore.

A few days later I saw he was in a relationship on Facebook. I couldn't believe it. How? I wasn't sure if it was even real. I assumed it was fake, but it turned out it actually was real.

I got angry; he played the fuck out of me just like Jody. I texted him and called him a cunt and told him that karma was going to get his ass.

He never responded back. He was in a relationship with a twenty-five-year-old girl. I thought that was so disgusting. He was in his early forties. She looked younger than her age and like a man.

How had he gotten into a relationship so fast, I wondered? I was also upset because I wanted a relationship, and he gave it to her... some little kid. That fucking asshole. It was on from there.

I started doing my detective work Scorpio style. Keep in mind, Souls, I was a Scorpio moon. Scorpios are natural detectives, and they are also very vengeful. They will always get you back and it isn't safe to play around with them.

So the revenge began. I made some phone calls and found out who Psalms' parole officer was. I made a report that he was drinking and starting fights at the bar, which was true. I was trying to get him in as much trouble as I could. Then I made a fake profile of him on the Plenty of Fish dating website, but on the gay side. I was giving gay men his number; I know they were blowing his phone up.

I started watching his girlfriend's page on Facebook and liking her comments and pictures. I didn't feel like I was doing anything wrong by liking her pictures. I never threatened her or messaged her. Besides, she wasn't my target.

Months went past and I got depressed. I couldn't understand why I kept getting played by men. I could tell I was never going to get a boyfriend. I was watching Psalms' page and my phone instantly started playing "Can't Hurry Love" by the Supremes. I knew the universe sent me that. *'How the fuck am I hurrying love? I'm in my thirties,'* I thought.

I was getting desperate, and I couldn't sleep. I hated God for allowing Psalms to do that to me.

I found a woman who did love spells for $400. She assured me it worked.

Weeks went past and nothing was happening. None of my love spells worked. I felt like when other people did love spells, it worked for them.

Then after it had been months, I became angry with the spell caster. "You have to wait," she said angrily.

The spell never worked.

I saw that Psalms' girlfriend was pregnant. *'That was so fast,'* I thought. I found his best friend on Facebook and friend-requested him. He knew nothing about me. I told him what happened between me and Psalms. His friend reported back that Psalms said he didn't care.

I told him I was doing magic on them. I did a breakup spell.

Psalms said it wasn't working. "It's making us happy," he told his friend.

I got more readings on them and did not like what I was hearing. One reading said they were happy and could possibly get married. They were also living together.

'*How did this loser get out of jail and get straight into a relationship and have a baby?*' He didn't deserve that. He already had a bunch of kids.

I sent Psalms a message on Facebook directly instead of through his friend calling him a child molester. He had changed his number, so it was the only way for me to contact him.

He responded by saying I was harassing him and that he was going to call the police.

I wasn't worried because he had no proof it was me. When I got my revenge on Psalms, I made sure I left no traces. Usually, I didn't care if I did leave traces. Somehow, I was always able to get out of trouble.

I couldn't figure out where they were living, but I knew in what area, so I called CYS on both of them. Psalms posted on Facebook like they didn't care. So I did it again.

I eventually left them alone until I saw an old message Psalms' girlfriend had sent me months before. It read: 'Leave me alone, bitch." I called CYS on them once again and then I left them completely alone.

I couldn't break up their relationship. It wasn't fair and I was crying. I still didn't want him to get away with what he did. I wanted him to die. I looked for other spells I could do. I found a jar and put his name on it and asked for him to die and then buried it. My friend helped me find the perfect spot. She agreed that it was the right thing to do after how he treated me. I had no remorse.

# Chapter 17:
# El Portal

I left my job because the coronavirus was going around. My dad insisted that I quit. He was worried I would get sick and so was I. I didn't know what was going to happen, or how I was going to pay my rent. I got angry with my dad because I didn't want to get kicked out of my home and then have to go to his house.

Work had been starting to get stressful before I quit. I was constantly being harassed by the clients. When one left, another one came in. I was outnumbered as usual. They were doing dumb shit like asking for shit they didn't need. They tried to get me in trouble by making false reports. They purposely refused to follow rules. I had never seen anything like it. I could tell I was being watched through the security cameras. When I came out of the door or off the elevator, there was someone standing there waiting for me. The majority of them were gang stalkers. They were using people who already had mental issues and had already been to my facility. They had given me problems before, but it was getting worse. I got to the point where I stopped interacting with them. They even followed me up and down the hallways.

In each group of people, there was a ringleader. One woman knocked on the office door and then walked away. She constantly asked for things. She said things to piss me off and started arguments. We ended up getting into a big one.

Another woman gave me problems. She was a big bitch who wanted to be a boy. Sometimes I forgot she was a woman. She faked a seizure one day to try to startle and scare me. I was in the office, and someone knocked on the door and said she was having a seizure. I went and looked and saw her violently shaking. I ran back into the office to go call an ambulance, but luckily my coworker stopped me. She went in there and checked out the situation. "It's not real," she said. I was so fuckin pissed she had done that, but I was pleased to hear three days later she actually had to go to the ER for real. She had an aneurism in her lungs. I had fun with that information when she got back from the hospital. I asked how she was feeling. They couldn't handle my smart-ass mouth and my sarcasm, and I made sure they weren't comfortable stalking me.

Another one who was nicknamed Steven Tyler because she looked just like him was bothering me too. I could tell she was the leader. She hated when I ignored her, so I knew exactly how to piss her ugly ass off. She was one of the ones that seemed to take the harassment personally. Like it was more than a job to her. She started out nagging about shit as the others did. Then I stopped doing things for her. She had borderline personality disorder too, so she was getting pissed. When she spoke, I ignored her. They tried everything to make my job stressful without a break. She was the worst one, but I was willing to fight.

But then the corona started spreading immensely.

I got a reading by a lady named Angel. She was a really good reader, and she was available any time I needed her. She said I would be moving in with my dad again.

I thought, '*Oh hell naw.*' I had already done that too many times before and plus, there was no way in hell I was going to live with that bitch again. She said I would be forced to move.

By that time, since I had quit my job, I didn't know what I was going to do. So, I came up with a plan to cuss Mouse the fuck out so my dad's house wouldn't be an option. Besides, I wanted to cuss that bitch out for putting that hex on me and getting that man to do it. Fuckin bitch. So I sent her a message that basically said fuck her and I *knew* what the fuck she did and that karma came back on her sorry ass. I was referring to when I did the breakup spell on her and my dad. Then I told her that I hoped she died, and I meant that shit too. Then I cussed out her daughter out as well.

My dad called me and tried to stand up for her and asked me why I sent her those messages. I kept telling him she knew why. I cussed him out too. I said this was between me and her. Then I said, "And what are you going to do about it?" See, I wasn't at their house. I could say whatever I wanted. I brought up the situation with her daughter getting him robbed. Then he hung up on me. I stood up to him and I was glad.

A couple of weeks later, I was still mad about the information I received. I decided to send Mouse a Ouija board. I was hoping she would be dumb enough to open it up and use it. I thought, *'Fuck it, let's send Ivy one too but say it's from Jody and send one to her son for a graduation present.'* I know, clever right? I was hoping he would open it and use it as well. So, I sent them both from online. I put Mouse's under a different name, but she would still know who sent it. My dad called me and told me to be careful because that was harassment. I didn't care though. I said, "Go right ahead." Ivy ended up sending hers back. Well, at least I tried.

At that time, I had reconnected with an old friend from high school, Penny. I did a few readings for her. We began to get a lot closer because she was experiencing a spiritual awakening, and I was trying to help her. I was going through a transition of my own. My powers began to increase. I was experiencing some kind of euphoric feeling after I ate food.

I met a shaman on Facebook. I was doing picture readings then, and he asked me to read him. I did it with no problem. We became cool after that. I asked a bunch of questions about spiritual matters. He had a deck of angel cards. I thought they were so cool. He did Enochian magic, which is angel magic. It is one of the oldest forms of magic and the most powerful. Well, that's what he told me. Since I was getting more connected with the angels, I wanted to get a deck.

I ordered it and it came with all seventy-two cards inside. All seventy-two angels. Did you know there were seventy-two angels? I sure didn't. Each card had a picture of one of the angels with their sigil on it. Those cards looked different from the cards I usually get. It came with a book that described each angel and what they represented. It also said who your guardian angel is according to your birthday. I was so excited to try them out. I did a few readings with them at first. Then I found my angels assigned to me including Michael. I felt a connection with them, especially an angel called Loulah who had a childlike energy. She was my birth angel. She looked like a ball of rubber bands with eyes all over it. I thought she looked pretty spooky, and she didn't have wings like I thought all of them had.

For some reason, she and Michael did not get along. Michael did not want her anywhere near him. At first, I had them all in the bed with me, but Michael would not have it. It got so bad that I had to separate them and put them in different rooms. Michael was in charge, and I would choose him over her. I took turns spending time with them. Michael really didn't like other energies beside him. I felt like they both were fighting for my attention. I loved them both. Once I was coming out of the shower and I felt an overwhelming feeling of love from Michael. I felt love from both of them.

I was so excited to have my cards. I just wanted to contact the angels and tell them I loved them so much. I took all the cards and put them on my altar and lit a candle. In the book it gave me a spell to say to contact the angels. I had no idea what I was doing, but I did it anyway. I didn't even think about it. I said the spell and left the candle burning.

The next day, I felt some energy in my house. Something was definitely different. There was a lot of energy by my altar where I had done the spell: a lot of masculine energy. I also noticed there was this white smoke in my room. I didn't feel any negative energy. When the candle got to the end, it was taking too long to go out so I snuffed it out. I noticed some of the angels were contacting me and I was glad to have them around me.

Then things started to get a little strange and the energy in my house was heavy. I decided to call Angel. I told her everything that happened. I told her I had snuffed out the candle. "Bitch, no you didn't," she said.

"It wouldn't burn out, I was afraid it would cause a house fire," I said. Everybody knows you never put a candle out during spell work. She told me to relight the candle and end the spell. So, I did what she instructed me to do. The heavy energy went away, and things seemed to go back to normal.

A week later, I tried contacting Archangel Michael and asked him if he could assist me with a spell. I did it right that time, because the first time I tried it, I used a seven-day candle when the book called for two taper candles and to place one angel card to contact. I called all seventy-two angels, and I never closed the spell; I left it open. With the second time, I used two taper candles, placed Michael's card in between, said the spell, and closed it. I never really thoroughly read the book like I should have.

After doing a reading, I saw Michael had not granted my request. I asked him to give somebody their karma for what they did to me.

A couple of weeks went by, and that heavy energy was back. It was a little strange but not too bothersome. I noticed one day there was an imprint on my closet door. I could only see it if all the lights were out. I thought, '*Wtf is that*?' It looked like a devil[3]. I said, "Wait a minute, that looks like the devil card from my deck." I grabbed the card, and the imprint matched[4]. I started to worry.

I contacted Angel again. All she kept saying was, "You done fucked up, Bitch. You done did it now."

"Omg, what did I do?" I felt horrible. I knew I was in big trouble. *'How did I do this? How was this able to happen?'*

I thought about it for a while and realized it was not my doing. Whoever Mouse was paying to do work for her must have done some spell to get me to open a portal in my house. I believed a domination spell was placed on me. I would never have done something like that on my own. I had never invoked anything before. Also, I thought it was strange I invoked all the angels at the same time.

Souls, I had *all the angels in my house*! That was some real shit. So, remember when I told you I sent the Ouija board to Mouse? I was sure the spell was her way of paying me back by getting me to open a portal in my house. Not only that, they sent demons to kill me. Yes, I know I told Mouse I hoped she would die, and I meant every damn word. That bitch put a nasty hex on me to keep me away from my dad which was fuckin ridiculous. Some people may think this was karma, but I disagree. I did not deserve this magnitude of punishment. Especially what that stank-ass bitch did to me first. Now I had all the angels and devils and demons in my house.

I didn't know what to do. I knew I had to close the portal and that was impossible. I knew I needed a lot of help. I was searching for people who could help me. The energy got even heavier in my house. I couldn't sleep. I felt the weight crushing me while I lay on the bed. I really didn't have anywhere else to go. I left all the lights on in the house because I was too scared of the dark. Angel tried to help as much as she could, but I had so many questions and I was running out of time. I was spending so much money at that point on readings. Angel said she would pray for me and get her friend to pray for me, but I could tell it was too heavy for her. I did some protection spells to help the energy in the house.

I noticed there were some little spirits inside of my candle holders stopping my candles from burning out. I took pictures of those little fuckers[6]. I was interested in what they were; I found out they were called

Tenko. They were Japanese demons. They had big noses and caused chaos. I had never experienced anything like that. I knew they could not kill me, but I wasn't sure what harm they could do. I would hear them jumping around in my living room. I told them to settle they ass down.

Angel told me that since Michael was there, he wasn't with the bullshit. He wasn't allowing shit to go down while he was there. The Tenko were afraid of him.

The spell work I was doing wasn't working. My candle glass was turning black. That usually happens when there are blockages. I also saw a man with a hat during one of my spells. His name was thin man. I had never heard of him until then. First, he visited one of my friends. She said she saw him in her dining room. She also said she got attacked by a demon on the same day. Then all of a sudden, there was a documentary on HBO about him. They said he got a little girl to kill another little girl.

I went out to lunch with Penny. I really needed to get out of the house. I told her all about the portal and what was going on. When we got back to my house, she really wanted to come inside and see what it was like. I wasn't sure if she was too scared. As we got closer to the entrance of my building, there was a figure laid out on the ground. I knew it hadn't been there before I left the house. "It looks dead," I said[5].

"I see that," she said.

"It looks like it was running. Like it got hit by car," I said. I was scared as hell, thinking *'Damn they on the outside too.'* I had to be inside with those creatures. It looked really creepy and had long legs.

As soon as we got inside the house, she was able to locate the portal right away. I wasn't sure where it was, but it was right by the window where my altar was. Penny said, "Wait let me look at the window." It seemed as though the creature had been on his way to my house, and something had killed it.

"Michael did that," I said with victory. I looked at my cards and I was correct. Michael had killed his mothafuckin ass. He had stopped him right before he got in my house, and it said he wasn't allowing any more demons inside. *'Wow, demons are real and the fact that I am seeing them is scary and incredible at the same time.'*

Penny continued to walk around my apartment. "It feels really cold in here." She could also feel when the energy changed as she went from the kitchen to the living room. It was not fun. There was an uneasy, heavy feeling that nobody should have in their home. It made me so uncomfortable, and I had to live there and figure something out and fast. I definitely did not want to move. Penny decided we should pour water and bleach on the demon print outside and then I should walk around it with sage and let it know it was not welcome here. We took a bucket outside and she poured the bleach water over the demon. I went around with the sage. She gave me a hug and left.

I couldn't even think in that damn house. It was so depressing. I could hear demons talking to me. They told me there was nothing I could do. I was talking to a guy friend through text and we said good morning to each other. I heard somebody say mañana. I was like, "Mañana." I knew it was Spanish, but I forgot what the word meant. I looked it up and saw that it said good morning. *'Damn, I got demons all in my conversation,'* I thought. I said out loud, "Ain't nobody talking to you." I wondered why it was talking Spanish. "Y'all gotta go."

I was up late one night because I couldn't sleep. I got a message from one of my Facebook friends. I didn't know him that well, but he seemed to be cool. He said spirit told him to contact me because I was going through something. He was a psychic as well. He described himself as a mystic. I explained to him what was going on. He did a reading for me and gave me instructions on what to do to get the spirits out my house. He assured me that sending love was the best way to go. It was very detailed, but one of the things he instructed me to do was to invoke the god Anubis. "You need an animal," he said.

I used a statue of a dog my dad bought me. I was told to put a love sigil on the dog that he created. Then to put one over the devil imprint. Once I invoked Anubis, I instantly heard it barking. I had always wanted a dog, so I picked it up and petted it like a real dog to try to calm it down. I put it right next to Michael's statue and realized it was barking at Michael. It was loud and he wouldn't stop. "Why are you barking at Michael?" I asked. I ended up moving Anubis to a different table. He stopped eventually.

I was hoping everything worked, but I was sadly disappointed. The demons were still in my house.

I went on Facebook asking several witches if they knew how to close a portal. I came across a witch who specialized in portals. She said, "You came to the right place." She said she could close the portal for me. I couldn't believe it; I was so grateful. She said she wanted to do it for free. There was no way I was not going to pay her for basically saving my life.

The witch didn't have any pictures of herself on her Facebook page. She was very mysterious to me. She didn't want to talk on the phone. We communicated through Facebook. She lived alone in a house, and she always sent me pictures of her cat.

I showed her all the pictures I had of the demons. At that point, there were black marks all over my floor[7]. There were three huge ones leading into my bedroom right where the imprint was on my closet door. They were burn marks. The demon was burning marks in my floor. I guess they were hoof prints.

She did some kind of magic and asked me what I saw in a tray. I saw a witch. That represented Mouse. She somehow redirected the magic. Whatever magic was directed at me would hit a candle instead. Then she told me to draw a number on my door and circle it and keep a crystal near me for protection. "Are you ready?" she asked. She transferred her energy from her house through the circle at my house. In just a few seconds, my house felt different. "How does it feel now?" she asked.

"It feels safe and calm," I said.

Then I heard something say, "Alert." She said she put an alarm around

my house so no demons would try to come in nor would anybody try to put magic on me. "You should be good now."

I paid her and thanked her.

A couple of days later, I saw more marks on the floor. They were all over. I contacted the witch again and she assured me they were on their way out.

A week later, everything was back to normal. No more heavy energy. The marks stopped. I could sleep in peace and go about my normal day. I was walking on eggshells at that point. I didn't want to do anything to reopen the portal. I was told by Angel not to do any candle magic because I was in jeopardy of it reopening.

The witch and I got to know each other. She told me she had a familiar. She showed me a picture of him. She was younger than me but seemed to be older. She said she wanted to protect my energy so nobody could locate it and she needed a box. Before I knew it, she had already left the store. She moved fast. Her energy was fast too. She did send me one picture of herself. She had the most beautiful long hair. She sent me a video of a portal she opened on accident in her house. She was also a teacher and mentor and had classes.

I had a dream about a gorilla, and I heard someone say, "I'm going to kill you, Brandi Wilson." When I woke up, I wasn't scared, but you know I had to call my reader Angel for a reading. She said it was Mouse and the person she paid to do work on me. I started seeing skull and crossbones, so I knew a hex was being placed on me. I was right: Mouse was trying to kill me.

I had a reading with the African priest for the second time. I shared with him everything that happened and everything I did. I could tell he was kind of upset with me. "What are you doing?" he said. "Why are you messing around with sigils?" He gave instructions on what to do, which was a little different than the first time. He told me not to invoke any more entities or work with any. He also asked, "Well did you move?"

I said, "No, I'm still here."

"Most people would have had to move," he said.

I didn't want to move but insisted that I had to. I knew if I did what he told me to do I would open that portal.

# Chapter 18:
# Pernicious

I met Nick through Penny. She referred to him as her witch friend. She said he had previously helped her get to the fifth dimension where he was. She told me they lit a candle, and she experienced a trance. She said he was able to answer her questions before she even asked them. I was excited. I thought, '*My turn!*' I wanted to try it.

I contacted him on Facebook. I told him what was going on with me and about Mouse attacking me. He assured me he could help. I instantly felt an attraction to him. It was a romantic energy, and I just wanted to keep talking to him. I didn't find him physically attractive, but he was so smart and knowledgeable. I was intrigued.

Then the sexual energy started to pick up. I heard my spirit guides say, "You're going to have sex with him." I didn't believe them. It had been three mufuckin years since I had sex, so I just blew it off. I was more focused on getting help.

He quickly became my mentor. We had a three-way conversation on the phone with me, him, and Penny. We talked about a lot of spiritual matters. We were all on the phone for at least three hours. We got on the subject of the universe having no time. I came to the conclusion that the universe was never created.

All of a sudden, it felt like my third eye cracked open. I felt like I was floating. I couldn't feel my feet touch the floor. It was like I wasn't on earth anymore and I had entered a new dimension. "Guys, what's happening?" I asked. They had no idea. I tried to describe it the best I could.

I continued to talk to Nick every day after that. "I want to talk to you every day," I said.

"I can try," he said.

That awakening process was a rude one. I felt alone. I felt like I was living outside of everyone else. It felt lonely too. The only company I had was them. I felt like they were my support system and like we created a triangle.

I got close to both of them. I loved them both as friends, but I felt a strong, passionate connection with Nick. I didn't know where it was going to go, and I didn't care. I didn't want Penny to feel left out or that I was going to completely disregard her for Nick. That definitely wasn't the case. I wanted her to be okay with us.

There were flies in my house. They were big and mostly surrounded the kitchen window. I knew they were from some kind of hex because Mouse had sent them before. I also came to the conclusion the flies were a computer program and so was I.

Penny came over to see the fly situation. "They are just sitting there," she said.

"I killed some of the flies, but it's almost like they allowed me to kill them. They didn't try to escape or anything," I said.

Penny looked around the house to see if she could find anything else.

I sprayed a lot of bug spray and got really sick because I couldn't handle the fumes. It was still really hard to get rid of them.

I talked to Nick, and he implied that someone was removing the protection that he had put around me. He said it was someone around me. I wasn't sure what he was talking about. He didn't want to say the person's name. "Come on now," he said. "There is someone around you who want you to themselves and doesn't want you to be with anybody else."

"What," I said. It became clear he was talking about Penny. "If anything, she would feel that way about you not me," I said.

Nick got quiet.

"Penny doesn't even like girls that I know of, and I like dick," I said. What he said didn't make sense.

Nick asked me to do a reading for him. I wanted to. I saw him having constant misfortunes in order to get his chair in the underworld. It was true, then: he was really the god he said he was. He had told me previously that he believed he was the reincarnation of a god from Greek culture. It wasn't that I didn't believe him, but seeing it in the cards is different.

He felt so relieved. He felt like he was going in the right direction. Everything he was doing was for a reason. I also saw a few women come up. I saw there were two women, and one wanted a relationship. He was trying to figure out who the women were. "That's Penny," he yelled.

I said, "Do she want a relationship with you?"

"I don't know!" he exclaimed.

I told him he had to choose between two women. One was Penny; the other was me.

He said, "You always gotta pick one."

I was really confused. I said, "Why, is she mad?" Penny looked mad in the cards. I told him to pick one and try having something with them.

He told me he had sex with Penny.

"What?" I gasped. It started making sense. "Why didn't anyone tell me?" I asked.

"I just met you," he said. "She should have told you."

It was a very weird situation, and I felt like I had no chance of connecting with Nick romantically after learning that.

We had a conversation about him not liking Penny in that way. "I want you. I want you, but I can't have you," he said.

I really wasn't sure what to say. We don't even talk all like that.

"Let us talk, bro," he said.

I had several conversations with Penny, and she swore she wasn't into Nick. I barely looked at my cards, so I didn't even pay attention or even care to read them. I was focused on Nick and the awakening process. Finally, Penny gave me the okay to talk to him. She said it was just sexual between them and she thought he was annoying. I was so relieved. I wanted things to be okay. Me and Nick had such a strong connection.

Nick was a mean and unhappy person. He would get attitudes with me sometimes. Even though he was like that, I tried to adjust. Then there were times he was so kind and sweet. "I feel like I could fuck up a whole bunch of people for you," he said. "You make me feel happy." I could tell he thought very highly of me.

We discussed everything. I told him about my sex life and how inconsistent it was.

"Oh, you're one of those virgin goddesses." He was referring to the virgin Greek goddesses. It didn't fully register, at first, how I connected with them until I did some research. I had never heard of them before. I looked up virgin goddesses and they didn't have sex or got married. It sounded just like me.

Nick told me he was the exact opposite of me sexually. Since I wasn't having sex, he was having a lot of sex. I knew he was a player, but that wasn't on my mind.

Nick understood me. He understood who I was. I appreciated that. I thought he was special too.

We were talking on the phone one afternoon and Nick had an attitude during the whole conversation. He was being mean, and I wasn't sure how to take it. I just wanted to get off the phone. After we hung up, I asked Penny if he was always mean like that.

"No," she replied, "he is never mean to me."

Soon after that, I got a text from Nick.

I asked him if he wanted to come over to watch a movie. He had asked several times before. I wanted to wait until I got used to him. I warned him that every time I met a guy in person, it went downhill after that. Since it was the first time we were meeting in person, I wasn't planning to have sex with him. Plus, I knew spirit wouldn't allow me to.

When he arrived, I felt very comfortable, and I gave him a hug. "You're so little," he said. He was tall and slender. I was worried I wouldn't find him attractive, but I did. We walked to my apartment. "This is nice," he said. "This doesn't look like a place where black people stay."

I told him there were a lot of black people who lived there. I noticed he had a small bag with him. I wasn't sure how long he was planning on staying. He took his shoes off before proceeding into the living room. I gave him a tour of the place. I also showed him where the portals were located. I told him I was worried that the portals would open when he was there because he was so powerful. He said the portals weren't completely closed.

"Yes, they are," I said.

"No, they are not," he said. "Energy moves; you can never really close a portal. It's quantum physics." He told me he lived somewhere where there was a portal open, and he had to move.

Nick felt like I wasn't taking things seriously enough. "You have demons coming through your walls, my nigga. You're in a dangerous situation," he said.

He was right. I was in danger. It wasn't that I wasn't taking it seriously, but there was nothing I could do about the situation.

Nick told me he was homeless for two years. He suggested for my safety I should move even if it was to a place I didn't want to go. I didn't want to hear that or to move.

We then went back outside so he could smoke. I showed him where the thin man was. "No don't step on it," I yelled.

"Why are you so scared," he laughed.

We walked up the street and I waited for the gang stalkers to start following us. It was weird because not one person came out. We went back into my apartment, and he showed me a tattoo he had. It was a tattoo of Anubis. "You invoked me," he said and started laughing.

Souls, remember I was doing spell work to close the portal and I invoked Anubis to help me? He was Anubis or he was one part of Anubis. Energy was able to split into different people. Nick was three gods in one body.

We watched the movie called "The Invisible Man". At first, Nick sat on the floor. I told him it was okay to sit on my bed. He quickly got up and sat next to me. He talked through the whole movie. He was so loud, and I kept thinking I would never go to the movies with him.

I started getting sleepy. I was on my way to falling asleep and he kept looking at me, but I was to too tired to move. I wasn't sure when he was leaving, and it was getting late. The movie was over, and Nick just sat on the bottom of my bed and leaned against the wall.

I lay down in my normal spot. "Do you want a pillow?" I asked.

He said, "No." He had some scarf he carried with him. He said it helped him spiritually. He covered his face with it. I was wondering when he was going to make a move.

I couldn't completely fall asleep, so I asked him to transfer energy to me. We touched each other's fingertips, and I could feel his energy go into my hand. It was so cool. Then we did a meditation together and I started seeing a vision. It looked like I was in China on a bicycle and then I saw a portal and I was too scared to go through it. I quickly opened my eyes. I told Nick what I saw.

"Why are you so scared to go through that portal?" he asked.

After that portal opened in my house, I wanted to stay far away from them.

I laid back down, and Nick curled up on the bottom of my bed and went to sleep. He stayed the night. I never had a guy stay the night at my house before; he was the first. I watched him as he slept and thought if he wanted to have sex, when he woke up, that it was okay. I thought about getting up and looking for my condoms to have them ready. It had been a year since I bought them. I didn't know where they were. I wondered why he hadn't yet tried to have sex, and I thought I would have to make a move.

Finally, it was morning, and he was knocked out and snoring and shit and I wanted him to get up. I slowly pushed my butt back against his penis and rubbed my booty on him. I faced towards him while his eyes were still closed.

He started to kiss me. He gently bit my bottom lip. When I kissed him, it felt like a dark basement. I got up and said, "Let me see it."

He pulled down his pants and I turned the light on.

"That's big," I said. I lied – it was smaller than I expected. He was tall so I had thought he would be bigger. I wasn't complaining though, I was just excited to have some dick back in my life.

I stared at it and took a lick. It was a nice-looking penis. I began to suck, gripping his penis tightly and not giving him any time to breathe. Spit ran down his penis and it was nice and wet. He balled his fist up and grabbed the bed sheets. "Oh, fuck," he said. I wondered if I was hurting him but since he didn't say anything I kept going. I also didn't want to take his dick out of my mouth to ask him. I moved my hand up and down. He tried his best to hold on. He then lifted his butt up off the bed. I didn't let that dick slip for one moment. I devoured it like it was my last meal.

I gave him a few breaks and licked the side of his penis very gently, but then followed it up with more spit and more powerful strokes with my hand. He couldn't stay still. I then made attempts to deep-throat his dick. I couldn't fit the whole thing in there, but I went down as far as I could. I chocked on it a couple of times, which I enjoyed because it made me produce more spit. The sensation of his penis in my mouth and on my tongue was divine. He moaned the whole time. I knew I was doing a good job. I moved my hand down in circular motion. I even tickled the head of his penis while still sucking it. He sat up because he couldn't stay down. I licked in every crevice.

After about twenty minutes, I was getting a bit tired so I sped up the energy so I could make him cum. He started to scoot back. He tried to run from me. Then he finally exploded in my mouth. When I was finished, he was really amazed. "Wow, that was different."

"Really?" I asked.

He then laid on the floor with his pants halfway on. "It still feels like you're sucking my dick. My toes are tingling."

I put my feet on top of his stomach just doing some weird shit, but he didn't mind it. He said that his butt was wet from me giving him head.

I laughed. That was the best blow job I had ever done. I didn't expect him to act that way and rave about it. He said he would always remember that moment. "You got somethin with you," he said.

"Well, it's been a year since I did it. I like doing it," I said.

"I can tell." He gave me a kiss on my forehead.

We then laid on the bed together. I still wanted to have sex, so I started backing my ass up against his dick again. At that point, I started to get hot. So, I took my pants off. Then I proceeded to take my underwear off. He helped pull them down. He leaned on his side and said, "You're gonna put it in." I could tell he was worried about hurting me.

We tried numerous times to get the penis inside me, but I was too tight. I softly caressed his face as he rubbed his penis back and forth on my clit. "You have to try putting it in," I said.

He got up and spread my legs open. He slowly tried to put his dick in. He got it inside and it hurt a little. He said he had to go inside soft because if it was hard, we would be unsuccessful. He was gentle with me, maybe a little too gentle. I appreciated it though. We made eye contact and he started to moan. I yelled the whole time. "Your dick feels so good in my pussy."

Then I fucked up and said, "Jesus." We both stopped and looked at each other. His dick started to come out and then I asked him to perform oral sex on me. He looked at me and smiled. He sat up and sat beside me with his back turned towards me. He began to lick my pussy backwards. He was licking downwards. It hurt a little bit because my coochie was sore from penetration. I couldn't handle his tongue – my vagina was too sensitive – so I told him to stop after a few minutes.

He got up to get dressed. He was bragging about how tight my pussy was and how he could feel all sides. He said that I was really wet, and he had pussy juice all over him. He sat on the bed and licked both of my nipples. He asked me to sit on his lap. He kissed me and then asked me to give him a hug. I hugged him and he said, "Aww." The alarm on his phone was going off and he didn't want to put me down, so he got up and picked me up with him. He sat back with me still remaining on his lap. He told me he had requested his Uber and he had to go. I threw some clothes on so I could walk him out, but I couldn't find my glasses. They had flown off somewhere. I walked him outside and he kissed me goodbye.

I couldn't believe I had sex again. I was happy about it. Later that day, he told me something bad had happened to him and he would call me later. I hoped everything was okay. He called me later that night and said, "We're just friends."

I wasn't sure why he was saying that. I wasn't expecting anything more. "Okay," I said.

He told me that someone had called CYS on him because he was asleep and didn't answer the door. Then he told me he got in an argument with his baby mom, and she wanted him to get out. I was confused as to why all of a sudden that was happening. I felt like I couldn't even enjoy the sexual encounter now because bad shit was happening to him.

"Do you think it's because of me?" I asked.

He said he thought about that. He told me previously that bad things happened if he had sex with the wrong person.

I felt bad for wanting to have sex, but I hadn't had sex in three mothafuckin years. I felt bad for him. He was feeling so down and sad and I wasn't sure what to do. I thought about letting him come stay with me. I knew I had to be careful letting men come to my house.

A couple of days later, I started getting STD symptoms. My discharge was really smelly, and I had more than usual. It felt like I was peeing on myself. I was worried, but I wanted to wait until I got tested. I decided to tell him anyway. He felt like a lot of bad things were happening to him at once. I told him, "Let's just get the results back first," but I convinced myself something was wrong. I wasn't sure if my coochie was adjusting to his energy or what. Then I started to get angry because I knew he was fuckin somebody else and that wasn't okay with me. "Why didn't you bring any condoms?" I asked.

"Why didn't I bring any condoms?" he said sarcastically.

"Yeah, I don't have sex so why would I keep them?"

"I didn't come over to your house for sex," he said.

"I never said you did." I knew I should have looked for those condoms. I felt so stupid.

"I was planning on coming to see you this weekend before you went to the doctor."

I wasn't sure if he was telling the truth or not. I told him that wasn't a good idea. I asked him if he was fuckin the other girl with a condom.

He said, "You already know the answer to that."

I said, "What about Penny?" Like, what was this guy doing? Just fucking everybody raw? He told me he fucked her with no condom too. I got really irritated. I was so scared there was a possibility I could have a STD again. Especially, since I just got cleared of the last one.

299

He started questioning me about who I had been with and the last guy that gave me an STD. I had just gotten checked a few weeks before and my HPV was gone.

He started acting funny after that, and I felt like he was ignoring me. That made me even angrier, so I went off on him. I called him a monster. I felt like that may have triggered him because people had made comments about his looks. I asked him if he cared about me and he said, "As much as I can." Like, what the fuck did that mean?

I said, "Okay, well maybe you should continue to fuck the other girl you fuckin, cause maybe you care about her." I told him I didn't want to talk to him anymore and he seemed to be upset about it. He sent me crying emojis.

The next morning, I sent him more messages and he responded, "Have a nice life, Brandi."

That pissed me off, so I told him to go to the doctor himself and get checked and that I wasn't going to tell him my results. I told him I wouldn't speak to him again. He insinuated that was a lie and that I would still contact him.

We texted a few times after that. He kept sending me videos on spiritual matters. He sent me an article about the seven sisters. They were Zeus' daughters whom he turned into stars. Nick felt like I was one of them. I assured Nick that he was right the first time and that I was Persephone. Nick completely stopped contacting me after that.

I told Penny what was going on. I told her I had slept with Nick and that it was probably a bad idea. I felt she had the right to know. I told her it was possible I had a STD. I thought I was being a good friend. She seemed to be a little concerned. It was weird we even had that conversation.

I got the test results back and they were negative. I was really surprised and relieved. My symptoms had gone away also. I told him, but he was still not responding to me. I apologized as well. I told Penny because I knew she was probably worried too. I was really stressed out, so I asked Penny if she wanted to go out to eat.

When she came to pick me up, she was acting strange. She had a gold ring with a green stone on it. She said her friend had given it to her, and she wanted to see if I picked up any energy from talking about it. I was very hesitant to touch it, but I did and felt a strong energy from it. "You can open and close portals with this," I said. I thought it was something positive.

We got to the restaurant and all of a sudden, she started saying how cute I was. Then out of nowhere, she started talking about her sex life. I wasn't sure why. So, I started talking about Nick and how he told me he didn't want a girlfriend. Then I started talking about our sexual experience.

Penny had sunglasses on and was acting weird. Then she said she was smoking weed and that's why she was wearing them.

"He was really gentle with me," I said. I was really sad about the situation.

She told me Nick had pushed her away, and I didn't understand why. I mean, if they were just friends why would he stop talking to her just because he was talking to me?

I felt like something more was going on. Something just wasn't right.

I got a reading done to see if Penny was doing magic on me, and I was right. The nerve of that fuckin bitch! I found out she did a separation spell on Nick and me. *'She's been doing stuff on me the whole time,'* I thought. She was putting bad energy on me, having me touch shit. Nick had even warned me, but I just hadn't seen it. I was too distracted by him. I tried to see why she was doing it. She wanted another chance with him and wanted me to go away. *'What the fuck!'* They could have been starting something. I was really confused. *'How dare this bitch betray me after all the help I gave her funky ass.'* That's why she had given me all those compliments when we went out to eat. I couldn't understand why, if she liked him, she hadn't said anything. She just expected me to figure it out. I helped her out a lot and that sorry-ass bitch did magic on me.

I was pissed. I made comments on my Facebook page about people doing shit behind my back. She had tried to insinuate she was going to get me robbed like she did one of her guy friends. She was trying to scare me and bully me the whole time. It had gone right over my head, and I had been too focused on Nick to see anything. I wasn't scared of her at all and was surprised she would even think that. She tried to say smart-ass shit, so I just blocked her and didn't say anything because I didn't know exactly what she was doing just yet. I wanted to kick that sorry-ass bitch right in her fuckin face. I wanted the bitch to run up on me. I decided I needed more information.

In the reading I got done, I found out Penny also put a love spell on Nick. I sent Ha the whole reading. I told him what she did, and I still got no response from him. I was really upset. I really liked him, and I was tired of the interference in my connections with men. It ended exactly at three weeks like all my other connections. I had no choice but to move away. I saw in my cards that they were going to get back together and start having sex again. I saw him apologizing to her and them starting a relationship. I got another reading as well. My reader told me their plan was to ignore me and start a relationship. *'Those motherfuckin bitches,'* I thought.

Penny texted me and said she was not sure why I blocked her but that it was my prerogative and she just wanted to see if I was okay. *'Who uses the word prerogative?'* I thought. The bitch was weird. I didn't respond. I knew she expected me to go off on her, so I decided to take another route and send her a picture of Nick's cum stains on my comforter. I had left the cum stains there as a little souvenir. I asked her if she knew how to remove cum stains from a comforter. "It won't come out," I wrote. It was war, and I didn't give a fuck.

*'If Penny and Nick wanted to date, why haven't they dated?'* I

wondered. They had been friends for a very long time. I remembered the reading I gave Penny. Nick was the guy friend she was getting closer to.

Nick was putting relationship memes on his Facebook to piss me off and make me jealous. He was implying that he and Penny were dating and that she always had his back. So, of course, I started talking shit too. I couldn't take it anymore.

I said, "Fuck it." It was my last hurrah. I decided I was going to call CYS on him and it would be the last time I would do that to people. I wasn't sure how to get revenge on Penny. The bitch didn't have any kids, and I didn't know where she lived. I called CYS and told them that Nick was doing drugs and leaving his kids home alone. The first part was true, but I wasn't sure about the other part. It was what he got accused of the first time they had been called on him. I was watching his Facebook page, and he was saying all this shit like he was happy, making indirect posts about Penny and acting like they were together. I didn't do anything to either of those motherfuckers. I was very angry, but I had also seen him talking to other girls as if he were single.

He was talking all this shit about me. After I called CYS, he made a post about somebody doing him dirty, but he did me dirty first. He claimed he didn't even like Penny, but he was back fuckin with her, so I felt it was only right to get him back. At that point, I didn't give two fucks. I was tired of that fuckin pattern repeating. He blocked me on Instagram. I didn't really care if he was going to do magic on me. Fuck him and her.

It was the day before Halloween. He made a post about not getting revenge on people, but he said on Halloween he was going to do something.

I made a new Instagram page and started following him and went back to sleep. In my dream I heard him call me "Miss Piggy." I had just gotten a new logo done. All of a sudden, I kept hearing his song in my head. It was the song he did that I really liked. I was hearing it all day. I just kept thinking about him. I started having sexual dreams about him. He was coming into my dreams every night. *'Oh great now he's dream walking. That mother fucker,'* I thought.

I tried to figure out what I was going to do. I masturbated twice in one day because I couldn't help it. The magic he was doing was making me want to have sex. That night he went into my dream and fucked me. He sat against the wall, and I lay down with my legs up and I could see and feel his dick going in and out of me. It felt so real because it was real. Then he picked me up and I sat on him, and I licked his neck. Then he got up to leave and somehow, I convinced him to have sex again with me. So, we had sex again. In the dream, the sex felt amazing, but I didn't want to have sex with him. It was rape.

When I woke up my vagina was sore, and I had cramps in my abdominal. I went to the bathroom to pee and there was a drop of blood in my underwear. That was fuckin ridiculous and against Universal Law. *'He's gonna pay for this. You're not allowed to this,'* I thought. I felt really violated. I did not want any sex with that man. He continued to come in my dreams and harass me. The dreams were all sexual and of us being together, but I didn't want him anymore; it was too late.

There was a guy I went to high school with who was friends with Nick. He appeared in my dreams several times too. In one dream, I was laying on the bed, and the guy started crawling on it toward me; he was trying to rape me. I screamed no and started kicking my feet. Then I woke up. He also sent one of his other friends into my dream, but I caught on and deleted his sneaky ass off of social media. I wasn't sure if his guy friends were witches or not. I didn't like being taken advantage of and I was being ganged up on. I stopped masturbating to Nick because I realized that was causing the sexual encounters in my dreams.

Nick started showing up in my dreams as other people, some people I knew and some I didn't. He would try to pull my pants off or get on top of me. Penny started showing up in my dreams too. I had dreams of guys picking her over me, which we knew wasn't true in real life. Nick picked me over her, and she got jealous. She was a jealous, ugly bitch who was miserable. He chose me. It was the first time a guy had chosen me first, but since she did a spell, it ruined everything. In the dreams I had about Nick, he wanted to have sex again. It was clear he wanted a relationship which was out of the question. A reader said he was trying to get my money; he wasn't getting shit from me. He was also doing psychic rape and it was wrong.

I also had dreams about Nick and Penny having sex. It was so disgusting. In my dreams, I would be laying in my bed, and I would hear noises so I would put my ear up to the wall and would hear them moaning and then I would wake up. Those motherfuckers were sick. I dreamed they were on TV and it said they were a couple. They started dancing around and I ignored the whole thing. I never looked at him once. He followed me around and then my friend Olivia showed up.

Olivia ended up coming back around in real life and in my dreams. She told me it was going to be hard to get rid of Nick.

In one dream, I was in a house with a group of men, but Penny was there. Somebody stole my purse, and I was looking for it. I saw Penny and Nick rolling around on the floor and then other people started fighting. I saw Penny in a room, and I said, "You betrayed me."

She said, "I had to," and she blew magical dust in my face.

My mentor Gaia was angry about what was going on. Her husband just so happened to be a very skilled dream walker. She asked him to help me. She also contacted her ancestors. Nick had fucked up. I was given instructions on what to do on my side. I also did spiritual baths which helped a lot until a girl I knew asked for a reading and asked how she could get some spell work removed. She then went back and told Penny and Nick. She set me up. They tried many ways to stop the work that was being done but I remained successful.

# Chapter 19:
# Year 2021

Olivia sent me an email asking if I could give her a reading. I was excited to hear from her. "Of course," I said.

She said she had lost her ability to read. She moved out of state and then she had moved back into town. "No prob," I said. I *knew* I could re-teach her. It took me only two times for her to be able to read again. We talked about working on ourselves. We tried to see how we could be better people. While in discussion, I remembered some of my childhood trauma.

I asked my mom what happened between her and my dad while she was pregnant with me. She explained to me that she had Crohn's Disease and she had been really sick, so she hadn't been able to care for me. I wasn't mad her. I honestly didn't care. She told me my dad left her. She said they planned to have a baby, but then he wanted to leave after I was born. She didn't want to get stuck with raising a baby on her own when she had two other kids.

Nick was still obsessed with me and obsessed with causing me harm. He was very persistent, but I had already moved on and was enjoying my life. He and Penny constantly were entering my dreams, but I was kicking their asses.

In one dream, Nick would not leave my house. So we started fighting and I kicked his ass and smashed his fingers in the door. I knew they were doing stuff by dreams and readings, but I really didn't feel anything. I could tell the magic they were doing wasn't working.

Nick even went into Olivia's dream one night. She had completely forgotten about it until we were talking on the phone, and she said, "I just remembered Nick came in my dream." She said he had been watching her for a while. Basically, he tried to get close to her to make me jealous and it hadn't worked. She said she told him to get out of her dream and kicked him all the way into outer space. He came back and apologized and gave her some flowers and candy. Olivia was able to control her dreams. After that he never went into her dreams again.

I decided to start a YouTube channel. I was getting over the Nick situation, and I just didn't care anymore. I felt like it was time to get out there and be seen. At first, I didn't want to show my face because I didn't feel like doing my hair and putting on make-up. I heard spirit tell me to show my face. So I started being on camera and reading. I really loved doing it and I was enjoying myself.

I got this girl to do a popularity and money spell for me because I wanted more clients. The spell worked like a charm. Before I knew it, I started receiving a lot more clients, which meant I started getting more money, and not just from the tarot readings. People started to like me more and I got more followers on YouTube and on TikTok. It was insane! I was definitely Poppin and in the spotlight. All I could think about was making money. I had never been like that before. My focus had never solely been on money. Then, I couldn't stop thinking about it and I was looking for new ways to make it.

I was sitting on my bed one day and I asked myself, "How can I make more money?" I decided to start a counseling business. The idea just popped into my head. I always wanted to do counseling, so I actually started it. I wasn't sure how I was going to do it, but I knew that was the right direction to go in. I knew I couldn't start a spiritual counseling business without a license and there was no way I was going back to school.

I talked to a couple who had done readings for me before and asked them what I needed to do. "You don't need a license or degree to practice tarot counseling," they said.

I wanted to incorporate tarot with counseling. I created a 30-day program to raise your vibration that also taught how to do tarot readings or do a birth card, past life, or deceased loved one readings. The counseling program was separate. The program also offered support, motivation, and positivity. The tarot would come in when I needed to see the overall energy. I really didn't need the tarot for the counseling part. I also offered vent sessions, where a client could talk and I just listened without any judgment. I guess sort of like talking to a priest. I started getting everything together.

Amidst starting my counseling business, I was also getting very impatient since I hadn't had sex in almost a year again. I refused to do any readings or any spiritual work until I was allowed to have sex. *'What the fuck is this*?' I thought. I couldn't have sex because I was doing spiritual work? Well that's what the cards said. The cards said I could have sex with one of my friends if I wanted to, but I had to stop reading cards. *'Fuck them cards,'* I thought.

I decided to have sex with a guy I had been friends with for about two years online. I had never met him in person. I knew he liked me and wanted to have sex with me. He was a nice guy and really supportive. He had a girlfriend though. I did care, but I also wanted to have sex really badly. I had a dilemma. I started talking sexually to him and then he offered to come over to my house and bring me lunch. I thought about it and then I felt bad. I didn't want to have sex with somebody's man. I told him it wasn't a good idea.

Some weeks went by and then I changed my mind. He told me he was on his way to a high school reunion that happened to be by my house. I thought it was okay to meet him outside. He wasn't able to make it to the event. I still wanted to have sex, so I got impatient.

He came over to my house. I met him outside, and he gave me a hug. When we got to my room, I turned the light on so I could see his face. He wasn't too bad looking in person, but I had to make sure I was somewhat attracted to him before having sex. I was nervous. I told him I had only had sex with two people. We got on the bed and started kissing. Then he took my underwear off and started giving me head. He did it exactly how I liked it. It was good.

He took his clothes off and his dick was small. Really small. He pulled out a condom and I said, "Wait." I had to get the kind I used for sensitive skin. He shoved his dick inside me. It hurt me a great deal. I started to scream but not in pleasure. I told him it hurt, but he continued. It seemed like he went even harder. It was not a pleasant experience.

When he was done, I was glad. I had felt an extreme amount of energy coming from my vagina, and I was relieved to get that out of me.

He started acting nervous. He kept texting his phone and going into the living room. He put his clothes back on and said he had to go.

"No," I whined. I wasn't finished. I wanted to have sex again and at least suck his dick.

He was acting funny though. He started to withdraw from me. I didn't know what the big deal was. I did not like that at all. I cussed him out and I think I hurt his feelings, but I didn't care.

I also sent his girlfriend messages on Facebook with a picture of the condom we used. I went in the garbage and found it and dug it out. I kept it in a bag just in case I wanted to do magic on him.

At my apartment, the portal was closed, but I was still seeing and hearing ghosts. I kept seeing dead little boys. I saw one out of the corner of my eyes. I saw the color blue, that's how I knew it was a boy.

I started hearing people's thoughts. All five of my senses got stronger. I could taste people's thoughts and what they had eaten previously. I could smell what lotion, cologne, perfume, or body wash a person was wearing, even when I wasn't around them. I could see colors more vividly and spirits more clearly. I could feel energy more intensely. My body was more sensitive. I could hear my body talking to me. I could read and hear energy a lot better. I heard thoughts and conversations. I heard ghosts and spirits. I heard my spirit guides a lot better. More dead people started to contact me: a lot of young children, mostly boys. When people died, they would contact me, and they wouldn't know where to go. I wasn't sure where to send them. I was able to manipulate energy and shapeshift. I could spiritually turn myself into different forms if I wanted to.

There were handprints on my walls and strange noises of things falling inside my apartment. I would see faces in the walls and ceilings.

I kept smelling something sweet in my apartment. I knew they made ice cream downstairs in my building, so at first, I thought it was coming from there. The smells kept getting stronger and stronger, then they changed. It seemed like it was coming through the vent, but I knew my bitch neighbor had something to do with it. Every time I talked on the phone or made a noise, I started smelling shit. The neighbor started making more noises. She was banging on the wall and throwing stuff. I ignored the bitch for a while but after months of that shit, I started doing shit back. I was so happy and content in my life at that point, but I was thinking, '*Fuck this.*'

I started making noise and slamming my door, but that's when the smells picked up even more. The smells were getting too intense, and I started feeling sick. I started looking for stuff to plug the vents up with. I put some clear tape over the vent in my room because that was where the smells seemed to be coming from. It seemed to calm down for a while, but then it started up again. I put duct tape and paper and cardboard over it. I tried several times and started to get tired of doing it because I was still smelling shit. It started to smell like chemicals.

Then it started to smell like gas, and I got worried, so I called the fire department. They came in and said they didn't smell anything. I couldn't sleep at night. The smells just kept coming and I wanted to vomit. I tried so hard not to leave my home. I moved my bed into the kitchen because I thought the smell was coming from my bedroom, but it was in the kitchen too. It was coming out of all the vents. I began to sweat and thought I might die in there. I complained to management about the smell. They needed to investigate first, so I stayed a couple of days at my work mom's house. When I got there, the gang stalkers were still bothering me. That's when I knew they had something to do with the smell.

When I returned home, I started smelling acid and my face started to burn. '*I know those motherfuckers didn't pump acid into my house,*' I thought. I left the house immediately and headed to the hospital. On the way there I noticed my face was red and it looked like it was burned. I couldn't believe spirit would let them disfigure my beautiful face. The doctors just said it was an allergic reaction. Thank goodness.

When I got back, the management offered me a new apartment to stay in, but it was $300 more. I had no choice but to take it. I was relieved to move. It turned out I liked the new apartment better and it was way bigger.

Soon, my neighbors started bothering me over there too. They were in with the gang stalkers. Everybody on that floor was a gang stalker. A girl neighbor had kids who would scream really loudly to bother me. There was constant slamming of the doors. All day I would hear them except when I was in my room. They knew when I was out of my room. I ignored them at first, but after the first couple of months, that shit was getting ridiculous. I wasn't reacting to anything but then I would go off. They would slam doors while I was taking a shower. I became immune to the door-slamming, and the kids screaming was bothersome only sometimes. Eventually, I was able to tune them out. The apartment was so big I could barely hear the noises anyway, and I stayed in my room most of the time.

I started working again at my old job but in a different house.

Nick was still attacking me, but I was able to set up an altar and get my ancestors in the house, and Gaia helped me with that. I started hearing music again, mostly in the kitchen. I could tell Nick was trying to get inside the house, but he was blocked. I could hear him screaming and crying trying to get in. *'This is crazy,'* I thought. My ancestors were helping keep him out. I learned how to do hex removals. Nick was throwing so many hexes at me non-stop. I was able to get them off and was able to keep him away for a while.

I found out my nephew was psychic too and more advanced than me. I had taught him how to read cards and he had learned really fast. He could read pictures well too.

Mouse continued to come into my dreams with her bullshit. She kept trying to fight me, but I kept whooping her ass. In one, she was sitting in my aunt's living room and her daughter was there. I went to punch her, and she blocked my punch. Then she said, "I blocked it," to her daughter. She seemed to be happy about it, so I grabbed her by her hair and pulled her to the ground. Then she started acting like a victim and my dad came and picked her up off the ground.

I wanted to contact Enoch out of the blue. I wasn't sure why. I asked Olivia to contact him for me because he had blocked me. She contacted him on Facebook. I could tell he was hesitant, but I was happy to hear from him.

The energy was exactly where we had left off. I realized he was a reincarnated god like me. We planned to go out on a date. I was so excited. A real date. Finally, somebody I really wanted to go on a date with. The feelings were mutual; it was so hard for me to find a connection like that. Out of all my connections with men, Enoch was the strongest and the most compatible. He was everything I was looking for. He was financially stable and attractive. Most of our conversations were about spiritual things. He was still in a relationship, though he had emotionally moved on. I wasn't sure what I was doing, but it felt right to do. I felt more comfortable with him that time around. I was definitely planning to have sex with him. We talked about it often. He even introduced me to his brother and his dad, although I wasn't completely comfortable with it.

On the day of our date, I got a text from him saying his baby mom/girlfriend read all of our text messages. She said she wasn't letting him go no matter what. He said he needed to deal with that situation first. I was fucking furious; I had only talked to him for a week. Things had been going so well.

I kindly said, "Okay," and told him I did not want to be involved in any three-way bullshit with him. I didn't deserve that.

He said he understood. He didn't even call me, just texted. I didn't even know he still had feelings for her. He was afraid to leave her and if he did, he felt like he was letting her down. I wondered why the last time it hadn't been a problem. He said he was so ready to leave her. I was mad at God. *'Not again,'* I thought. This was confirmation even more to me that I wasn't getting into a relationship. They wouldn't even let me be with another god. They had set me up again.

Angel told me during a reading that Nick was blocking all my relationships and being a fuckin hater. There was always an excuse about why I couldn't get a relationship. Something was blocking me. *'That's bullshit,'* I thought, *'that's a lie.'*

I knew I wouldn't talk to Enoch again, so I thought, *'Fuck it.'*

A couple of days later, I sent him a text that said, *'Fuck you.'* I meant it too. Of course, I had to follow up with a call to CYS. I also did a couple of other things, but I could tell it didn't affect him. If I couldn't even be with someone on my level, then what the fuck? I knew he was a soulmate or twin flame or something. He knew it, and I knew it. *'What kind of life is this?'* It was so miserable having this pattern done to me repeatedly. We went our separate ways.

The gang stalkers continued to repeat the same fuckin scenarios over and over again with different people. I bought several books about gang stalking, and it confirmed everything I was thinking. I noticed that going to the police was a waste of time because they were in on it too. One of the books I read confirmed they had a stinky smell, a sulfur smell. They were demons and extraterrestrials taking over human bodies. They were all really odd looking. Nobody could help me, not even god himself. How long was this going to continue? It had already been three years.

# Chapter 20:
# Hoes Love God Too

I wanted to get my hair done so I reached out to a girl on Facebook, Fiona. She happened to read tarot cards as well. "I would love for you to teach me more," she said. She was a nice girl and really positive. I had thought about doing classes to teach others and I thought it would be a great opportunity with her.

She came over to my house. She talked a lot, and she told me she was a Sagittarius. I got along with Sagittarius people pretty well. She was already really good at reading cards. I just gave her a few more tips. I noticed she was staring at my breast. "Do you like girls," she asked. "No I replied. Fiona told me she bisexual and it didn't bother me.

We started to hang out more and became besties. I told her all about the issues I was having, and she told me all about hers.

She came over one day to read cards and when she left, I started picking up sexual energy from her. I thought that was weird.

Later, I called Fiona and told her about it. She told me she got some sex oil from a local witch. The oil had great reviews online. This oil was supposed to bring you a romantic partner. I knew I had to get some immediately. I started to use the oil. It smelled really good, and it had glitter in it.

Fiona came over and said she was really stressed out because she was talking to so many men. She attracted men very easily. She was still connected to her ex-boyfriend who she couldn't let go of. She also was having problems with getting clients for her businesses.

I had just started doing meditations, so I tried one out on her. She laid on my bed and I told her to relax. I started to touch her on different spots of her body. I touched the bottom of her leg, and I had a vision. I saw me and her kissing. I started to giggle because I had no idea where that came from.

"What?" she said.

"Nothing," I said. I just ignored it.

After I was done we gave each other a hug and then she left. I began to have strange thoughts about Fiona: sexual thoughts. I didn't even find her attractive. Fiona wasn't ugly but I definitely was not attracted to her.

While Fiona and I were talking on the phone, she was telling me about her sexual experiences with women. She then went on to tell me how oral sex should be performed. "You are supposed to lick around the clit. Women only come that way," she said.

Even though I disagreed, I listened to her. She liked talking about sex a lot. I could tell she was hinting at eating my coochie or wanted to pursue me in that way. As she talked, I got slightly turned on. I wondered what it would be like if she ate my coochie and if I would even be open to it. We ended the conversation and began to text each other. She mentioned she thought about us doing stuff.

"What kind of stuff?" I replied.

"You know, like nasty stuff," she said.

I giggled to myself. I couldn't believe she was saying that stuff to me. I told her I thought about her watching me as I showered.

She said, "My thoughts are a little more nasty than that. I think about eating your coochie and stuff like that."

I paused for a second. I could feel my pussy pulsating a bit. I could tell she was kinda nervous telling me that. I felt like I should at least give it a try. I told her she could come over and we could discuss it. I also told her I had more of a romantic energy towards her, but she had more of a sexual energy toward me.

"I don't know about that," she said. "I never heard of that." Romantic energy and sexual energy go hand and hand.

She agreed to come over. "I just want to make sure everything is mutual," she said.

The next day, I was a little worried and I tried not to panic. I wasn't sure exactly what was going to happen. I was open to talking about it, but was I really going to let this girl perform oral sex on me?

She told me she was feeling a little sick and she had a cold and asked if I was okay with her still coming over. I was cool with it. I told her I would let her know when I was on my way home from the store. She never told me when she was on her way. I thought maybe she changed her mind. I talked to her later that night and found out we had a miscommunication. "I thought you were coming over," I said.

"You never said you were home," she said.

We agreed she would come over the next day. "Let's watch a movie," she said.

"Yeah," I said. "I will bring some snacks with me."

She wanted me to try her popcorn with a chocolate combination.

It rained that day. I went to the store and bought a few snacks too. It was a perfect day for a movie. She arrived with snacks in her hand. I was nervous, but she didn't seem to be. "What do you want to watch?" I asked.

"Let's watch something scary," she said.

We sat on the bed together. We watched the movie, and we shared snacks. When we were done, we both sat back against the wall at the bottom of the bed. I looked at her to see if she was going to make the first move. Then I got more comfortable, and I laid down next to her. She acted normal, so I moved closer to her. I started to rub up against her and still, she did nothing and continued to watch the movie. I just laid there for a moment. I rolled my hand down her back touching her butt and then I placed my hand on her vagina and began rubbing it. She began to rub on me too. "I wish I wasn't on my period," she said. She asked me if I wanted to kiss her.

I started to laugh. Was I really going to kiss this woman on the mouth? I said, "Ok," and she leaned over and kissed me. It felt weird. It didn't feel romantic at all. It was too soft and too much female energy. I kissed her again. It felt like I was kissing my sister.

We both took our shirts off and exposed our breasts. "Your titties are not small," she said. I had always thought they were tiny for some reason.

Her breasts were huge. They had to weigh ten pounds each. I stared at them and then began to suck on them. "I don't feel like anything," I said.

"You're not supposed to," she said, "I feel it."

I began to suck on the other titty.

She smiled at me. "Would you be ok if I ate your coochie?" she asked.

"We can try," I said. I took my clothes off and lay down.

"Open your legs," she said.

I was very hesitant. I felt like I was at a gyno appointment.

"How can I eat your coochie if you don't open your legs?" she asked.

I slowly opened my legs.

She started to examine my coochie. "You have a nice coochie," she said. "Your hole is not small."

My vagina was very small and tight; it must have opened up after I had sex with my guy friend. She began to lick on it. I didn't feel anything. I just lay there and made random noises. When she was done, I was disappointed. I hadn't gotten any pleasure out of it. I started to think something was wrong with my vagina.

"Did you like it?" she asked.

"Yeah," I said, but I wasn't telling the truth. "I didn't really feel anything. Maybe something is wrong with my coochie."

"Girl, you got a small clit that's why."

That was true. The experience was nothing like I had expected, and I felt like I wasted my time doing it. Fiona said she was surprised any of it happened.

We got dressed and Fiona's ex-boyfriend texted to see what was taking so long for her to come over.

"Stay here," I said, "stay at my house."

Fiona wanted to stay, but she had promised her boyfriend she would be at her house. She was also talking to a guy in jail. She told me she decided to get in a relationship with him because she felt bad for him. He texted her too that night. "Who is Brandi?" he asked. "Why are you still at her house? Is Brandi gay?" As she read the text messages to me, we started laughing.

We then pulled out our tarot cards and started reading. I asked what the purpose of us having sex was. The cards said it was so I could learn about my body. "I can teach you how to have sex," Fiona said. "I'm really good at it. I know what men like. I wish I had a dildo. I would fuck you with it."

I wasn't into dildos. I didn't like anything fake. It reminded me of not having a real dick and a real man.

We looked at the cards some more and they showed us having sex again. She left for the night, and I took some time to register what happened.

I had just got off work and it was around 12:00 am. I was excited to see her again. I hopped in the shower and made sure I was fresh. She let me know she was on her way. She greeted me with a pink sweat suit on. She just got her hair done and she wore it out. I turned the TV on and turned it to American Horror Story. She lay at the end of the bed. "Why don't you lie down here with me?" she asked.

"I lay up this way," I said.

"Let me come up there then." She came to the top of the bed and lay down beside me. We leaned toward each other and started kissing. This time, we used our tongues. "That was a good kiss," she said.

We took our clothes off. She had lingerie on and showed it off for me. It was red with lace. I thought it was nice, but it wasn't a turn-on for me. She pulled her vibrator out. I lay down and opened my legs. She began licking my coochie, but I still didn't feel anything. She then inserted the vibrator. Then I started to feel some kind of pleasure.

"Good, your clit is starting to get hard," she said. The vibrator was not big, but it still hurt a bit. At that point, she was licking my coochie and using the vibrator at the same time. The way she was licking my coochie was like how they did it on pornos. I didn't really enjoy it, but the vibrator was okay. "Did you cum?" she asked.

"I think so," I said. I might have cum a little. It wasn't intense enough to know.

I sat on top of her and pulled down her bra and began sucking her nipples. Then I tried to fit as much of her breast in my mouth as I could. I knew she would enjoy the way I maneuvered my mouth and tongue. She laid down and took her underwear off. Her coochie was huge. It was the biggest coochie I had ever seen. *'Dear God,'* I thought. It was the size of the grand canyon and it had hair on it too.

I scrunched my face up and turned my head. Fiona put her hand down by her vagina and said, "You don't have to do anything you don't want to do."

I really didn't want to, but I had already said I was going to do it. Plus, I wanted her to like me and continue to like me. I looked at her coochie with disgust; there was wet stuff coming out of it.

"Taste it," she said.

I shook my head no. Then I slowly put my hand out and touched some of the vagina wetness. *'Eww, I can't believe there's some on my hand.'* I put my finger in my mouth, and it was nasty just like I had thought it would be.

"Put your finger in it," she said.

Uh-uh. I shook my head no. I didn't feel comfortable sticking my finger in her vagina or with the whole situation.

"Yeah," she said, "Just put your finger in it."

I decided not to do that, and I leaned forward toward her vagina. '*I can do this*,' I told myself. I began licking her clit and it tasted salty as fuck. It was strong. It was strong enough to clear one's sinuses. I decided to spit on it so it would clear away the taste and it did. After that I didn't taste anything. I moved downwards and licked the whole coochie. I was curious about what the inside of a coochie was like, so I decided to stick my tongue in the hole. It was a weird feeling I really couldn't describe. I heard her moaning. She took a while to cum. She pushed me on my forehead to get me to stop.

"That was bomb," she said. "You did really good."

I smiled. I wanted to do a good job. We then decided to bump coochies. I sat on top of her, and we started to rub up against each other. She was much bigger than me, three times my size, so it was difficult to get our coochies to connect. I kept falling to the side and falling forward. I started sweating after a while. I ran out of breath and decided to take a break. "Try sitting on top of me," I said.

She tried and it still didn't work. My coochie kept hitting her leg. We tried some more positions. I tried leaning off the bed while she stood up and put one leg over me. I felt immense pressure that became painful. I couldn't bear her weight on top of me.

We got back on the bed, and I began to suck on her nipples again. I told her to bend over that time so I could eat her coochie from the back. She bent over with her wide ass in front of my face. I noticed how large her asshole was. I was flabbergasted. I had never seen such a large asshole in my life.

After about twenty minutes, she said she couldn't cum that way and that she needed to lie down. She did, and then I continued. She came again. "I usually don't cum twice," she said. "Where do you get all this energy?"

Later she asked, "So did you like?"

"It was okay," I said.

She said I was sucking too hard at times.

"Why didn't you say something?" I asked. I definitely didn't want to hurt her.

We discussed how we definitely preferred to have sex with a man. I preferred a dick in my mouth. I felt like eating coochie was like being on a vegetarian diet when I was more of a meat eater. It wasn't satisfying giving nor receiving oral from a woman. It was missing something.

We both lay down together and cuddled. I pulled my hand down her back and over her butt. I noticed she had hair on her butt and all over her body. She was really hairy. She took up most of the bed and I had little space left. I hung slightly off the bed with my naked body while she fell asleep. She started to snore so I couldn't fall into a deep sleep.

I finally started to drift off and I felt her kiss me on my cheek. She tossed and turned. Then she got up and told me she wanted to go get some snacks and that my bed was uncomfortable. She got dressed and we hugged each other before she left. I couldn't believe what I had just done. I had eaten a girl's coochie.

The next day I noticed a woman I worked with staring at my coochie. Every time we talked I saw her looking down there. *'What the fuck is going on here?'* It got to the point where I started feeling uncomfortable. When I turned around, she looked at my butt.

Fiona said that was happening because another woman could tell I had been with a woman.

My feelings for Fiona started to grow. I couldn't quite understand why she wanted to have sex with me but didn't want to date me. Why was this pattern continuing to happen? People were just wanting me for sex and nothing serious. There must still be a love hex on me. I didn't want a relationship with Fiona, but why wasn't I getting commitment in general. I started crying. I texted Fiona and asked her. Why didn't she have any feelings for me? I could tell she didn't have feelings for me because I had bought her flowers, and I didn't like her reaction. For some reason, I just wanted to buy her stuff.

"It takes me a while to really like someone," she said.

I thought she liked me; that's why I even had sex with her.

Fiona said she looked back in her messages and that she never mentioned anything about liking me. She said she didn't know what I was talking about and that she never led me on and that it was my fault for feeling the way I did.

I recalled something different and felt like she did lead me on.

She started being very mean and dismissive towards me. She pretty much didn't want anything to do with me after that.

That pissed me the fuck off. So basically, she didn't have any feelings for me and she wasn't interested in continuing the friendship. My heart started to hurt. It was the first time I actually felt pain in my heart. '*How many times can a person be rejected in life*?' I thought. I was being rejected by everybody, even people I didn't like that much.

I got a reading with Angel, did some research, and found out what was really going on. I found out Nick had done a gay spell on me. It made a lot of sense, because I usually didn't have any interest in women, and during that time, I had started feeling more attracted to other women.

I asked Angel why Nick was doing this, and she said it was because he was gay, and he wanted me to feel comfortable about it. I had the idea Nick was bisexual from some things he had said, how he walked, and just his energy. One time Nick had asked me if I wanted him to flat iron my hair. I thought that was strange.

I was also having dreams about having sex with other women and I was seeing their coochies. I didn't like how coochies looked and I thought they were disgusting. I had never seen them in my dreams

323

before.

I realized it was after Fiona and I started using that sex oil that my feelings changed about her. "It was the oil," I said. "This is fucking crazy. That oil made me like her." I wasn't sure why it made me like her instead of her like me. She is the one who wanted to have sex with me in the first place.

Also, Olivia had given me a reading earlier in the year. She said a guy was coming into my life and I was going to have some crazy sex with him and that the guy was hairy.

It was Fiona! The cards kept showing me a guy, but it was actually a woman. The cards tricked me and set me up.

I was so angry with Fiona. I felt she had used me for sex and my services. I sent her a request for money I felt she owed me. She kept declining it. I did a lot for her. I did several meditations, I did a money spell, I did a court spell for her boyfriend, and I paid for dinner. I paid for her dinner after she told me she was getting low on cash. She told me she was going to go to a shelter to stay. She lived with her parents so I wasn't sure if they were kicking her out. I tried my best to help her like I would any friend.

I paid a spiritualist to do a spell on Fiona because I couldn't do this particular one myself. I wanted her to think about me all day every day and dream about me. I also wanted to hex her. I didn't want to ruin her whole life – just her love life. I wanted her to know what it was like not to have any partners.

The dream spell was successful, and I could tell because I started dreaming about her. The hex wasn't working out – I started getting nerve pain. I have no idea why I kept trying to hex people when it just made me sick. I started to get pissed off. '*That fat bitch,*' I thought. I had to undo the hex because the pain was getting worse. I looked at my cards and asked about the hex and I got a card with Archangel Gabriel on it, which meant she was protected.

I tried to do a spell to make her want to have sex with me so I could reject her. I used some of the sex oil again. I started seeing a devil. I must have opened some portal. The devil had a woman tied up with hooks in her. Then the devil started staring at me like, 'What are you doing in here?' I knew once the candle was done burning it would go away.

A few days later, I noticed I could make a portal come out of my third eye and the world looked different.

I wanted revenge and I wanted to get back at spirit for doing that to me once again. They used my own friend against me. I would had never seen a woman coming.

I was all out of ideas, so I decided to call CYS. She didn't have any children, but her sister did, so I called about her children. While I was at it, I reported her baby sister too. I called a funeral home about her boyfriend. I pretended to be her and said I needed to make arrangements.

I had one of my friends call her and act like she was her boyfriends' other bitch. They got into a bad argument and it made Fiona and her boyfriend break up. It was like the perfect storm. She could not keep up with the conversation, she was getting put in her fat ass place. I could tell she was hurt that he was seeing another woman, which was probably true. My friend read the fuck out of her and pointed out that she was a broke ass bitch, and she had no clients for her businesses.

'She deserves all of it,' I thought, 'after what she did to me.'

I was just about to hop in the shower when I heard a knock on the door. There were policemen standing there. I was served with PFA papers. I rolled my eyes.

"Do you know Fiona?" the officer asked.

"Yes," I replied. "She owes me money."

"Don't contact her for any reason," they said.

I took the papers and went back into my room. "I can't believe this bitch filed a PFA on me," I said to myself. I called Angel, one of my readers, with the news.

"Oh my god," she said.

My previous reading told me she wasn't going to file on me. The cards had been wrong again. I started to read the things Fiona accused me of in the papers. Most of it was lies. I was a little nervous because nobody ever filed a PFA on me or taken me to court. I was mad at God for letting that happen to me because Fiona had started that shit. I felt like God was taking her side.

Angel looked at some cards for me and said Nick was actually the cause of this. Ugh, I was so tired of that black fuck. That had become his nickname after a while. My friends just naturally started calling him that. The cards said Nick did a spell that would make me like Fiona so she could turn around and stab me in the back and take me to court. It made sense. I thought it was strange that I was going to court with him for the same issue.

I was really nervous the day of court. I wasn't sure what was going to happen. I did my court ritual before I left the house. I caught an Uber and before I got out of the car, the driver asked me, "Can I give you something?"

With irritation in my voice, I said, "Yeah." I usually didn't take things from strangers. It was some piece of paper, and my intentions were to toss it in the garbage. I looked down at the paper and it had a website on it. It said: peacewithgod.net. I was stunned. I went to the website, and it was about Jesus and God. *'This is definitely a sign,'* I thought. I knew something good was going to happen and I was protected.

I sat in the chair worried. Hours passed. I saw Fiona come down to go to the bathroom. I turned my head. *'Fuck that bitch,'* I thought. I got up and moved to another seat so I couldn't see her.

I had a vision of me leaving court with a smirk on my face.

A woman called my name, and I walked over to her. She said she wasn't on either party's side. She tried to get me to sign papers to get the PFA extended. *'Hell no,'* I thought. That would make me look guilty. I told the lady, "Absolutely not." She walked away, and I sat back down.

Finally, they called my name to go into the courtroom. We were the last case left. Fiona walked in after me. The judge started going over what she had accused me of. Fiona just stood there looking just like penguin from Batman. She was shaped just like him. She said that I had threatened to kill her. She had a few Facebook posts I had posted about her. I had insinuated I was going to kill her, but I was smart enough not to mention her name. She said I was mad at her because she ended the relationship. That was not true. I had ended our friendship, and I had text messages that proved I had asked her not to talk to me again. I could tell she was unprepared. She didn't know what she was doing. She did bring up some things I had done but she had no proof. Fiona started getting angry. "Why didn't you just sign the papers like everyone else did?" she shouted. She was referring to the extended PFA papers.

When I had gone to court with Nick, they gave him a no-contact agreement. That's not what they had offered me. I already knew I wasn't signing shit. I told the judge I wasn't signing anything because she was lying.

She told the judge I was trying to extort money from her.

I was like, "What? If I wanted to extort money, I would have asked for more than $300. I would have asked for thousands."

She didn't even have any money. The judge decided to drop the case and not grant the PFA. I was relieved and happy. Fiona, on the other hand, was pissed.

"Wait, can I ask one more question?" she asked the judge.

"No," he said.

I laughed silently to myself.

Fiona sat out in the waiting room like a brat, mad that she lost. I waited for the judge to give me some papers in another room. I saw Fiona leaving and she was talking on the phone. "Why don't you just move on?" she said. "She has a mental illness, and I'm going to take her to court again." She was just mad, and I didn't give a fuck. She should not have taken me to court in the first place, and I had wiped the floor with her ass. The mental illness talk didn't bother me at all. She should have read her cards on me. I already knew I was crazy.

On my way home I had a vision that she was crying in her car. *'Wheeeew that was a close one,'* I thought. God did have my back. She wasn't God's daughter after all like she thought. She had claimed to be God's daughter after we got into it. She never mentioned God to me before but apparently she thought she had some kind of close connection with him. God's daughters weren't sluts, I thought.

I soon found out Fiona paid a man to do a money hex on me. I thought she was so jealous of me because I was financially stable. I never tried to stop her money. I only tried to help her get more. After some research, I also found out that her parents were millionaires. If her parents were millionaires, why was she going to a shelter. This bitch was lying. I was furious and decided to take her ass to court this time.

We went back to court, and she signed a no-contact order. I wanted her to get more than that, but my free lawyer said that was the best option.

My money started to slow down, and I wasn't getting as many customers. Fiona had gotten a new job that supposedly paid a lot of money. I was swole, not because she had a job, but because I felt like God was blessing my enemies. I knew the money spell I did for her worked. I felt God had used me to help her. *'Why didn't he just do it himself. The Fuck,'* I thought.

I started having unpleasant dreams about Fiona. I had to get my friends to help me with spell work to block it and to get my money flowing again. It did work but whatever hex it was kept sticking to me. I was doing spell work back-to-back and it would work but then I would have problems again. I kept doing spells on her so she wouldn't get a boyfriend. The cards said, her karma was that she wouldn't get into a relationship for a while and I mine was that my money would slow down. So I didn't want her to have a boyfriend and she wanted me to be broke. The case was closed.

Souls, Fiona was another part of "The Hero's Journey", she was the temptress, just like Mahogany. If I'm correct, I had two temptress scenarios, which means I may never get out of this journey because it seems to be repeating itself. How is that possible? The fucked up part was a great friendship was ruined because of these stupid patterns I keep having. I felt like I was forced to have sex with Fiona just to fulfill some journey I never asked to be apart of.

# Chapter 21:
# The Judgement

There was a scheduled court date for me and Nick again. I went, but he never showed up. I was irritated. I went all the way down there for nothing. My case got called first.

"Are you still having problems with him?" the judge asked.

"Yes," I said.

"He never showed up to the last court date," the judge said. He was found guilty of harassment.

"Will this go on his record?" I asked.

"Yes," the judge said, "and he will have a fine. If he doesn't pay it, he will spend some time in jail."

I couldn't believe it. It was actually happening. *'There is a god,'* I thought. I didn't have to show any proof or hardly say anything, and he had gotten charged. It was so effortless.

When Nick found out, he was pissed. He sent me a message saying I would be punished.

I thought long and hard about who I could get to help me with him. I thought of Mahogany because she knew how to dream walk but I wondered if she would be open to talking to me. We did leave off badly. I hadn't completely forgiven her either, but I needed help.

I sent her a friend request on Facebook. She quickly accepted it. "That looks like my Brandi," she said. She was happy to hear from me!

I told her about my situation, and she offered to meet up to talk. I was a little bit nervous because it had been a while. "I'm not far from you if you want to meet up now."

When we met, I saw her standing there and saw that she was as petite as I was. She still looked the same. I went up to her to give her a hug.

"You look beautiful as always," she said. "You don't look like you been touched by the sun or the wind." I think she was surprised at how good I looked after surviving her attacks.

It was a little awkward at first. We began to catch up about our lives. She was married and had several other men she was involved with. She told me she was into BDSM and I was very surprised and a little confused. Then I thought that was something a Scorpio would be into. She also told me she was into it with some guy. "I don't like to fight, Brandi. I always win, and a win for me equals a death."

I took a big gulp. Then I remembered she almost killed me. I wanted to know why she attacked me all those years. As I told her about all the attacks and dreams I had about her she seemed to be concerned about how long they lasted.

"I don't know what happened," she said. She tried to make it seem like she didn't do anything to me but we both knew she did.

"I thought you were trying to kill me," I said.

She stayed silent. I then caught her staring at my body. We talked about what happened right before we fell out. "You probably thought I was leading you on, and I wasn't trying to do that. I was interested in you. I just didn't know how to go about that. I knew you were sent to me for another reason, but I didn't want to hurt you. Then she said, "I'm open to everything now. Open to dating women."

"You're married, and I'm traditional," I said.

"I'm not traditional," she said. Clearly, she wasn't. She had like five boyfriends on the side.

After a long conversation, I gave her a hug again. I wanted to kiss her; I wanted to piss my spirit guides off and I could tell that gay spell was still affecting me. I asked her for a kiss.

"What kind of kiss?" she asked.

I said, "Just a little kiss."

"Ok," she said. We both locked hands together and kissed. It felt too soft and feminine. It felt like when I kissed Fiona.

"It doesn't feel like boyfriend and girlfriend," I said.

I was disappointed as I walked back home. I felt like I was trying to make myself like women, and it wasn't working. I looked in the mirror and noticed I had broken out into hives from kissing her. I think I was allergic to her. It was weird.

I stopped talking to her shortly after that but then, a few weeks later, I decided to contact her because I was bored. I asked if she wanted to date me.

"Yeah," she said. "I think this would be good for us."

We had something weird going on. We shared romantic and sexual energy but did not want to have sex with each other even though her sexual energy was so strong. She was a triple Scorpio sun moon and rising so the force was strong. We decided to have a non-sexual relationship but she would send me naked pictures of herself. I just laughed. It was just odd looking at the female body. Our connection lasted for three days because it wasn't a real relationship to me.

"I knew you were going to do this," she said.

I think we both knew that we didn't like each other in that way enough to be serious. We liked men. Though the energy was there, the dick wasn't.

I didn't think she was serious anyway and didn't know she would be upset. I felt bad. "Thanks for dating me," I said.

Mahogany and I tried to stay in touch with each other, but it just wasn't the same. I knew she would end up hurting me again and possibly do magic on me too. I didn't want to go through that.

I moved back in with my dad, and I wasn't happy about it. My dad kicked Mouse out of the house and Angel did some magic to help with that. Mouse kept coming by though. I didn't want her over there. I had seen in the cards that she and my dad were trying to get back together. I was not having that shit. I sent her some unfriendly messages and she continued harassing me in my dreams. She told me I needed some dick. It had nothing to do with dick; I was there for revenge. I was doing a lot of magic to keep her away from the house and to stop her from doing work on my dad.

Mouse kept driving by the house and I couldn't catch her, so I told the police she was harassing me, which she was. We ended up getting a court date. I was tired of going to court, but I had to. I started taking pictures of her every time she came by. We first went to court for a PFA protection from an abuse order. She looked very nervous, and she should have been. She filed one on me too, but I didn't care. The judge granted both of them. After that she stopped bothering me. I didn't have any more dreams.

I wasn't done with her ass yet though. I filed for harassment. When we got back to court, I explained what happened and showed the judge a picture of her. Mouse barely said anything at first. "What are you doing over at her house?" the judge asked her.

"You should see the messages she sent me," Mouse said. "She said she hopes I die."

"Do these messages have anything to do with this incident?" asked the judge.

"No," she replied.

"Ok then. You have been charged with harassment."

I couldn't believe it. "Again," I said to myself. "I won again!" It happened so fast just like it did when I went to court about Nick.

Mouse's ugly face wrinkled up like she wanted to cry.

I was so happy and relieved. Finally, justice!

I had a dream about Nick again. We were at some house and going into a room to have sex. Nick pulled his dick out for me to suck it. I then saw a weird black energy bouncing around the house. Then I woke up.

I felt a stabbing pain in my vagina. I curled up into a ball. All I could do was cry. I had been raped again. It hurt so bad, worse than before. The cramping in my stomach was also more intense. *'Why doesn't God stop him?'* I thought.

I gave up at that point and called Angel. *"He's raping me"*, I said. I knew Angel wasn't sure what to do but Angel found out she had a unique gift. She could do magic in an unusual way. She did some magic to make Nick go away and to change his focus.

I went on his Facebook and saw that he finally got into a relationship. I wasn't sure if it was with a man or a woman, but I was happy for him since it had been so long since he had been in one.

Everything Angel manifested was coming true and all her magic was working. I was just glad because he finally started to leave me alone.

All the dreams went away. I was able to sleep peacefully.

Then one of my high school classmates got murdered. It was an unfair situation. My abilities had increased so much that I could see dead people instantly, so that classmate started coming around me. I felt so bad for him. I started letting him sleep in the bed with me at night. I started to feel energy from him like he wanted a relationship with me. I thought that was weird. I told him no several times.

We became closer and I gave in. We ended up being in a relationship while I worked on getting him justice. We dated for a month. He was kind to me and treated me better than most men. I could see him so clearly and feel him so strongly. He asked me for food, particularly candy. I had a good time with him. His sexual energy grew stronger and stronger. I thought it wasn't a good idea to have sex with a dead person, but I gave in. I imagined him on top of me and I started to masturbate. After I climaxed, I started to feel nerve pain like I was electrocuted. *'I knew this was a bad idea,*' I thought. '*I knew this relationship couldn't continue. This man is dead.*'

I tried hard to stay away from him and send him on his way to finish the death process, but it was difficult. I had sex with him a few more times, then I decided to end it.

A few days went by and I started seeing George Washington. At first, I saw the four founding fathers just walking around and not paying me any attention. Then George started looking at me and talking to me. "What the fuck do he want?" I said to myself. I was opposed to talking with him, but then I got the same energy like he wanted a relationship with me. '*Why does he like me?*' I thought. George wore a war uniform. He would come in my room and hang it up and sleep in the bed with me. '*What is happening?*' I thought.

After a couple of nights, me and George were in a relationship. He followed me to work. He would look out for me along with other war vets. He even told me to go to a museum where he was at. He called it a date. He promised me I could have his home in Virginia. I learned about him, and I also learned how sexual he was. The sexual energy was so strong I couldn't resist. I could feel George on top of me as I masturbated. I imagined George going in and out of me. Then he began to eat my ass. I had no clue how freaky Mr. George Washington was. He wanted to have sex all day every day.

After speaking to Angel about it, she did not approve. "Girl, what the hell are you doing? That man was a slave owner."

She was right. What was I doing having sex with an old-ass white man, who owned slaves, and who was dead?

"Oh no, girl," she said. "I don't think that's him."

"What do you mean?" I asked.

"I think it's a demon."

Maybe she was right. Something was wrong.

She asked her cards why I kept getting romantic offers from dead people, and she said it was because of some spell I did. I did a spell on my dad so we could start getting along and it must have backfired.

I had a hard time getting rid of George after that. He just wouldn't go away. Finally, I started to ignore his mothafuckin ass.

A month went by and I read online that a rapper was killed. He instantly appeared on my bed. "What happened to you?" I asked. I saw him crying blood and holding his head. "OMG did you get shot in the head?" I did more research and saw that he had. I felt horrible. What was going on in the world?

The rapper decided to stick around, and I again started picking up romantic energy from him.

*'No, not again. I'm not getting involved in this way,'* I thought.

He started to wipe blood on me and do really weird things. I wondered what he wanted from me. He convinced me to be in a relationship with him too. I promised myself I wouldn't have sex with him and that it was probably a demon. He came across stronger than any other dead person before. We would hold hands and I could actually feel his hand. I heard him burp and fart. It was so real. I then noticed the rapper started being aggressive with me and arguing with me.

"That's not him, girl," Angel said.

I wondered why God didn't just send me a real person that was alive. *'Why they got to be dead? This is not a real relationship.'*

Me and my dad were not getting along. In fact, it was the worst it had ever been. He was doing things I didn't approve of, and I was trying my best to save up so I could get the hell out of there. But I couldn't find a job. I was out of work for two months, and I kept seeing that guy doing magic on me in my cards.

Then my dad kicked me out of the house, and I couldn't believe it. I called Angel for help as I walked on the dark streets. I walked to a nearby hotel and was angry because I had to spend a lot of the money I had saved to move. I hated him. I figured all this drama had something to do with the hex that was placed on me. I stopped talking to my dad after that.

My health got worse. I began to break out in rashes. All the magic I was doing was making me sick and I began to lose a lot of energy. I tried so hard to stay afloat. There was a lot going on.

I thought I had opened another portal. There were dead people and creatures walking around everywhere. I tried to close it myself, but I ended up going back to the girl who closed my portal the first time.

"There is no portal. You have an evil entity attached to you," she said.

I wasn't surprised. I got something put on me every year and I was tired of that shit. Apparently, the person Fiona paid attached a demon to me so I would have bad luck. Not only did it fuck up my money, but it made unfortunate events happen to me. *'That's why my dad was behaving in that manner.'* It all made sense.

"I can take it off for you," the lady said.

"Thank you so much," I said.

She removed it and money came in for me instantly. I was finally able to be financially stable again.

I started to realize tarot cards and doing magic spells wasn't doing me any good. It was causing me harm. After doing spells and trying to go into other people's dreams, I realized I was causing myself severe headaches.

I decided I was done with magic.

Then the cards kept telling me my soulmate was coming but he never showed up.

Years of waiting, crying, and being in pain... I couldn't do it anymore. I was done. The cards had lied to me for many years. I came to the conclusion that I wasn't getting a partner in this life and there was nothing I could do about it.

At the end of the day, nobody really won.

So I decided to retire from doing tarot cards and practicing magic.
Souls, you've been asleep way too long.
It's time to wake up.

# Conclusion

**W**ell, Souls, that's my story. My real, honest, and true story. I've been writing this book on and off for five years. It has been a long journey. It was hard because I got attacked many times while trying to finish.

I endured a lot of trauma due to the harassment of demons that never seemed to end. I always wondered why I was chosen, and I realized it was the kind of energy I carried. I have a very rare form of energy that no other being possesses. I never said that I was perfect. I had a lot of fucked up shit done to me but I have done some fucked up shit as well.

Things you should know:
Mostly all the people who attacked me with magic had a Scorpio placement for their sun, moon, or rising.

I wasn't raped by Jody, but I was attacked/raped by the demon he invoked, which was caused by the hex that was placed by whoever Mouse paid. Most of my sexual encounters were demons.

I was raped by Nick in my dream because of the spell I did with the sigils. I invoked that demon.

All my romantic partners were brought to me by magic somehow. Most of my betrayals came from women over a man. A lot of betrayals started after I started reading tarot cards.

I found out I was a Scorpio moon and rising. This explains the overwhelming amount of sexual energy, me being so vengeful, yet so powerful and gifted. Before I retired from doing magic, I was able to defeat the gang stalkers and make bad stuff happen to them. I was able to stop Nick and Mouse from coming into my dreams. I was able to manifest very well and was on top of my game.

Don't get it twisted, just because I retired, I can still be very dangerous when fucked with, but I am moving on from this life and hopefully into a more peaceful one.

I'm happy I told the truth and got my story out.

## Final Notes

Whoever decides to deface this book or try to change or distort it will have a bad fate. The Most High has sealed this. Selah

I block all physical attacks and spiritual attacks that may be thrown at me, my family, my friends, and anyone in my blood line. I ask the Most High to protect us all. Selah.

# Reference

Here are pictures taken during my life, especially showing spiritual activity and my journey.

**Growing Up:**
*These are not referenced in any specific chapters.*

1.

2.

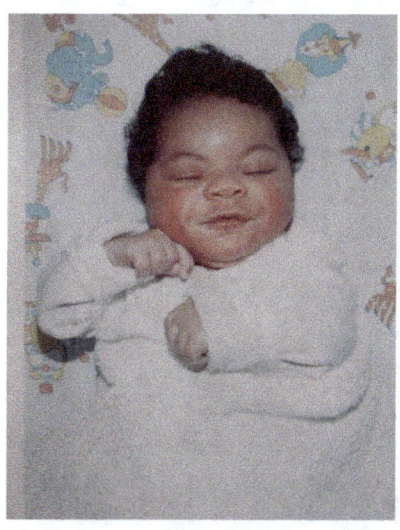 

3.

4.

5.

6.

7.

8.

9.

10.

11.

## Photos of Spirits and Spiritually Related:

1. Demon Eyes in My Hair from Chapter 6: All Bitter No Sweet

2. Witch I Discovered After an Egg Cleansing

3. Devil Imprint from Chapter 17:
   El Portal

4. The Devil Card with the
   Imprint (see above)

5. Hat Man

6. Long Thin Man from Chapter 17: El Portal

7. Long Thin Man Dead on the Street from Chapter 17: El Portal

9. Tenko Japanese Demon Mask

8. Archangel Michael from the Angel Cards from Chapter 17: El Portal

Ruby Lane

Japanese Vintage Konoha
Yamabushi Tengu 天狗 Mask of...
$126.00*

This Japanese vintage Tengu 天狗 mask dates to the early
to mid 20th century, between the 1920s and 1950s of the
Showa period which was from 1926 to ...

Visit

## 10. Tenko Spirits in the Candles
### from Chapter 17: El Portal

## Demonic Faces Watching Me:

1. Demon Face in the Mirror

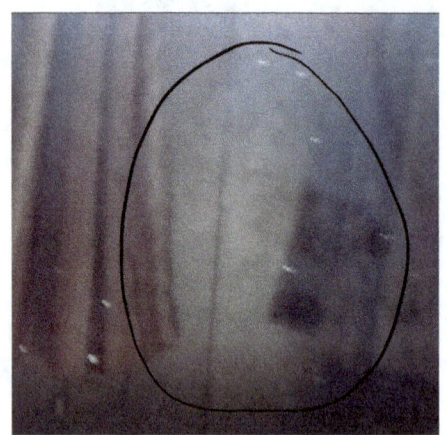

## 2. Demon Face on the Ceiling

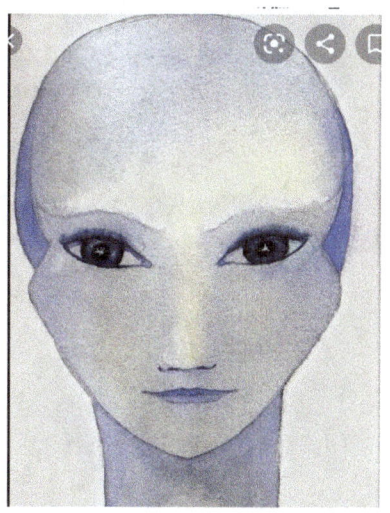

## 3. Demon Face in a Candle

## 4. Demon Face in the Clouds

## The Cemetery Photos:

*From Chapter 14: Serpents in the Shade*

1.

2.

3.

4.

5.

## Car Accident Photoshoot:

1.

2.

3.

4.

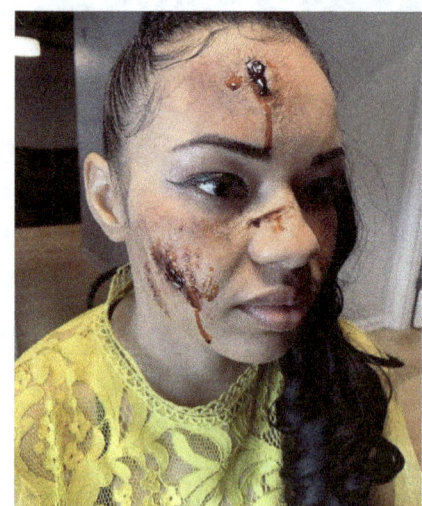

5.

6.

7.

## Other Photos From My Life:

1.

2.

3.

4.

5.

6.

7.

8.

# No Filter Spiritual Counseling

If you would like to talk to me and receive my proprietary and exclusive Divine Elevation Therapy, reach out to me at *nofilterspiritualcounseling.com*.

# Thank You

Thank you so much for reading my story. Would you take a quick minute and write an honest review on the book page? I would really appreciate it and it helps me reach more people.

Go to: *amazon.com/dp/B0CY4FMLGG*.